DATA WAREHOUSE AUTOMATION

DATA WAREHOUSE AUTOMATION

A Pragmatic Guide to the Easiest and Fastest Development of Your Data Warehouse

Martin Gandalson

Copyrights and Trademarks

ISBN 978-1-7178-2990-0

Table of Contents

1. Introduction and Scope

Congratulations! If you are reading this, you probably plan to build a data warehouse (DW) or have already done so. Utilizing recent technology, small companies can finally build a data warehouse at a very affordable cost, and keep the design (and the data!) in-house. Large companies can now build and maintain their data warehouses better than ever before: faster, cheaper, more secure, and more agile. In fact, in this hands-on guide we will show the step-by-step development of an actual data warehouse prototype, using free-trial tools.

This is a practical hands-on guide, and we will stick to the relevant topics that are important to someone who actually wants to build a DW as soon as possible. We won't be pontificating on academic positions, nor fluffing up the word count. We assume that you are more anxious to roll up your sleeves and get started than to debate theory with purists. Yet at the same time, we will detail the necessary planning that you must conduct in order to maximize the success of your data warehouse program. Along the way, we will identify and avoid the common pitfalls that can lead to failure.

The steps detailed in this guide can be used to build any data warehouse, data mart, or webhouse.

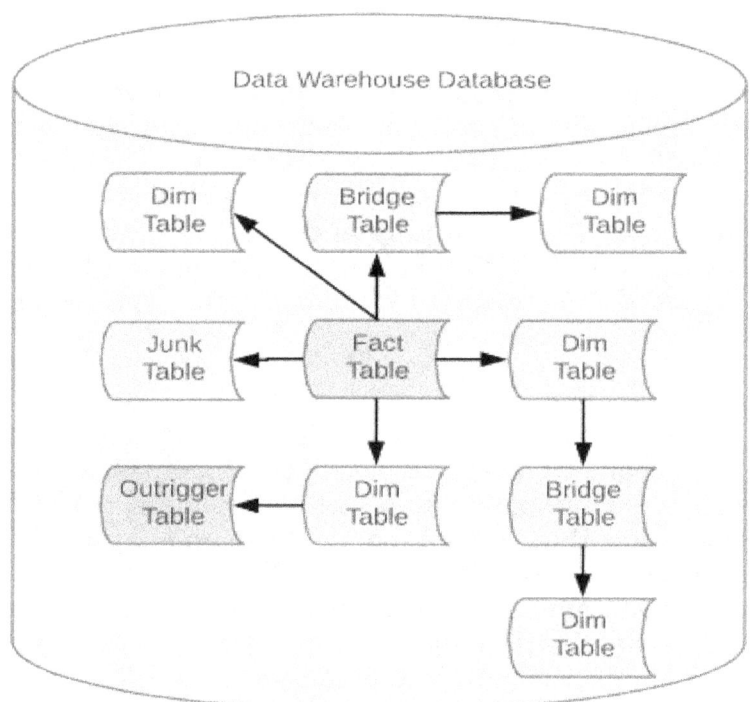

Illustration 1: Typical Star-Schema Data Warehouse

How This Book Is Organized

Dear Readers, I know that some of you will anxiously skim through the "planning" sections and eagerly jump right to the step-by-step construction of a DW. All I ask is that you at least read the "Strawman" exercise of Chapter 3, before diving into Chapter 5 to build your warehouse. You will find that this exercise accelerates your DW development.

In Chapter 2, we will start with a fast review of the benefits of data warehousing, as well as the benefits of using data warehouse automation (DWA) tools. We look at what's so great about data warehouses, and why it would be crazy not to use an inexpensive DWA tool.

In Chapter 3, we walk through the Proposal Phase, where you build your business case for data warehousing and develop a program plan for the pilot development and first year of operation. Readers most anxious to start building may be tempted to skip this chapter. If you do, please at least skim through the Strawman exercise, and pay particular attention to advice on security and privacy.

The short Chapter 4 introduces our plan in developing a Rapid Prototype.

Chapter 5 provides a very short overview of the goals, structure, and high-level tasks needed to build our data warehouse. Although there is a teeny bit of "theory" in here, it provides the overall context so that the subsequent detailed steps in later chapters make sense. Hey, even if you were building an IKEA cabinet, you would still look at the intro picture and description before jumping to step 1.

In Chapter 6 and the following chapters, we will build a data warehouse, hands-on step-by-step, in specific detail. Such detail, in fact, that you can reconstruct our examples perfectly yourself in your own databases. We are able to do this by using a free-trial DWA tool (Data Warehouse Wiz, from https://www.DataWarehouseWiz.com), which facilitates greatly accelerated data warehouse design. You do not need to be a data warehouse expert to wield this powerful tool. Moreover, you can follow these same steps to build your own data warehouse rapid prototype from your own data sources, all while using a 100%-functional free-trial tool. The later chapters provide details on using advanced features of the DWA tool, such that, by reading through to the last chapter, you will have the knowledge and instructions needed to build not just a mere prototype, but *any* star-schema data warehouse.

2. Benefits of Data Warehouses and Data Warehouse Automation

Technical Benefits of DW

You are likely familiar with the great potential benefits of DW, but let's do a short recap.

> **Data Warehousing Technical Benefits**
> - **"Standardized", Centralized, and Organized store of your company's data**
> - **Facilitates end-user productivity**
> - **Reduces time-demands on critical resources (human and hardware)**
> - **Provides fast query performance with minimal query design labor**
> - **Keeps history**
> - **Provides a single source of the truth**
> - **Enables data augmentation**
> - **Standardized format facilitates data mining/AI/ML/Predictive Analytics**

A data warehouse is an agile long-term asset with open-ended and flexible purposes. The most salient benefit is a "standardized" structure that enables data consumers to easily slice and dice data in any way imaginable. This allows data consumers to create ad hoc or unplanned reports with same-day execution, often in minutes. Usually a web client is set up to allow point-and-click report generation through generic queries. The web client (or other user interface) often allows the report consumers to create their own reports, without involving essential I.T. staff. This leads to greater end-user productivity and less burden on critical staff resources. Also, the data warehouse is built on a separate dedicated reporting platform, thus reducing burden on the sources (such as transactional databases in the company's critical operations).

The data warehouse structure is designed to provide fast report query performance, while requiring only minimal report query design labor. This structure is a "standardized" type of data model, such as the popular star-schema dimensional modeling. The architecture itself leads to fast performance in execution of report queries (SELECTS). It facilitates the design of "generic" query formats which can be used on any dimension/etc. It also provides a huge jump start for any new data analysts in your organization: anyone familiar with the popular star-schema architecture can join your company and be productive on the first day! By contrast, training a new person on your source operations databases often takes months.

The data warehouse retains a time-stamped history of your data, even when your source systems over-write or truncate their data.

The data warehouse provides a single version of the truth for your enterprise-wide systems. Previously, your data consumers may have struggled with inconsistent report results stemming from disparate systems or time-phasing dependencies. Such problems can be eliminated through use of an enterprise data warehouse, which holds centralized, coherent, consistent data.

The data warehouse facilitates easy data augmentation.

The organized and standardized structure of the data warehouse makes it much easier to feed generalized data mining techniques. Feeds to artificial intelligence/machine learning processes are much simplified.

Before implementing a data warehouse program, a typical company's data analysis systems are characterized by:

- Long delays in report development
- One-time reports or report queries that break over time
- Hand-crafted reports developed by highly-skilled, overburdened IT staff
- Data-cleaning may need to be done within the report, and also within

every report of the same type, or within a customized process to be run before the report

- There is a need for detailed documentation of all inputs/outputs of each report, and yet there still remains a risk of miscommunication of these parameters between report consumers and report developers

- Some reporting needs go unfulfilled

- Reports are developed only for subject areas specifically requested

After successful implementation of a DW, this company's analysis systems are characterized by:

- Reports can be quickly developed for any and all subject areas of the company

- Essential staff is freed up because report development requires much less skill

- Reports can be developed by the report consumers themselves with a small amount of training

- Reports can be developed same-day, often within the hour

- The data is in a "standardized" structure, so columns of each table (dimension, fact, etc) can be documented once, and used for all reports. This results in much less documentation required for report parameters, and much less risk of miscommunication of these parameters, particularly if the report consumers themselves develop their own reports.

- Data-cleaning is done only once, during the staging ETL. Report creators do not need to worry about cleaning.

- Report queries have a very long useful lifetime and are much less likely to ever break

Business Benefits of DW

The technical benefits are impressive, but what are the actual business benefits that enable you to meet business goals? The business benefits are more specific to your particular organization. Some common business benefits are listed here, and will be described in more detail in the later section "Building the Business Case".

Typical BUSINESS Benefits of Data Warehousing

- **Better business decisions**
- **Greater organizational efficiency**
- **Greater efficiency in the future cost of reporting**
- **Increase in market share**
- **Increase in sales and/or profitability**
- **Improvement in service effectiveness and efficiency**
- **Optimization of inventory and order fulfillment**
- **Enterprise-wide accountability**
- **Prerequisite for Artificial Intelligence/Machine Learning/Predictive Analytics**
- **Perceived value of company**
- **Ability to discover opportunities that would not otherwise be found, such as: sales niches, developing markets, product/service optimization, operating efficiency.**

Technical Benefits of Data Warehouse AUTOMATION

Given that you want to develop a DW, should you use data warehouse automation (DWA) tools? Recent developments have made this a no-brainer: The question is no longer "should you" but now "Which DWA tool(s) should I use?". While the answer to this is largely dependent on your individual situation, we will examine some of the benefits we expect from our DWA tools.

Data Warehousing Automation (DWA) tools are now easily affordable for even small companies. Even more exciting, DWA tools are now friendly enough to use totally in-house, avoiding the brain-drain of using costly outside consultants. Using DWA, even a small company with a single DBA can successfully—and affordably—build a data warehouse completely in-house. And a large company can bring total management of its DW back in-house, with all the great benefits of security, privacy, talent retention, and corporate knowledge retention, along with a significant drop in life cycle cost.

In some cases, DWA can be used to save face and salvage a failing DW even late in the game. This is sometimes possible by quickly refactoring the dysfunctional DW from the inside out, while using the insights that were learned during the original project.

Let's take a look at the pros and cons of using Data Warehouse Automation tools, and then see how recent developments in this market have virtually eliminated the down-side.

DWA benefits
- **Saves Time and Money: Reduces schedule, labor, and costs throughout the entire DW life cycle**
- **Reduces Risk, Improves Quality: DWA tools automatically produce consistent, tested, high-performance code**
- **Friendly: Tools can be used in-house, and do not require DW specialists**
- **Agile, Flexible, Adaptable: quickly and easily adapt to changing business requirements**
- **Excellent for DevOps and teamwork**
- **Facilitates rapid prototyping**
- **Easy deployment to dedicated servers, or to the Cloud**
- **Greater confidence and consistency: less testing required**

First and foremost, a data warehouse automation tool dramatically reduces development time and labor costs. It's Fast. This immediately leads to increased productivity, reduced delay of production systems, and a large reduction of manual effort. This also enables rapid prototyping like never before. This first benefit is a game-changer all by itself, but DWA holds many other advantages.

DWA tools produce tested, high-performance code in a consistent and methodical way. This reduces risk while improving quality. The tools incorporate best practices, common conventions, and naming standards. This facilitates efficient and successful teamwork.

DWA goes hand-in-hand with agile development methodologies, as well as the DevOps approach to smoothly integrated development and operations phases. The radically fast development and tool-coordinated methodology are conducive to agile module assignments in a team environment. The flexible nature of the tools allow developers to quickly adapt to changing business requirements. Data warehouse support can be shifted to ops staff with far less training. Maintainability is improved.

DWA tools are friendly and do not require data warehousing specialists. These tools can be used in-house by I.T. generalists, avoiding the need for expensive consultants. Subject matter experts are able to devote more time to reporting and data analysis, instead of tedious ETL coding.

Data warehouse automation tools ease deployment to dedicated servers, or to the Cloud.

Much drudgery is relieved by using DWA:

- Tedious requirement gathering
- Building data models, then schema and databases
- Mapping sources to targets
- Specification and design of transforms
- Hand-crafting ETL

- Manual testing of ETL
- Loading initial start-up data

Now let's look at the historical reasons against using DWA.

Spin-up Time:

Does the time required to learn the tool exceed the time-savings of using it? This is extremely unlikely, as most recent DWA tools are friendly and easy to learn. Novice warehouse developers will gain huge time-savings when using a DWA tool. While it is possible that a seasoned data warehouse developer may experience only a modest net time-savings in using the tool, the many other benefits of DWA will far outshine the meager investment in spin-up time required. Also note that most tools provide a mechanism for customization by an experienced developer. So even if you want to test out a clever new idea by customizing an ETL process, you still benefit from being freed up from the drudgery of the rest of the design, and you still benefit from viewing the code that the tool writes, as a helpful comparison. Your customization generally can be plugged into a hook in the DWA tool's overall solution. Win-win.

Cost of the tool license, and fees of any consultants needed to use the tool:

While it is true that early entries in the DWA market were quite expensive and pushed costly consultant fees, this is no longer true across the entire market. There are now DWA tools that are both inexpensive and friendly enough to use in-house.

Can an expert in the underlying native database tools (SQL Server, etc), by using the latest features, create higher-performance code than the DWA tool achieves?:

This is a fair criticism. There is a lag-time before new features of the underlying DB tools are incorporated into the DWA. Also, the DWA will avoid depending on a latest-version of the underlying DB tools, in favor of providing a more generic solution. It is also true that product support is better at the underlying-tool level than the DWA level. So the expert may be able to code higher performance, by using the latest features of the underlying tools. However, as noted above, the DWA *allows the expert to make this customization*. The expert still benefits from the DWA by escaping drudgery, easing teamwork, and all the other previously-mentioned benefits. Again, a win-win.

Is the DWA tool overkill?:

Overkill occurs when cost exceeds benefit. New DWA tools are low-cost and easy to learn, so their benefits far exceed their costs and it is not overkill.

In summary, using a DWA tool to develop your data warehouse is now an important factor for success. Most DW professionals would say a DWA tool is an essential necessity. The downsides of the past are no longer true.

Why An Expert Database Architect, Who Plans to Design Revolutionary Customized Code, Should Nevertheless Use a DWA Tool Anyway

It's simple, really. Suppose all the world ran on gas-fueled automobiles, and I want to invent a revolutionary ELECTRIC car. For my first prototype, I would most definitely take a gasoline car, remove the engine, and concentrate on designing/integrating my super innovative electric motor. I would most definitely not reinvent the wheel, literally. I would not waste time debating departing from standards like which side the driver sits on.   So get an appropriate DWA tool that will free you from the drudgery aspects of development, allowing you to focus on your revolutionary customizations within the clearly marked boundaries you set. You will not need to explain the DW's every detail and every line of code to every member of your DevOps. Instead, you present your high-level architecture, and point to the DWA tool for teamwork, standards, best practices, patterns, and conformity. You will need to go into detail only on your clearly-delineated custom module, where you can focus on your revolutionary code.

Agile Development

DWA is used throughout the DW life cycle, and in most cases never really ends, as the DW itself grows like some kind of living organism, with no planned "completion" date. These growth changes may result, quite likely, from intelligence garnered by use of the DW itself. For example, mining the DW may reveal a hitherto unknown correlation between a market segment and an overlooked product feature; the company moves to explore and capitalize on this discovery, which includes collecting more detailed information about these market and product areas, which necessitates changes in the DW and its sources. Agile Development and DWA go hand-in-hand. Even widely-accepted Best Practices tend to slowly morph over time, adapting to changes in technology. Develop small modules quickly. Deploy early and frequently. Welcome changing requirements from your data consumers and other interested parties, and implement these new requirements sooner rather than later.

3.   Proposal Phase

Perhaps you are anxious to start building your DW prototype and would like to remind me at this point that I promised to "stick to the relevant topics that are important to someone who actually wants to build a DW as soon as possible". Yet I also promised to maximize success and avoid pitfalls. Planning is a necessary step. Even if you are a CEO/Owner, and answer to no one, you must make a plan for success. If you don't visualize the business benefits, they are unlikely to magically appear. Luckily, in most cases the necessary planning can be done quite quickly.

⚠ *PITFALL: Building a DW without planning specific and realistic business benefits.*

Every company/organization has its own procedures for proposing and authorizing internal projects and programs; however, incorporating the steps below into your process will greatly aid you in creating a low-risk proposal/plan for developing a data warehouse. Each of these steps will be discussed in detail in the following sections.

1.   Identify Your Subject Matter Experts (SMEs)
2.   Planning Your Business Case
3.   Sketch a Strawman
4.   Evangelize and Secure Buy-in at All Levels
5.   Select a Short List of Vendors/Products
6.   Plan for Security and Privacy (Now!)
7.   Create a Rapid Prototype/Proof of Concept
8.   Choose Winning Technology and Tools
9.   Plan Schedule & Budget for the DevOps Pilot Phase
10. Plan any Organizational Impact
11. Plan Training

Your proposal will detail schedule & budget for a pilot project (the first deployment of an agile data warehouse), *and will also* outline an ongoing multi-phase DW *program*.

Identify Your Subject Matter Experts (SMEs)

What is an SME? Why do I need them? Why is this the first step?

Your subject matter experts are your in-house staff that are most knowledgeable about the story of your data:

- Where to find it
- How to access it
- What it represents (including data definitions)
- Where it came from
- How your current reporting systems work
- How your information systems work

They are usually in an Information Systems department or an Information Technology group. They have titles like Data Analyst, Database Designer, Systems Architect, Database Administrator (DBA), Business Analyst, Systems Programmer, etc. You need them because they have all the answers about the story of your data, and because they are essential to efficient development of the DW. This is your first step because it makes all the following steps faster and more optimal.

 PITFALL: Blindsiding your SMEs or other critical staff.

Your task is to assemble a small working group of SMEs to provide the expertise for smooth sailing through the rest of the proposal-phase steps. Note that "experience in data warehousing" is *not* a required skill for an SME. While this skill is certainly a huge asset if you can find it in an in-house SME, it is not essential and by far not the most important. Buy a good book on the subject and pass it around your group to familiarize them with overall goals and techniques, but it is not necessary to become an expert in the design theory. Plan to use an inexpensive Data Warehouse Automation tool (such as the free trial at DataWarehouseWiz.com) to automatically write the DW code and to implement best practices in the design. Later chapters of this book will show you how to build a data warehouse step-by-step hands-on, with minimal theory. For general theory, we recommend "Star Schema: The Complete Reference", by Christopher Adamson[1] or the classic "The Data Warehouse Toolkit", by Ralph Kimball and Margy Ross[2].

Planning Your Business Case

Your business case will start out as a rough draft, and you will refine it as you follow the proposal steps below. At this stage though, you should make a first attempt at specifying the expected business benefits of your DW program. Planning for these benefits is an essential part of your business case. By the end of the proposal phase, these business benefits must be clear, specific, and realistic. They should also be quantified wherever possible, and to the greatest degree possible. More DW failures are caused by a lack of realistic goals for business benefit, than for any other reason.

A DW that does not live up to its business case, and meet its written objectives, will almost always be viewed as a failure. Sadly, this DW may avail real--but unforeseen--benefits without getting due credit: It remains a designated failure. Just for fun, and as a cautionary tale against poor planning, let's take a fast look at some poor (but common) DW business cases that sometimes lead to complete program failure.

Avoid: "The Bridge to Nowhere"

This case is based solely on technical benefits without specifying any business benefits. Lacking any real business goals, this all-too-common case has the highest failure rate. If you have not visualized specific business benefits, can you really expect them to magically appear?

Avoid: "Lottery Ticket"

This case is not based on anything at all, other than a gut instinct or peer pressure. "Just do it". The gut instinct is probably correct (great potential opportunities exist in DW), but to act on it without further definition of business objectives is foolhardy. Often stemming from the misconception that a DW is self-justifying, this case too is likely to fail. Yes, it is possible that the DW team will blindly stumble into a significant benefit; however, this is much more likely if you are actively looking for it!

Avoid: "Robotic Replacements"

"The DW will reduce our operational information systems costs, and will cut our I.S./reporting costs by xx%." This is another common justification which is completely unfounded. How, exactly, will these cost reductions be accomplished? Answer: They won't be. Not gonna happen. Building a DW is not like replacing humans with robots; you still need everybody you had before--plus more.

Avoid: "Art Collection"

This one is a CEO's showcase for bragging rights. "And on this wall, I've mounted our DATA WAREHOUSE, which I purchased for $1.5M from elite designers BigBucks Consulting Inc." The only benefit is if investors/etc are impressed. Don't expect anything more from it.

Avoid: "Pin the Tail on the Donkey"

An outside consulting firm convinces a CEO/CTO to award them a DW contract while keeping his in-house I.T. department completely in the dark (under the pretext that staff would "resist change"). After this successful blindfolding, the consultants spin the exec around and tell him which way to go. It winds up a financial success—but only for the consulting company. Yes, this really happens. Don't be that guy.

⚠ PITFALL: Bypassing your SMEs or other critical staff.

Good: "Basic and Applied Research"

We've looked at some bad ways to begin a DW program, so what is a good way?

Forget trying to treat it like a typical information technology project, and approach it more like a scientific research program.

⚠ *PITFALL: Failing to recognize that a DW is more like a Basic Research Program than an ordinary I.T. project.*

Firstly, recognize that, unlike a typical project, a DW has no end date. It is, rather, an ongoing program with multiple phases of progressive deployments, characterized by business requirements that change over time. Similar to R&D.

Consider the three forms of research, as defined by the Organisation for Economic Co-operation and Development:

- *Basic research* is experimental or theoretical work undertaken primarily to acquire new knowledge about observable phenomena and facts, not directed toward any particular use.
- *Applied research* is original investigation to acquire new knowledge directed primarily towards a specific practical aim or objective.
- *Experimental development* is systematic effort, based on existing knowledge from research or practical experience, directed toward creating novel or improved materials, products, devices, processes, systems, or services.

This is exactly how the most successful data warehouse programs work!

The *DW itself* is akin to *Basic Research*: it is an organized and categorized collection of all knowledge known about a particular subject. In our case, the particular subject is our company, its environment, and its market.

Data mining in the DW is akin to *Applied Research*: we tease out patterns from the DW in an effort to discover methods & opportunities to further specific company goals. For example, we may be seeking ways to garner market share, increase profitability, or improve our services & efficiency.

The third analogy, to *Experimental Development*, is a bit of a stretch, but let's continue with it anyway. Next, the company needs *projects* (the "development"), not part of the DW *per se*, to take advantage of the methods/opportunities discovered from the data mining. So if our data mining has discovered a way to garner market share, then we need to develop a marketing campaign, or whatever, to seize this opportunity. It is only within this third phase that most of our business benefits are truly realized. Yet this was only made possible by the data-mining/applied-research, which in turn was only possible after the DW/basic-research. And that is an important moral-of-the-story that you gain from these analogies. Use this to frame a successful business case.

So the majority of the business benefits do not magically appear just because you developed a DW. Yet in the hands of a data analyst, business analyst, or motivated CEO, the targeted use of the DW will reveal methods & opportunities to achieve business goals. And then you do the work to implement these methods and seize these opportunities, finally realizing the business benefits. [Note: "finally" can come quite quickly. One company closed a $1.5M sale that happened directly as a result of discovering the opportunity through their one-month-old DW.]

Thus, a DW program is in many ways similar to classic research & development (R&D) programs, which are notoriously difficult to manage, especially in terms of predicting return-on-investment (ROI). While the DW program manager has some advantages over classic R&D (peer successes demonstrate that golden opportunities likely exist in your data, and the subject matter is well known), quantifying the benefits in a cost-benefit analysis is still quite difficult. One rule-of-thumb is that the more data you have, the more likely you will mine golden opportunities from it. A newly available way to reduce risk is to simply minimize the cost side of the cost-benefit analysis for the initial pilot. Only a few years ago, many companies needed about $1M just to deploy their initial pilot DW (materials, licenses, fees, and labor). Now, using cloud services like AWS, and development-accelerating DWA tools like DataWarehouseWiz, companies can deploy a pilot for a few thousand dollars or even less. Lower cost means lower risk, and when the pilot proves itself by revealing opportunities, this return justifies the next phase of progressive agile development & deployment.

None of this is meant to dissuade you from developing a DW. On the contrary, there is more motivation than ever before. From the daily news, we see a constant flow of success stories. We see exciting accomplishments, like finding planets outside of our solar system, that stemmed from the use of data warehouses. In the cost-benefit analyses, the costs have never been lower and the benefits have never been greater. Yet to maximize your chances for success, you should:

- Determine business benefits that are realistic and probable

- Include in your pilot, not only the development of the DW, but also its use (data analysis) in efforts to bring about these benefits

- Use agile development methods, and make frequent deployments to production of rapidly-developed small modules, while using the DW continuously to mine benefits starting at the earliest deployment

- Control your risk by controlling costs, especially in the pilot and first agile deployments. Focus initially on the "low-hanging fruit": the fact tables and data marts that will most quickly, and most likely, lead to significant benefits

With that pep talk, you should now start on your first draft of potential business benefits for your business case. You must conceive benefits that are appropriate for your particular business, of course, but it is helpful to review some typical ones. Let's take a closer look at the DW business benefits of Chapter 1.

Better business decisions

The DW provides increased accuracy and availability of your company's data, which in turn facilitates better-informed business decisions. The "single source of the truth" aspect of DW also improves consistency and accuracy, and therefore also the quality of decisions. The "History Retention" aspect of DW allows you to include complete knowledge of your subject's history in your business decisions.

Greater organizational efficiency

The DW's greater end-user productivity and reduced time-demands on critical resources (human and hardware) leads to an increase in efficiency and a resource multiplier: you can accomplish much more with existing or meagerly augmented staff.

This is not the same as saying the DW will result in operational cost reductions in the I.S. department. Although this may be a fairly common justification put forth, it almost never comes true. Instead, the greater efficiency comes from increasing the numerator (reaping greater returns), not from decreasing the denominator (the operational costs). Truth is, your overall operational costs will almost certainly increase. You will not be doing "more with less"; you will be doing "an order of magnitude more with only a modest increase in costs", even though that does not roll off the tongue very well. You are not replacing anybody with robots. All the staff that you needed to run your operational systems will still do so and will still be needed. Plus, it is likely that you will need two to nine additional staff for the DW. The benefit comes from the huge increase in your organization's overall output and productivity. The DW will create an additional operating cost, but hopefully will reap benefits many times the investment. Any reduction in operating costs will not come from eliminating skilled I.T. Staff, but from cost-reduction insights mined from the DW.

Reduction in the future cost of reporting

This reduction, in the *future* cost of reporting, is attained in the overall life cycle of the information-delivery systems. Here we make the case that, *without* a DW, our reporting costs on our legacy systems are projected to grow dramatically: perhaps exponentially, but at least linearly. In many companies, this is a very realistic projection. Furthermore, in the alternative scenario *with* a DW (after its initial development expenditure), these reporting costs flatten or at most grow very slowly. Thus, with the DW we anticipate saving substantial money from the future costs that would have been incurred otherwise. This is analogous to "saving" money with store coupons, or when we go shopping for a quart of Product X, and the store claims "You save 50% on the gallon size!". We spend more now, but we "save" a significant portion of the future cost if it is true that we would have consumed that much product anyway. That's right, this benefit of a DW is basically a Savings Coupon for (almost) Unlimited Reporting, If You Buy Now! Seriously, this is a common and substantial benefit that most companies can realize. Another advantage of this benefit is that it often can be quantified more accurately than most.

Increase in market share

Using the DW to discover ways and opportunities to increase market share, perhaps by setting strategic price points or through targeted marketing campaigns.

Increase in sales and/or profitability

Using the DW to discover ways and opportunities to increase sales and/or profitability, perhaps by finding up-sell/cross-sell opportunities, by developing markets, or by using targeted pricing. DW applied to collections activities can increase recovery while reducing overall collection costs.

Improvement in service effectiveness and efficiency

Especially important to non-profits and government agencies, this benefit is using the DW to discover ways and opportunities to improve the effectiveness and efficiency of the organization's services, thus producing a force-multiplier in the organization's overall efficacy.

Optimization of inventory and order fulfillment

JIT manufacturing, JIT inventory, minimize order fulfillment delays.

Enterprise-wide accountability

Provide enterprise-wide visibility and accountability among autonomous profit centers. For example, a conglomerate of diverse subsidiaries can finally view unified and consistent reports, down to fine detail, of all activity across the entire enterprise. This yields benefits of better management and opportunities for vertical marketing and cross-marketing.

Prerequisite for AI/ML/Predictive Analytics

The standardized format of the DW (star schema) facilitates data mining, and prepares the data for artificial intelligence, machine learning, and predictive analytics. In fact, building a DW is almost always a prerequisite for these advanced techniques. Using your DW as a step toward automatic data mining with AI/ML opens the door for a force-multiplier of all the previously-described benefits.

Perceived value of company

Operating a data warehouse may increase company valuation in the eyes of investors. For many companies, their databases are their greatest asset. Many small companies are being purchased simply for their databases. A data warehouse makes the value of the databases much more evident.

Once you have chosen your goals for business benefits, you are ready to sketch out a strawman plan.

Sketch a Strawman

Before you do anything else, including any more planning, take two days or so to chalk out an architecture strawman. The strawman is a high-level architecture plan, perhaps scribbled on a whiteboard or shared on a team collaboration board, accompanied by a spreadsheet of ballpark calculations and snap decisions. It has components with just enough detail to gain confidence that the DW can be designed within a certain schedule and budget, that basic functional and business requirements will be met, and that there are no technological gaps that would hinder development. The strawman does *not* need to be optimal, just plausible. Nor should you agonize over decisions at this point. The point of the strawman is to prove that it *can be done*, to offer a plausible solution that *would work*, and to provide a baseline solution **against which all other solutions can be compared**. Note that since there is no preconceived end date, the schedule and budget are estimated generally for a deployment of a functional warehouse according to the data sources as they currently exist. Separate long-range DevOps efforts should be budgeted for the operation and agile growth of the DW.

Following are step-by-step guidelines for sketching your strawman. Each of these steps could easily be argued over for several months, with heated debates over what is most optimal. That is not what you want for the strawman. You want to quickly—very quickly—determine a *plausible* solution, so that you have a baseline solution to show and talk about. You will introduce it as a strawman for discussion purposes, not as your proposal for a final architecture. As other ideas are considered and debated, you now have a base solution to compare with. This greatly accelerates the debating process. There is no loss of face if large sections of the strawman are replaced by better ideas; it is only a strawman and will have served its purpose.

Identify what data will be included in your warehouse

Bottom line: the big boss wants ALL OF IT. Every bit of data from your operations databases, excepting those "temp" tables that you bulk-loaded last year and never got around to dropping. The real question is what to include first, in the first data mart. Eventually, the DW will include all data available.

Identify the type of schema you will implement in the end-user warehouse

Bottom line: Star-schema, because that is the most common in use today. Kimball, and conformed dimensions. Because that way, every newcomer joining the DevOps teams can spin up quickly on your DW: "Oh yeah, it's a star-schema with conformed dimensions. Got it." If you (or the SME) are not familiar with data warehousing, buy a Kimball book[2], or download educational materials from the internet. Note though, it is not necessary that you become a data warehousing expert. Your DWA tool will handle the tricky details of coding the DW processes to best practices. You need only learn the basic concepts of a star-schema warehouse.

This document herewith will give you the highlights of data warehousing principles, but--in keeping with our objectives of pragmatism and conciseness— will not discuss much theory and rationale.

Identify the underlying DBMS technology for your warehouse

If your company already uses a good database management system (DBMS), and therefore has licenses and trained people, then that is probably your choice for the strawman. If not, and your data sources are rather small (< 10 GB), then start with the free version of Microsoft SQL Server Express Edition. [Some Advantages: 1) Free, 2) Very efficient Change Data Capture, 3) Helpful SQL Agent job scheduler, 4) Powerful SSIS & SSAS] Otherwise, choose a DBMS that is supported by both Amazon Web Services (AWS) and your choice of DWA tool. Note that the full Microsoft SQL Server is available as a managed service on AWS, and that this forms a cost-effective scalable solution for small through huge data warehouses. Microsoft SQL Server is a popular choice for DBMS due to its consistently high level ratings in performance, security, and availability.

⚠ *PITFALL: Tediously building a DW without help from a data warehouse automation tool (DWA).*

Identify your DWA tool

Choose a tool that:

- supports your DBMS
- is cost-effective
- is friendly enough to learn and use quickly in-house
- provides the key time-and-labor saving features without cornering you into relying on high-priced consultants or expensive ETL run-time licenses.

Additional features can be very helpful, but not if they come at the cost of eliminating one of the above four bullet points. A DWA tool that meets these requirements very well is Data Warehouse Wiz, from DataWarehouseWiz.com. This delightful DWA tool also offers a 100%-functional free trial period that is long enough to develop your first data warehouse.

Plan your client interface

How will your Data Consumers view reports? How will they create or order reports? What analysis tools will be available to them? If you plan to use AI/Machine Learning/Predictive Analytics, what type of interface will facilitate? Your wonderful new DW will produce big benefits only if you provide a friendly and powerful client interface to your Data Consumers (analysts, execs, managers, marketeers, AIs, etc).

A good strawman candidate for the analysis tools is Microsoft SQL Server Analysis Services (SSAS). This powerful and popular business-intelligence tool can easily aggregate and cube your DW data, and slice it and dice it in every imaginable way. Your star-schema DW is in the perfect format for SSAS to data-mine. And, of course, it plays very nicely with SQL Server DBMS. SSAS supports the popular R and Python programming languages for machine learning. SSAS is available in the cloud through AWS and Azure.

Most DW implementations include a web client interface for data consumers to create and view reports, and to visualize the results. This is a web app that the data consumers reach through their favorite web browser. It often includes visualization features such as charting and graphing, perhaps via a third-party charting package. Usually, the reports can be downloaded as spreadsheets.

Scope out disk storage space

Scope out the amount of disk storage that will be needed for your staging and warehouse databases. Make your first guesstimates overly high to see what ballpark you end up in. Begin by assuming you will use all source data (as in Strawman Step 1) and adding up the current storage requirements of your present sources, to get a total number of GB or TB. Now double that, to account for extra storage needed for denormalization, meta data, SCDs, and additional indexes. Double again, to account for storage needed by both staging and warehouse databases. Guess at the yearly growth rate of your data, and add in growth for at least the first year. When estimating growth, remember that many DWs are designed to hold all history forever, as opposed to transactional DBs which are often trimmed to a fiscal year and/or overwritten by newer information. Therefore, your DW will tend to grow faster than your transactional DBs.

On the side, scope out an additional server to hold database backups, with disk storage equal to the current total estimate (this assumes that backups of both Staging and Warehouse will compress 50 – 67%, but that you will always retain the latest two backups, and have extra room for the backup-in-progress). If you plan to implement high availability by duplicating the warehouse db, add in the required storage. If you want a separate 100% functional test/QA platform—which is highly desirable—double your totals once again. If you have better methods available to guesstimate, then by all means use them—but in general, guess high.

Scope out your target platform

Now examine your total guesstimate of required disk storage. Do you have that much space accessible to servers that are licensed with your DBMS? Or maybe you can add that much disk-space and stay within budget? [Note, however, that it is highly recommended to place your Staging and Warehouse on a server separate from your critical operations, so that there is no contention for resources.] If your answer is a confident "Yes", then you have a reasonable solution in hand.

Otherwise, price out a solution in the cloud, in Amazon Web Services (AWS). I hear you saying "What?...Wait, can we talk about this?". Remember, we are quickly sketching out a plausible strawman at this point, not delaying to determine the perfect optimal solution. Building your own physical server licensed for your DBMS, with access to big disk-space, can be a very expensive front-loaded cost that requires very detailed and accurate estimates of CPU demand, RAM, disk subsystem and size requirements projected over three years, not to mention DBMS license requirements which sometimes dwarf the hardware cost. **AWS has none of these problems.** AWS supports six major DBMS's, with the licensing costs rolled into the monthly "rental" fee of your virtual machines. You can begin by renting a lean configuration with the minimal CPU, RAM, disk, and DBMS required for today and today only. This solution scales easily and seamlessly. When you need more (CPU, RAM, etc) you simply pay for more and get it promptly. If you find that your configuration is overkill, you can downgrade to less and pay less. You are even less committed to a particular DBMS, since you did not lay out huge license fees. You can take your guesstimate of total disk storage size, along with your other guesstimates (CPU, RAM, DBMS), and quickly estimate AWS costs on the AWS website. Even if you intend to build your own physical servers in the long run, it may well be beneficial to start your first DW deployment on AWS (or your favorite cloud) and shake out all the details there, thus leading to solid detailed projections on your requirements for rolling your own servers. AWS even offers free and reduced-cost cloud solutions for a trial period which is long enough to develop your first DW. AWS is a low-cost and extremely low-risk platform for your DW prototype.

Another good cloud option is Microsoft's Azure cloud services.

Identify Security and Privacy Plan

Plan your methods of security and privacy now, before creating your first database table or designing your first web page. Done early, security planning is fairly straight-forward. Done late, security planning can be incredibly expensive or nearly impossible to get right.

⚠ *PITFALL: Postponing planning for security and privacy.*

The details are specific to your case, but here are some things to consider:

- Role-based DBMS access. Usually helpful to define distinct roles, such as Developer, Data Consumer, ETL Process, DBA. Each role is allowed only the minimum privileges needed for the task.

- Data Consumers, the end users, generally only need read access to the warehouse database.

- ETL Process, the scheduled process that you will design (via your DWA tool!) to load new data into your warehouse, generally needs read access to Sources, and read/write/execute to staging & warehouse DBs.

- Developers, the staff using the DWA tool, generally need read access to the Sources and owner-access (read/write/create/drop/execute) to the staging and warehouse databases.

- DBAs, the database administrators, need complete admin access to monitor and maintain the databases. Each DBA should have a unique username for login.

- Never share logins for any DW users. Promptly disable logins for anyone who terminates from the company. Promptly disable logins for outside consultants/partners/etc after their contracts are complete. Never give outsiders admin/root access, nor the ability to create additional usernames.

- Consider using database encryption. SQL Server includes the seamless "Always Encrypted" capability since the 2016 edition.

- Will your user interface include a web client? Use HTTPS, TLS1.2, login authentication, and password security (latest standards for hashing/etc).

Consider whether IP security is appropriate. Separate access from IoT (Internet of Things). Create the Login Page before any other part of the user interface, and make it rock solid secure. Then create a Template Page to be used for all other pages to be developed. Ensure that this template page requires that the user be logged in through your Login Page, and that the user's session has not expired. Make the Template rock solid secure and require it to be used by your developers for every other page.

Identify your highest priority data mart(s)

This data mart will consist of a single fact table and a few dimensions. This first data mart should be important enough that it justifies the cost of DW development, at least through deployment of this first module. For many companies, this first data mart centers around sales transactions.

Scope out schedule and budget

Scope out the schedule and budget for the prototype, your first data mart. Estimate materials & services costs based on your strawman. Try to allow at least one to two weeks for designing the prototype with a DWA tool, even though it is possible to complete this within days or hours. It is better to use this first experience to carefully analyze the results of each step, and to fully understand how each step works. This also allows time for recursive improvements as you gain knowledge during this phase.

Now estimate a second schedule and budget, for the first year's DevOps. This will include materials & services costs for the first year, including hosting of a DW with the full data scoped out in the strawman step 1. Add in development labor estimates for the full DW. A typical DWA tool user can average three to seven DW tables per day, through design and testing. Add in one or more data analysts (or other data consumers) that will extract the true benefits of your DW by using it.

Evangelize and Secure Buy-in at All Levels

During your planning, you should recruit supporters from all levels at your company/organization. Seek out SMEs, decision makers, and data consumers.

Use your business case and strawman to sell your concept. Get buy-in from key players.

Select a Short List of Vendors/Products

Don't restrict yourself to using solely one tool. Rather than finding the "perfect tool that does it all", it is better to examine candidates that cost-effectively fulfill major functions. Compile a short list of products that may be helpful and are worth evaluating.

Plan for Security and Privacy (Now!)

Hopefully, you have planned for security and privacy within your strawman. In any case, make firm plans now, before beginning your rapid prototype. Done early, security planning is fairly straight-forward. Done late, security planning can be incredibly expensive or near impossible to get right. This cannot be stressed enough. Many companies have been embarrassed, and opened to financial risk, because their "demo laptop" allowed a data breach.

⚠ *PITFALL: Trusting an outside entity (vendor, partner, consultant, etc) with access to the bulk of your precious data.*

Another important consideration of your Security & Privacy plan is the limitation of exposure to outside entities, such as data-warehousing consultants, partners, or vendors. Outsiders will routinely ask for full access to all of your data and systems. They will ask for administrator/root access to all your Source systems. They will want to "profile" all of your data, often copying it off-site to their own servers, sometimes in foreign countries. They will say that this is both routine and necessary. Don't fall for that. *None of these things are necessary.* Also, ensure that all outside parties sign a non-disclosure agreement. Any outside parties should be given only logins created specifically for them, and said logins should have the minimum privileges necessary for the job, and never the privilege of creating other logins. Never, never, never admin/root privileges. Also, the logins should be deactivated upon completion of the contract. The outsiders do not need access to all of your data. Your in-house SMEs can do the data profiling, and do it better. The outsiders never need to download your data to their own systems, and certainly not to a foreign country.

Create a Rapid Prototype/Proof of Concept

Starting in Chapter 4, we will go through detailed step-by-step development of a rapid prototype. Should the prototype be built during the proposal stage? Or is the prototype part of the first-year efforts proposed? This is largely a question of cost & time. In the past, a prototype took so long and cost so much that it had to be budgeted and proposed as a project in itself. Today, however, prototypes can be built so fast and cheaply that they have become part of the planning process in proposals.

Choose Winning Technology and Tools

After building one or more prototype(s), and evaluating candidate tools, chose your winners. Revisit and revise your strawman, turning it into a detailed proposal plan.

Plan any Organizational Changes

Within your proposal, forecast the DevOps team for your DW. Plan for developers, maintainers/DBAs, data analysts. Maybe this is all just one person in a small company, but make a realistic plan anyway.

Plan Training

Plan training for the data consumers that will use your DW to gain the true business benefits.

Plan Schedule & Budget for the DevOps Pilot Phase

Revisit the schedule and budget of your strawman, to create a detailed first-year schedule and budget proposal.

4. Step-by-step Construction of a Rapid Prototype

Construction of our rapid prototype will be enabled by a DWA tool called Data Warehouse Wiz. This inexpensive tool has a fully-functional free trial period, which will allow you to actually build your own prototype by following these steps, without any financial commitment.

Data Warehouse Wiz (DWiz) is a software tool for the creation, loading, maintenance, and modular augmentation of data warehouses and data marts. By using this tool, you can dramatically reduce the development time needed for these tasks—especially in the ETL (*extract-transform-load*) processes required for both your end-user data warehouse database and the intermediate staging database.

DWiz provides the following benefits:

- Saves Time and Money: Reduces schedule, labor, and costs throughout the entire DW life cycle. Automates the tedious coding processes.

- Reduces Risk, Improves Quality: Automatically produces consistent, tested, high-performance code.

- Friendly enough to be used by in-house I.S. Staff, without the necessity of DW expertise, thus freeing you from reliance on outside consultants.

- Agile, Flexible, Adaptable: quickly and easily adapts to changing business requirements. Eases change management.

- Excellent for DevOps and teamwork.

- Facilitates rapid prototyping.

- Easy deployment to dedicated servers, or to the Cloud

- Greater confidence and consistency: less testing required

- Robustness: DW load errors are often caused by Source changes (e.g., schema changes) that were made without proactive thought to DW ramifications. These can be detected and handled gracefully. Most importantly, loads can be resumed efficiently and effectively (after error resolution) with no corruption and no data loss.

The latest downloads for Data Warehouse Wiz—software and manuals—are available from DataWarehouseWiz.com .

Don't make your development all about a mad race against time, thinking that this will make it more impressive. Using the DWA tool will already result in impressive schedule & budget savings over hand-crafting or outsourcing, and you won't gain anything by racing to shave off a few more days. It is much more important, when building your very first small data mart module with your DWA, to scrutinize each step of the way to thoroughly understand it. Your first working data mart module is likely to consist of one fact table and a few dimensions. While using the DWA for this first module, take the time at each step to understand what the tool is doing for you and how. In the staging and warehouse databases, look at the tables being created and examine how the stored procedures are coded by the DWA. See how source change management is handled, and how slowly-changing dimensions are handled, for example. Once you understand exactly how the tool performs its duties, you can trust it and fly through the development of all similar parts of your DW. When you come to a point of using other capabilities, perhaps the design of an Outrigger or Junk Dimension, then study these carefully during the first use.

5.   Overview of Data Warehouse Development Goals

The goal of DWA is to facilitate the design and maintenance of data warehouses and data marts, with the least amount of development time and labor. A good data warehouse is an extremely valuable tool for both the marketing and operational units of a company, providing the ability to run ad hoc reports on any element of the company that is covered by the warehouse/mart. Yet many companies are put off by the possibly onerous task of building a data warehouse. DataWarehouseWiz (DWiz) enables a company to perform this task quickly and efficiently with internal assets.

Much has been written about the design of data warehouses, with the most popular design strategies being those promoted by Ralph Kimball[2], or variants thereof. DWiz facilitates the design of a star-schema data warehouse that is compliant to the Kimball principles of dimensional modeling. Yet it also allows you to intentionally make exception from these principles, if and when you want to. You are always in the driver's seat. DWiz will help you throughout the design, generating the software code, but will always allow you to view, edit, augment, or override this code.

It is strongly recommended that you build your Warehouse in a separate server from your company's transactional databases, so there will be no competition for resources. You will also build a Staging database, preferably on the same server as the warehouse. This Staging database will handle all ETL (*extract-transform-load*) operations for the warehouse; it will host the collection and assembly of data from your company's source databases, and will handle the processing and transform of the data to a form usable by the warehouse. This version of DWiz assumes that you will build your Staging and Warehouse databases with Microsoft SQL Server (any version).

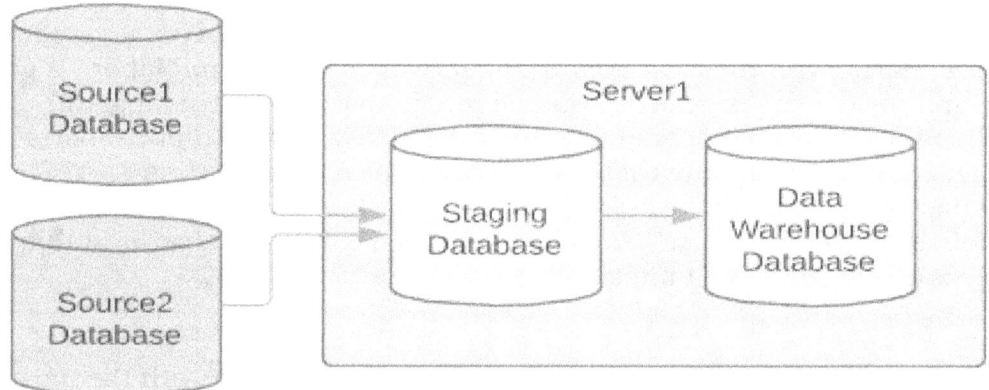

Illustration 2: Databases Needed for the Data Warehouse

As shown in the above diagram, in building your warehouse you will be concerned with three database areas:

- The WAREHOUSE, your desired goal of a powerful reporting platform
- The SOURCES, one or more existing databases (or files) that hold the raw data from your company's operational transactions
- The STAGING database, where we input differential raw data from the Sources, and transform it to forms usable by our desired Warehouse

Warehouse Database

The very basic star-schema warehouse begins with a Fact table and multiple Dimension tables. Fact tables hold "the numbers", mostly additive facts about transactions, some non-additive facts such as datetimes, and foreign keys to various dimensions. The Dimension tables hold all the other descriptive info about a particular dimension. So if you had a large stack of sales invoices, and wanted to make a data warehouse, you would probably create the following warehouse tables:

- Customer Dimension table, holding customer name, address, phone, etc.

- Product Dimension, holding product name, description, specs, etc.

- Salesperson Dimension holding employee name, etc.

- Date Dimension, holding the dates of sales with date-part columns (month, year,etc.)

- Invoice Fact table, holding rows with foreign keys pointing to the above tables for each line item, along with the sales price paid, cost-of-goods (for accounting) and any discount amounts.

So the Invoice Fact table forms the center of the star, and each row can be thought of as a point of intersection of all the dimensions. This very basic warehouse would facilitate a wealth of reports useful to sales, marketing, and inventory.

The following illustration shows the types of tables found in a data warehouse. These types include:

- Fact table—the central point of your star schema, holding mostly facts and measures (along with foreign-key pointers to the dimensions)

- Dimension table—a table that links to a Fact table, and holds attributes which describe points along a particular dimension

- Outrigger table—a table that inscribes another new outrigger dimension upon a Dimension table, which then allows fast searching of the new outrigger dimension within both the base dimension and, through it, the fact table

- Junk table—a table that efficiently collects miscellaneous "junk" (typically low-cardinality fields uncorrelated to any dimension)

- Bridge table—a table that establishes groupings, and in so doing resolves a design problem of a many-to-many relationship of a desired dimension by linking the one-to-one relationship of a grouping

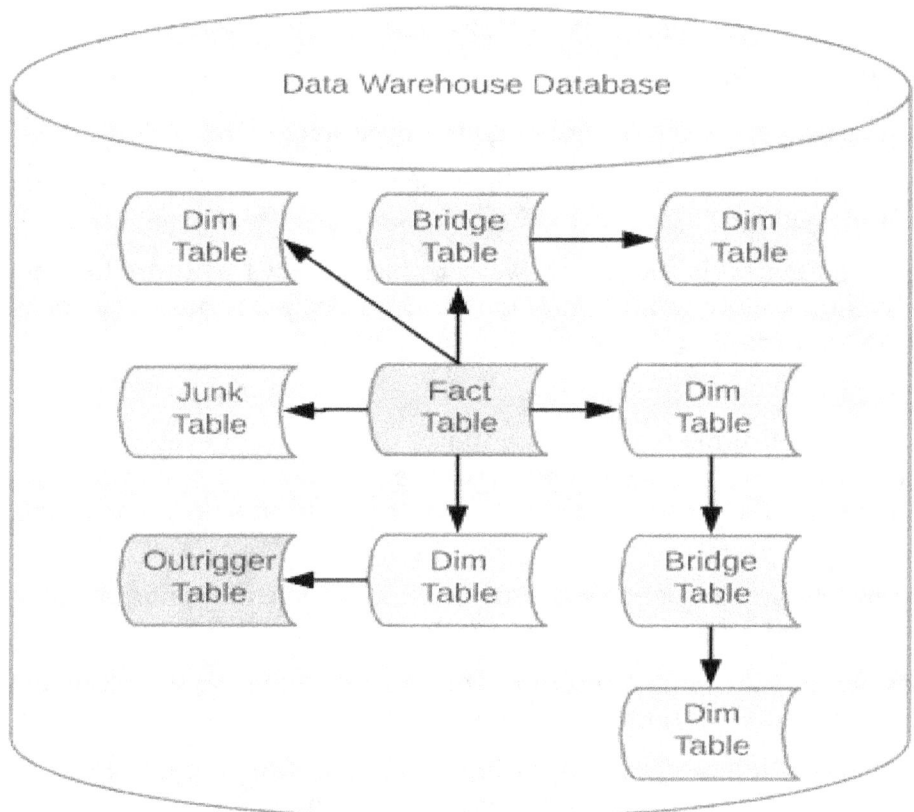

Illustration 3: Types of Tables in the Data Warehouse

Fact tables tend to be "tall and thin", meaning they have many rows (often millions, billions, or more), but each row uses as few bytes as possible. This is accomplished by restricting the Fact table to only two types of data:

- facts (Especially additive facts, such as counts, costs, prices. Sometimes dates.)
- foreign-key-pointers to the other tables (mainly Dimensions).

In contrast, Dimension tables tend to be "short and wide", with far fewer rows than the Fact tables, but with each row typically being wide with many de-normalized descriptive columns. These columns contain attributes with everything you would want to know about the dimension entry, in easily-understood forms. This enables the end-user to quickly and easily construct report queries that are also fast to run.

As the warehouse grows, various other types of tables may be desirable, such as Bridge, Outrigger, and Junk tables. These other table types are sometimes used to structure warehouse data in a way that facilitates high-performance reporting queries even while the basic dimensions are growing huge.

Staging Database

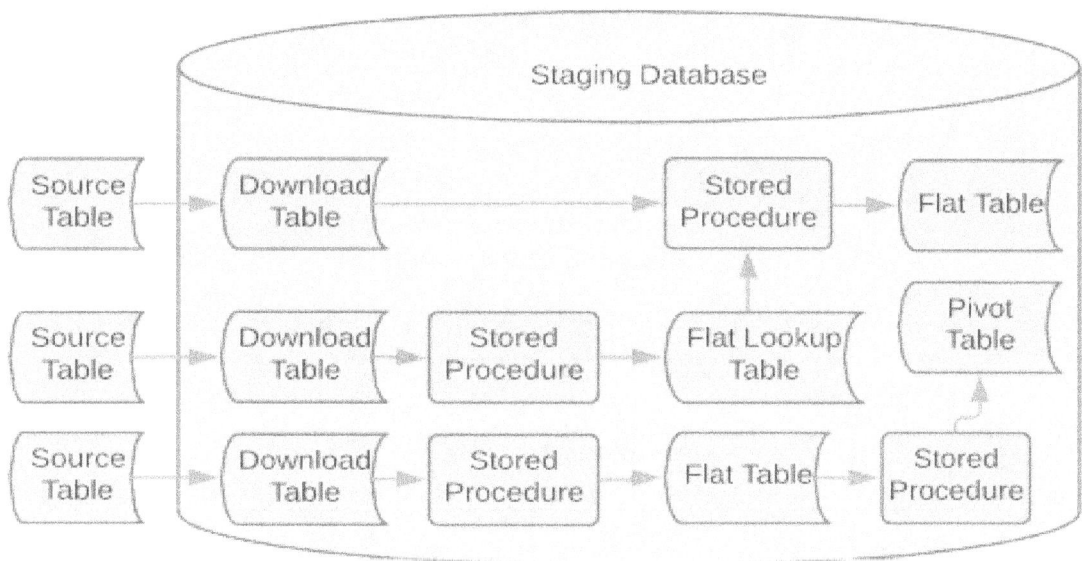

Illustration 4: Types of Tables Found in the Staging Database

The above illustration shows the types of tables found in the Staging database. Within the Staging database, we need:

- DOWNLOAD tables--to capture the data from your sources. A given

Download table has a one-to-one relationship with a table in your Source DB.

- FLAT tables--to assemble the transformed data in preparation for going to the warehouse. Each Flat table requires a Flat Procedure to feed it.

- Possibly PIVOT tables—to pivot certain source row data into new Flat column data. Each Pivot table requires a Pivot Procedure to feed it.

- Possibly helper tables, such as lookup tables, to assist in the transforms.

Source Database(s)

The Source tables typically come from your company's transactional operations database(s), as shown in the illustration below.

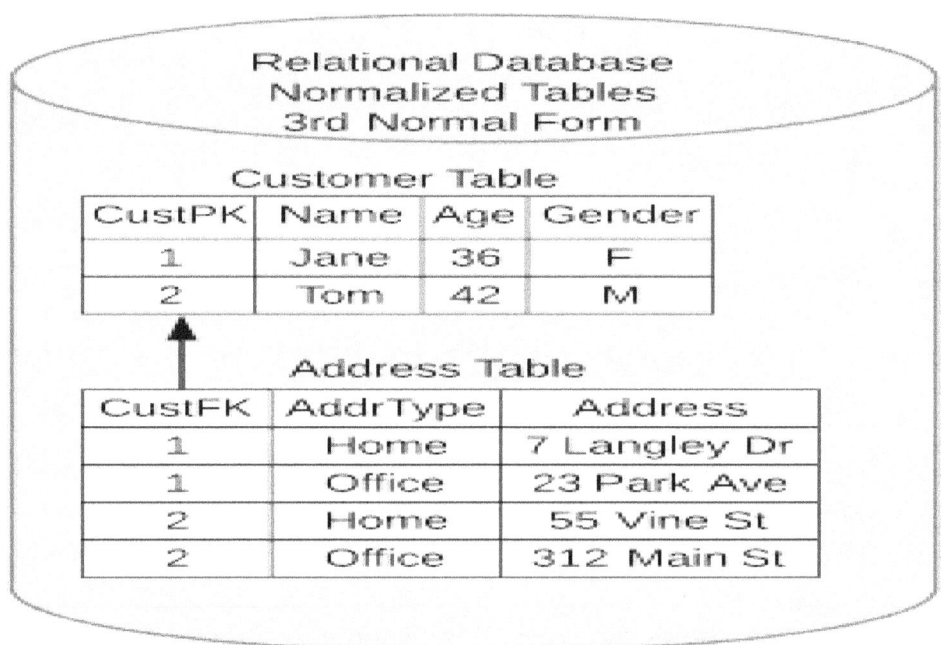

Ilustration 5: Typical Source Database in Normalized Form

Source tables are often in 3rd Normal Form, which is great for your operational DB, but not optimal for data warehousing and reporting. The task of the data warehouse ETL engine is to replicate and transform the data from your Sources into a standard data warehouse form, which is optimized for reporting.

ETL Groups

Constructing the data warehouse is typically done in modules that we term "ETL Groups", as shown in the next figure. An ETL Group may be thought of as a "project".

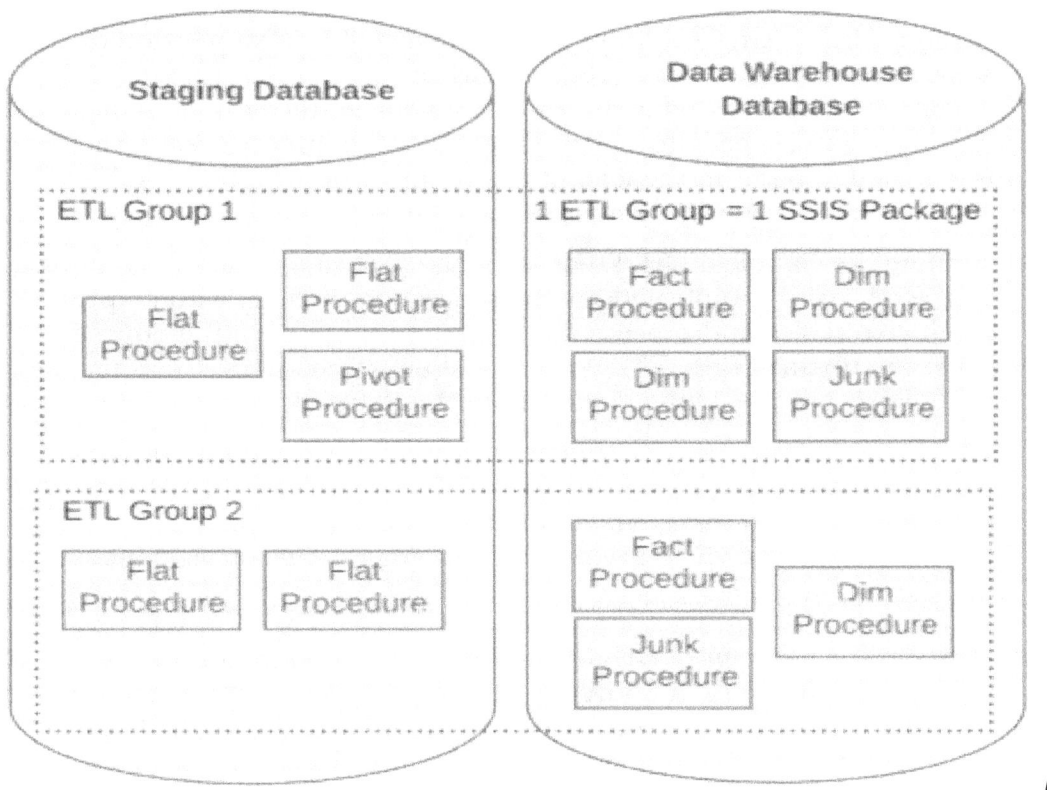

Ilustration 6: Visualization of ETL Groups

Each ETL Group will ultimately become a process that can be scheduled as a SQL Job in SQL Server. The agile development of an ETL Group (project) basically consists of these steps:

1. Creating an empty ETL Group.

2. Defining table schema for all the tables needed in the staging and warehouse databases. From these definitions, DWiz will write the code to create these tables, including meta-data columns for maintenance, but will not fill any data at this point.

3. Defining procedures to transform the Source data into forms usable for the warehouse. From these definitions, DWiz will write efficient code for the procedures, but will not execute the procedures yet (no data will be filled yet).

4. Compiling the ETL Group. DWiz will compile the complete ETL code for the group into a single SSIS package (preferred) or a single stored procedure (slightly easier). DWiz will write code so that this module can be run standalone. This includes code to efficiently extract changed data from the Sources, code to execute the transform procedures in the proper order, code to perform the load of the staging and warehouse tables, and code to maintain the warehouse.

5. Running the compiled ETL Process for the first time. This first run will be much larger than normal, as the process must start with empty warehouse tables and process all the current data from the Sources. Subsequent runs of the ETL Process will be much shorter, as they only need to process the changed data from the Sources.

6. Scheduling the process. At this point, the ETL Process can be scheduled like any other SQL Job, independent of DWiz. In fine agile development style, you can then use DWiz iteratively to add new tables and functionality to your ETL Process, or to design the next ETL process.

You start by defining an empty ETL Group for your intended purpose, such as "ETL_Invoices". Then choose a Source table that is rich in facts, such as "Invoices", and use DWiz to make a Download table for it in Staging (e.g., "DownloadInvoices"). Next, in the Source, determine all the related tables that will provide information, piece-wise, for dimensions--such as "Customer", "Product", "SalesPerson"--and make Download tables for them. Realizing the warehouse Dimension tables are intentionally denormalized, you often need to download multiple tables for a single dimension, such as source "Customer" and "Address" and "Phone" tables that will ultimately lead to a single "Customer Dimension". Each Download table has a one-to-one relationship with a single Source table. The Download tables are truncated at the beginning of each run of the ETL Group Process, and typically only the changes in the Source tables are then downloaded (dependent on the chosen Change Management method). Thus the "*Extract*" part of the ETL Process captures changes in the Source DB and puts them into the Download tables.

Next you will use DWiz to define the Flat tables, which stage the de-normalized data for all warehouse tables (Dimensions, Facts, Bridges, Outriggers, Junks). To define a Flat table, you need to look ahead to what will be needed by the end-goal warehouse tables. Each Dimension or Fact table typically will draw from a single Flat table. This being the case, you will define Flat tables that each combine elements from one or more Download tables. After the Flat tables are defined, you will use DWiz to define a Flat Procedure for each one, using the versatile Flat Procedure Definition Page form to specify any necessary joins (of Download tables) and any transforms on the data. Thus the Flat Procedures perform the "*Transform*" part of the ETL Process. Unlike the Download tables, the Flat tables are not truncated during the ETL Process, instead accumulating the complete history of the subject data. The goal of a Flat table is to stage all the data needed for a particular warehouse table, in the format required by the warehouse table, such that loading of the warehouse table can be efficient and straight-forward.

Once the Flats are designed, you use DWiz to define the Dimension tables in the Warehouse, and to define a Dimension Procedure to feed each one. Then use DWiz to design the Fact table and a Fact Procedure to feed it. At this point, the ETL Group can be compiled and tested as a self-contained module. It is important to note that this ETL Group Module can be run as a scheduled task (perhaps nightly, hourly, or every 15 minutes), independent of DWiz. You do not need to start DWiz in order to run the ETL module. Upon successful testing of the ETL Module, DWiz can be used to augment it with further tables and capabilities, or another ETL Group can be designed to run separately. You can add capabilities such as Bridges, Outriggers, Junks, Pivots, and Snapshots.

When a compiled ETL Group Module is run, it performs all *Extract-Transform-*

Load operations for that group:

- The **Extract** part of the process extracts data (typically delta changes only) from the Sources and fills the Download tables. Each Download table is a one-to-one pipeline from a Source table.

- The **Transform** part of the process, which is performed mostly in the Flat Procedures. This transforms and re-formats data from the Download tables, staging the results in the Flat tables. A given Flat table, which is in the de-normalized form favored for warehouse tables, may draw and transform data from multiple Download tables.

- The **Load** part of the process then determines what changes are needed by the warehouse tables, and loads them from the Flat tables. As the transformations have previously been accomplished by the Flat Procedures, a given warehouse table is typically loaded from a single Flat table.

- When the ETL Group Process is compiled and run, the data flows in stages:Download tables will be loaded from their corresponding Source tables/files, directly one-to-one.

- Each Flat table will be loaded with processed/transformed data from one or more Download tables--not necessarily one-to-one.

- Then the warehouse tables--Dims, Facts, Bridges, Junks, Outriggers, etc--will be loaded with data from Flat tables.

- In several places, Stored Procedures will be used to handle these ETL steps. These Stored Procedures handle all processing needed to fill and maintain the Flat tables and the warehouse tables (Dim, Fact, Bridge, Junk, Outrigger). Stored Procedures are small programs of SQL code that are embedded in the database itself. DWiz will write the Procedures for you, but will always give you an opportunity to view and modify the code if you wish.

Steps Needed to Design Any Data Warehouse

With the following steps, you can develop *any* data warehouse.

Start by creating empty Staging and Data Warehouse databases. Run DWiz and connect to your operational Source DB. Use DWiz to view the Source DB, and select a source table (such as Sales) to provide facts for a new Fact table in your first new data mart. DWiz will design a Download table in the Staging DB to capture the data changes of this table. Just click on this source table in DWiz, then complete a short simple form, and DWiz will create the Download table and design efficient Extract coding for the ETL. Downloading can be done incrementally using Change Tracking or Change Data Capture. You also have the option of downloading the whole table from the source database. DWiz automatically adds meta-data columns needed to track changes.

⚠ PITFALL: Choosing an inappropriate grain, or implementing inconsistent grains.

Next, decide on the grain, which is the lowest level of detail that will exist in your new Fact table. Note that often you will need to join multiple Source tables together to produce one de-normalized Fact table. For example, many company Source transactional DBs have separate tables for SalesInvoices and SalesInvoiceLineItems. These will be joined together to produce one de-normalized SalesInvoiceFact table, which will have the grain at the lowest detail available: each table row will correspond to a single line-item of an invoice.

Now, view your Source DB again and choose what tables will be needed to flesh out your Fact table and also to form the related Dimension tables for your star-schema data mart. Then use DWiz to quickly form Download tables and ETL for all your chosen tables. For example, if you have chosen Sales for your fact table, then you will also want to Download tables related to Sales, such as customer & customer info tables, sales employee tables, product info tables, and vendor info tables.

Next, use DWiz to form Flat tables in Staging that will have the de-normalized (flat) schema that will be needed for your warehouse Dimension tables. You can use DWiz to create these Flat tables by clicking the closest Download table, to use as a template, and then filling-in a simple form for the Flat table design.

DWiz automatically adds meta-data columns needed for tracking changes. In the same way, create a Flat table for your fact table, making sure to include a foreign key column for each of your dimension tables. Ensure that each Dimension maintains consistency with the grain of the Fact table.

Now use DWiz to design the "Transform" part of your ETL, which takes the differential input from the Download tables, applies transforms as needed (joins, filters, format changes, cleaning, and any other desired processing), and stages the output to your Flat tables. DWiz will design a SQL stored procedure for each Flat table, based upon your selections and inputs to a form called a "Flat Procedure Definition Page". After writing the code for a stored procedure, DWiz will display the entire source code (with nothing hidden) and even allow changes, before committing the new stored procedure to the Staging DB. DWiz automatically handles all meta-data columns and writes efficient code for the differential updates to the Flat tables. DWiz offers powerful options in the Definition Page, so that it can write robust and efficient code for you. DWiz can even write code to pivot tables for you—a common need for data marts.

Next, use DWiz to design and create your warehouse tables, starting with the Dimensions, and ending with the Fact table. You create these warehouse tables by clicking the closest Flat table, to use as a template, and then filling-in a simple form for the warehouse table design. DWiz automatically adds meta-data columns needed for tracking changes.

Now use DWiz to design the "Load" part of your ETL, which takes the differential changes from the Flat tables and loads the updates to your warehouse tables. DWiz will design a SQL stored procedure for each warehouse table, based upon your selections and inputs to a form. After writing the code for a stored procedure, DWiz will display the entire source code (with nothing hidden) and even allow changes, before committing the new stored procedure to the Warehouse DB. DWiz automatically handles all meta-data columns and writes efficient code for the differential updates to the warehouse tables.

Finally, use DWiz to assemble all the ETL code into one efficient SQL Server Integration Services (SSIS) package. This package is your "ETL Process". [As an alternative option, DWiz instead can create a single ETL group stored procedure instead, which serves as the ETL Process.] When designing this ETL Process, DWiz automatically sequences all the parts of the ETL, from "Extracting to Download Tables" through carefully ordered "Loading to the Warehouse Tables". Congratulations, you have completed a first data mart of one business area. The first time that you run the ETL Process (SSIS package or group stored procedure), it will download the entire contents of your selected Source tables, and completely fill the new Data Warehouse/Data Mart. Thereafter, each scheduled run of the ETL Process will extract new/changed data from the Source, transform the staged data to formats conducive to data warehousing, and efficiently load the differential data into your Data Warehouse to keep it up-to-date. Schedule the ETL Process to run on a regular schedule, such as nightly, hourly, or every 15 minutes.

Test and experiment with your data mart. Deploy it to your production platform. Open your first small data mart to actual data consumers as early as possible. Encourage your support group to use the new DW and welcome suggestions. Data warehouses tend to be most successful when data consumers participate early in the agile development cycles.

In fine agile style, you can make improvements and expand to cover other business areas—DWiz will assist you at every point, making the design changes easier, and automatically downloading/processing the minimal data necessary to accommodate the design changes. For each new Fact table that you create, you must define the grain and maintain consistency with any relationships to existing Fact tables. You should conform the dimensions such that, when a dimension is related to multiple Fact tables, the exact same Dimension table (and its keys) can be used by the various Fact tables and in each case "mean the same thing". So, for example, if both the Sales fact table and the Inventory fact table use a "product" dimension, then you should use one single Product Dimension table which is shared by both and which is accurate in both cases.

As you build out and expand your DW, you may find it beneficial to add advanced warehouse structures such as Bridges, Junks, and Outriggers. DWiz can guide you through (and write code for) the use of these advanced structures.

6. Installation and Setup of Tools Needed for a Rapid Prototype

Installation and Setup entails three tasks:

1. Installing the DWiz App.

2. Creating empty databases for Staging and Warehouse.

3. Reviewing the Global Settings to ensure that the defaults are satisfactory.

Installing the DWiz App

This section includes summarized instructions for a typical installation. If needed, please refer to the Data Warehouse Wiz Installation Manual for more detailed instructions. The installation manual is available from DataWarehouseWiz.com , where you will also find the latest downloads for Data Warehouse Wiz. Note: When installing DWiz, it is not a requirement to use the same server as your staging/warehouse DBs. Normally installation involves the following steps:

- Create a free online account at https://www.datawarehousewiz.com

- Order a Free Trial or Paid License activation token. This token will be sent to your email address.

- Download the app installer from https://www.datawarehousewiz.com

- Run the installer

- Run the newly-installed DWiz app, click on the menu item Help->Activation, and enter your activation token (see illustration)

Illustration 7: Help Menu in the DWiz App

In addition to the Data Warehouse Wiz app, you will need access to Microsoft SQL Server, where you will create new staging and warehouse databases for your project. It is highly recommended that you create these new databases on a separate server from your company's main transactional databases, so they do not compete for resources. If you do not have a server handy for your prototype, consider using the cloud services of Amazon Web Services (AWS). Specifically, look at Amazon RDS for SQL Server, currently at the following link: https://aws.amazon.com/rds/sqlserver/ . The AWS solution is particularly attractive for rapid prototypes, as it allows you to instantly obtain a SQL Server platform without committing to expensive hardware nor expensive licenses. It even offers a free year for small (< 20 GB) SQL Server databases.

In a pinch, it is technically feasible to use a good desktop PC or laptop for your rapid prototype DW. Don't expect high performance, but if you have the required disk-space, it is possible to go this route for prototype experimentation. Download the free version of SQL Sever Express from this link: http://downloadsqlserverexpress.com . The free version only allows databases of less than 10 GB. Also download the free SQL Server Management Studio tool.

You will also need database access to the source databases, your company's transactional databases. In the case of large source databases, it may be advisable to do the initial development and first load of the staging/warehouse by using a copy of the source databases, and then redirecting the ETL connections to the actual source databases afterward for nightly (or periodic) updates. To do this, you would backup a source DB, then restore the backup to a new location (the "copy"), possibly on the same server as your staging/warehouse DBs. After completing the initial development and load using DWiz, you would then redirect the ETL connections in DWiz to the original source DB for the nightly updates (see the section "Connection Strings" in Chapter Compiling an ETL Group). DWiz will never attempt to write to any of your Source databases, with the sole exception being if you instruct DWiz to load the example Tutorial source tables into a source database.

Create Databases

Begin by creating the empty staging and warehouse databases. Open Microsoft® SQL Server Management Studio (SSMS) and create DWizStaging and DWizWarehouse. You may substitute other names for these databases; if so, substitute your names consistently for DWizStaging and DWizWarehouse throughout this document. SSMS allows the easy creation of databases by right-clicking "Databases" in the Object Explorer and then selecting "New Database...".

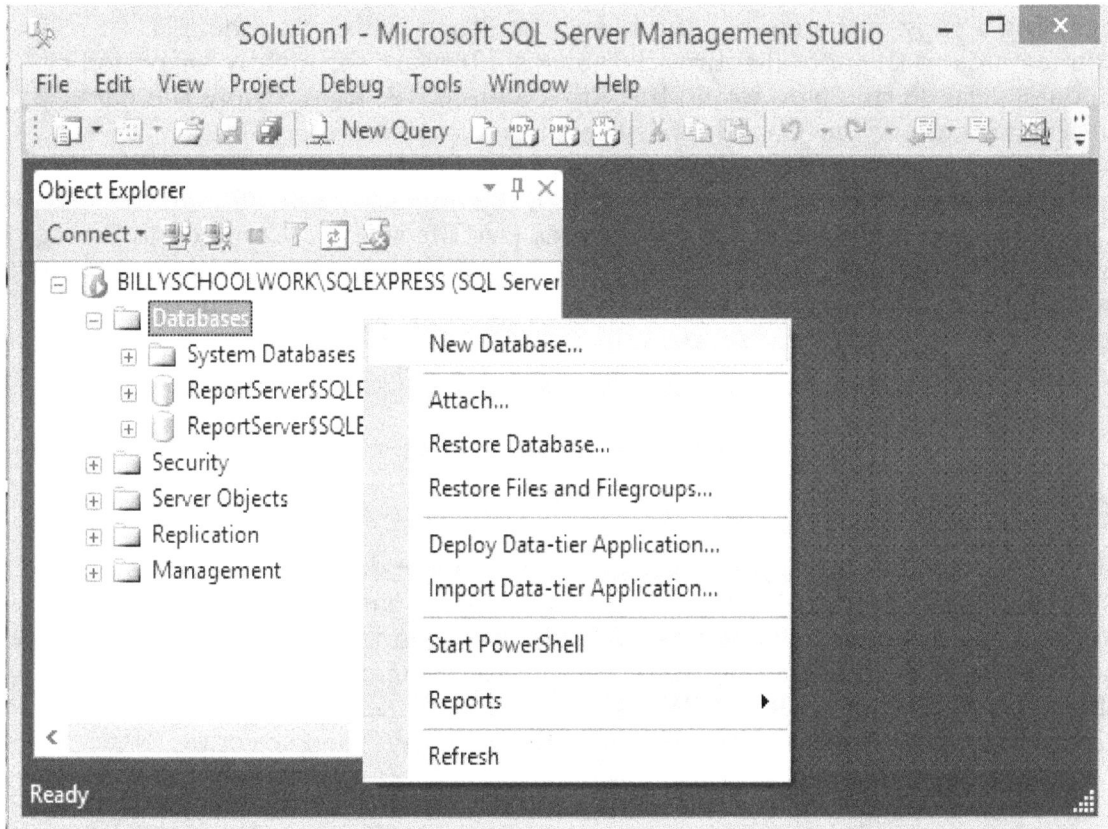

Illustration 8: Creating Databases in Microsoft SQL Server Management Studio

After creating DWizStaging and DWizWarehouse, create a third empty database called DWizSource. For the step-by-step development of a rapid prototype in this document, we will work through the examples of the DWiz Tutorial, which will use DWizSource as the pretend "company source database". We will pre-load DWizSource with a Tutorial Source DB provided by DWiz. As we work through these examples, you may re-create them exactly with your own copy of DWizSource. Also, you may connect to your actual company Source databases and perform the steps on your real source DB, building your real DW. Also, note that you can use your DWiz app to create multiple warehouses: you can create a set (DWizStaging, DWizWarehouse, DWizSource) for the following examples, and a second set (MyCompanyStaging, MyCompanyWarehouse) for use with your actual company sources.

Start Data Warehouse Wiz

When you start up the DWiz app, it will display a Welcome page which describes the status of the app, as shown in the following illustration. If the app has not yet been Activated, follow the directions to obtain your Free Trial or Paid Subscription.

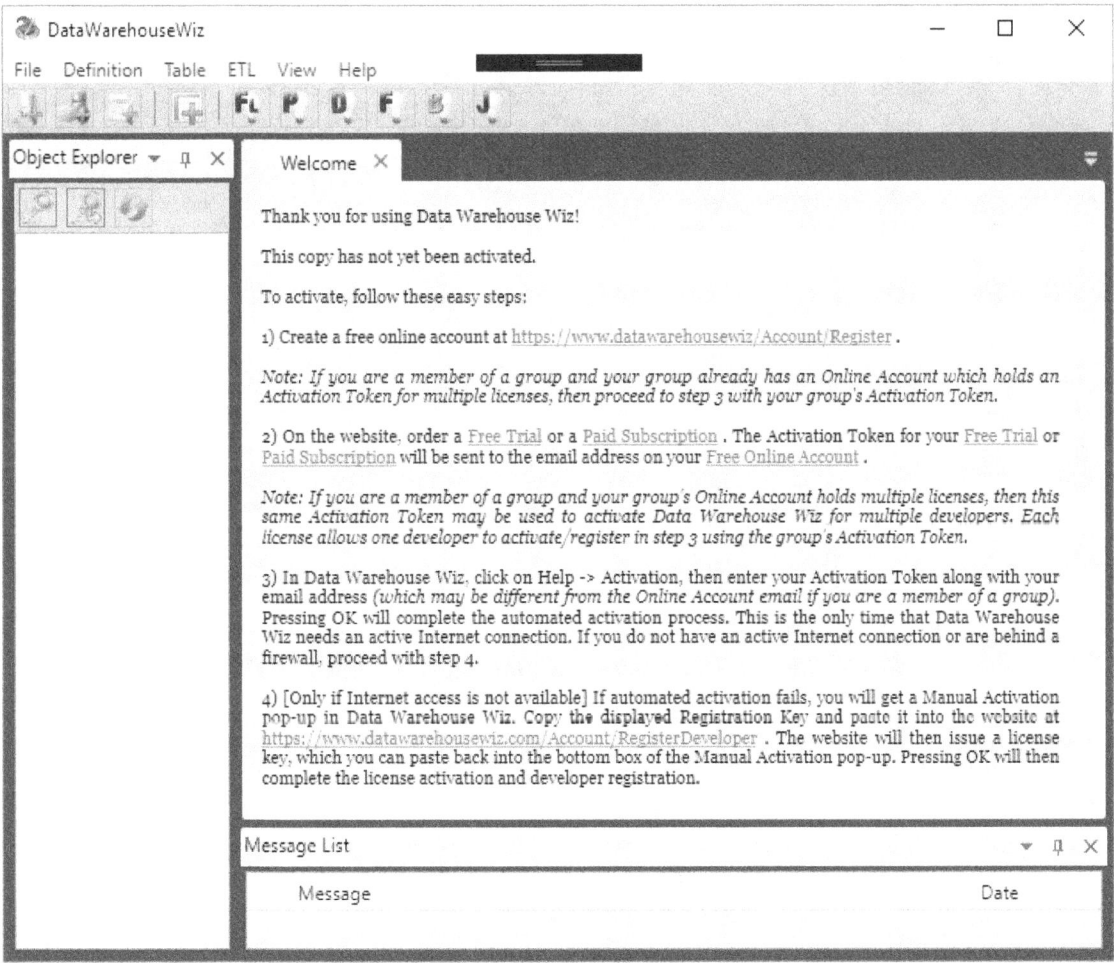

Illustration 9: The Welcome Page

Connect to the Databases

After opening Data Warehouse Wiz, connect to the Staging/Warehouse databases by clicking on the "Key" icon 🔑 (or by selecting File-->Connect to DW):

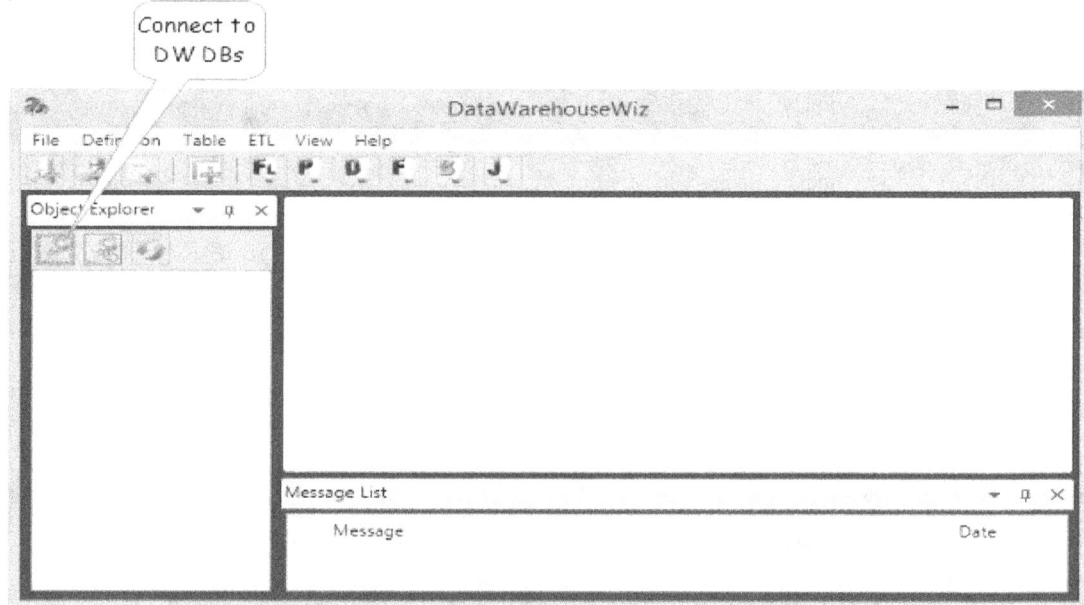

Illustration 10: Connecting to Staging & Warehouse DBs

From the popup window, enter connections to DWizStaging and DWizWarehouse, the empty databases that you created in the previous section. Then press Connect:

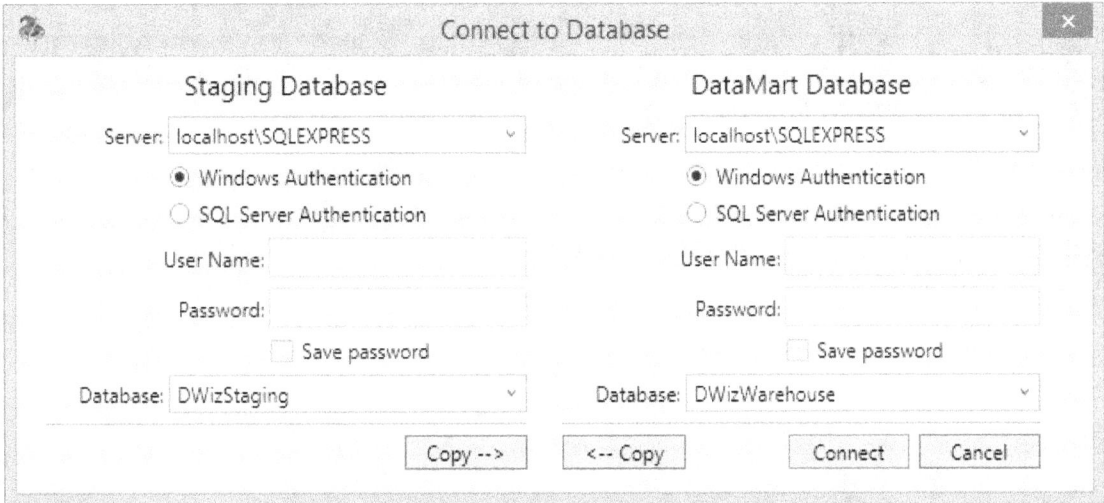

Illustration 11: Connect-To-Database Pop-Up

The first time that you connect to the Staging db, the app will ask to write metadata tables to it:

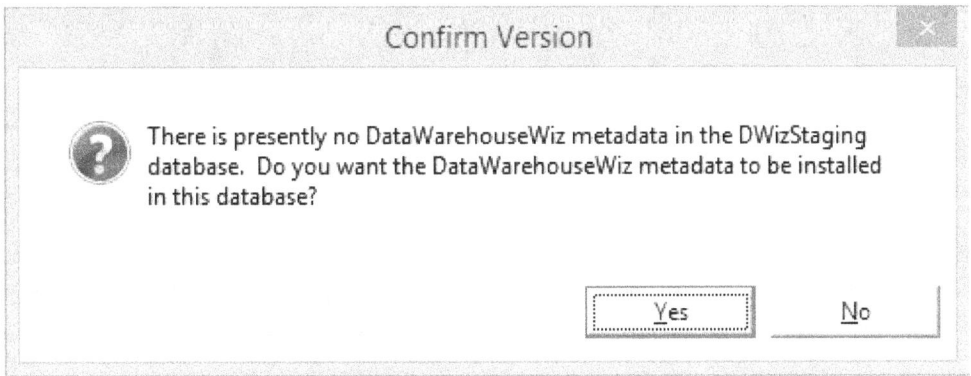

Illustration 12: OneTime Initialization of DWiz Metadata

Please select "Yes" to create these metadata tables. These tables will hold your project data for ETL processes that you will create through Data Warehouse Wiz, and are required for operation.

Next, connect to your first source DB or database copy (DWizSource in the example) by pressing the Key/Green-Arrow icon ⚿ (or by selecting File-->Connect to Source):

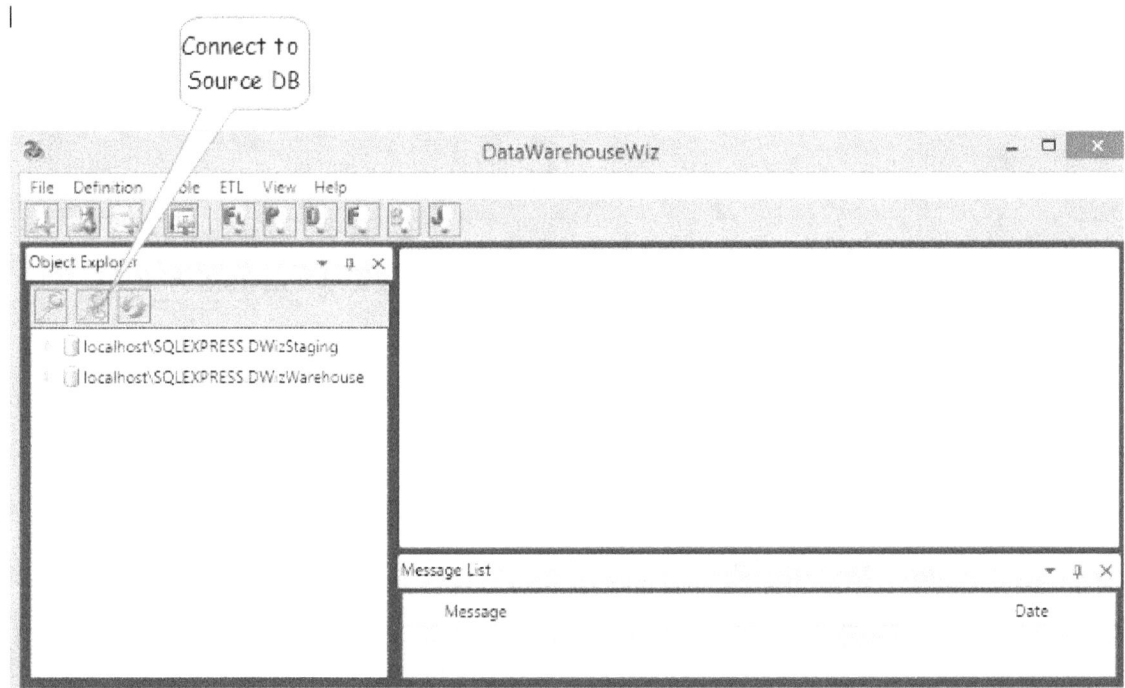

Illustration 13: Connecting DWiz to a Source Database

For your source DB, you would normally open your company's main transactional DB or a copy thereof.

At the popup menu, enter the connection to the source db and press Connect:

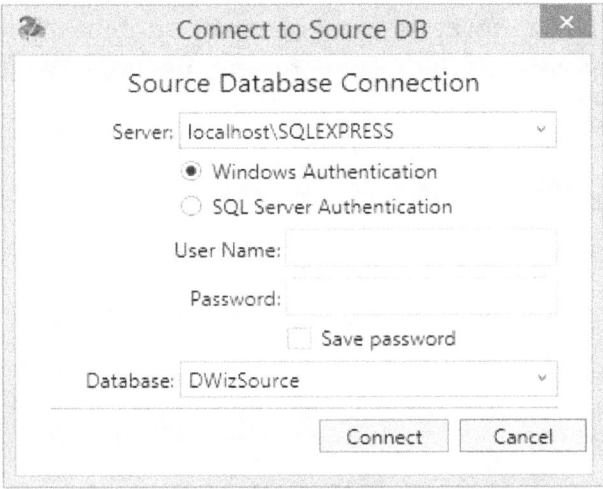

Illustration 14: Connect-To-Source-DB Pop-Up

If you wish to work through these step-by-step examples exactly, then connect to the empty DWizSource that you just created. After connecting to DWizSource, click through the app's top-level menu to Help->Tutorial->Install Tutorial Tables. The app writes the tutorial tables to the DWizSource database. This database then becomes the "source" DB for the tutorial exercises, posing as the "operational database" of a small company that wants a data warehouse.

Introducing DWiz Main Controls

The following is a quick introduction to the main controls of Data Warehouse Wiz.

DATA WAREHOUSE AUTOMATION

Main Window Controls

- The illustration below shows the major control areas of the DWiz main window. In DWiz, hover your mouse over an item to view the helpful mouse-over tool-tip. Major areas are:Menu BarConnection ButtonsGlobal Button BarObject Explorer

- TabsPage AreaPage ButtonsTab Button Bar

- Message List

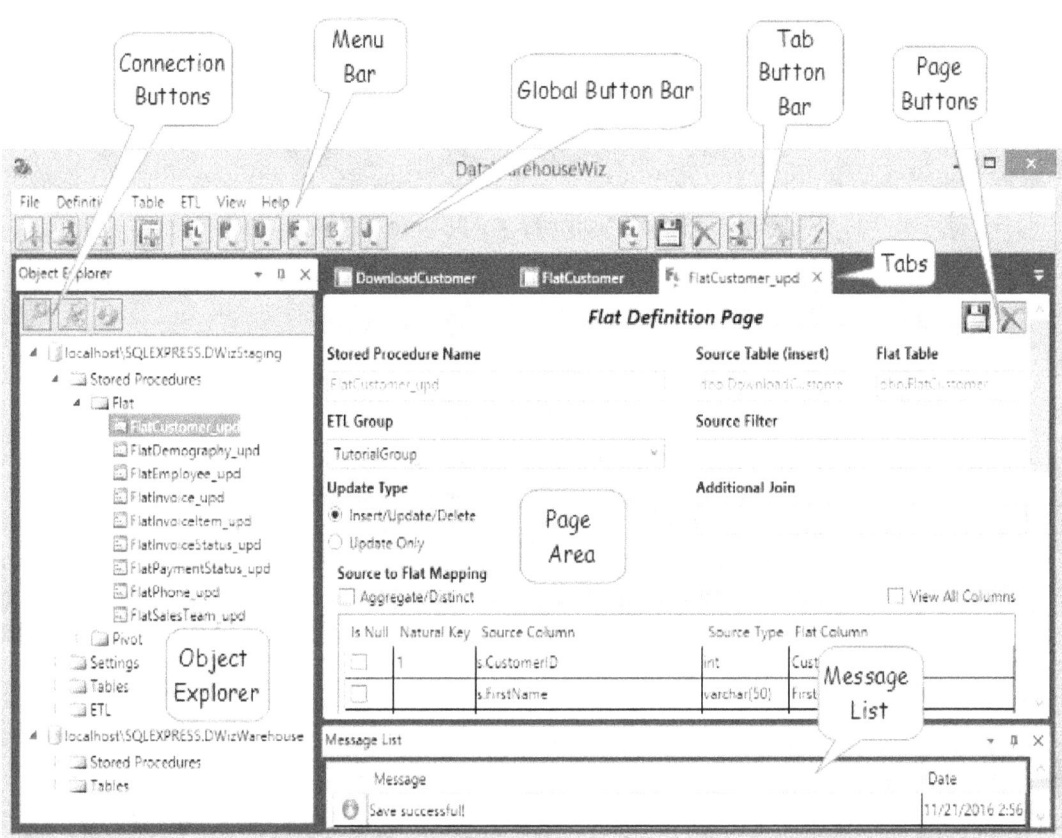

Illustration 15: DataWarehouseWiz Control Areas

Menu Bar

The first time that you start DWiz, you will use the "Help" menu of the Menu Bar to activate your free trial or paid license. After that, the Menu Bar allows you to create tables and procedures "from scratch"--but it is much easier to use the capabilities of the Object Explorer! [See Object Explorer, below.]

Connection Buttons

After activating your free trial or paid license, your first task will be to connect to your Staging and Warehouse databases (see Installation). You will need to connect to these databases each time that you start up DWiz. You can connect to your Source DBs via the Connect To Source button. When you connect to a DB, it will be shown in the Object Explorer. The Synchronize button is also in this area (blue arrow swirls).

Global Button Bar

The Global Button Bar allows you to create tables and procedures "from scratch"--but it is much easier to use the Object Explorer! Hover your mouse over any button to view the helpful tool-tip describing its use.

Object Explorer

This is where most of your table and procedure designs will start. Right-click an item to use it as a template for the next item in your design. You can use a Source table to provide the starting schema template for a Download table. You can modify the template any way that you want, but this starting point saves you from tedious typing. You then use the Download tables as templates for Flat tables, and the Flat tables as templates for Warehouse tables. In this way, you can quickly "walk" through a fast-prototyping design from your source DB through to the final data warehouse.

Items under the Object Explorer, such as tables and procedures, normally have a tiny blue icon on the left. If the icon turns yellow, this indicates a Warning (such as "An item has changed in your design which would necessitate the recompilation of either that item or one of its dependencies"). Red icons indicate an Error that must be corrected. View Warnings and Errors in the Message List area. The illustration below, under "Message List", shows a yellow-icon warning and a red-icon error.

The Object Explorer may be set to dock, float, or hide as desired.

Tabs

When you open an item from the Object Explorer (or Menu Bar or Button Bar), a new tab appears in the Tabs, and the page opens in the Page Area.

Page Area

When you open an item from the Object Explorer (or Menu Bar or Button Bar), the page opens in the Page Area. The page Area is a form specific to the item (table, procedure, etc) that you are working on.

Page Buttons

The Page Buttons are located in the top right section of the Page Area. These buttons are related directly to this one page. Most pages have a "Save" button (icon is a floppy disk) and a "Delete" button (icon is a red "X"). When you hover the mouse over a page button, the tool-tip help text will appear.

Tab Button Bar

The Tab Button Bar holds buttons that are directly related to the open tab/page, some of which may be redundant with the Page Buttons for convenience sake. When you hover the mouse over a tab button, the tool-tip help text will appear.

Message List

The Message List displays messages (Success, Error, or Warning) when a page is Saved or Compiled. The Message List may be set to dock, float, or hide as desired. The following illustration shows a message in the Message List that resulted from an error detected in a Flat table.

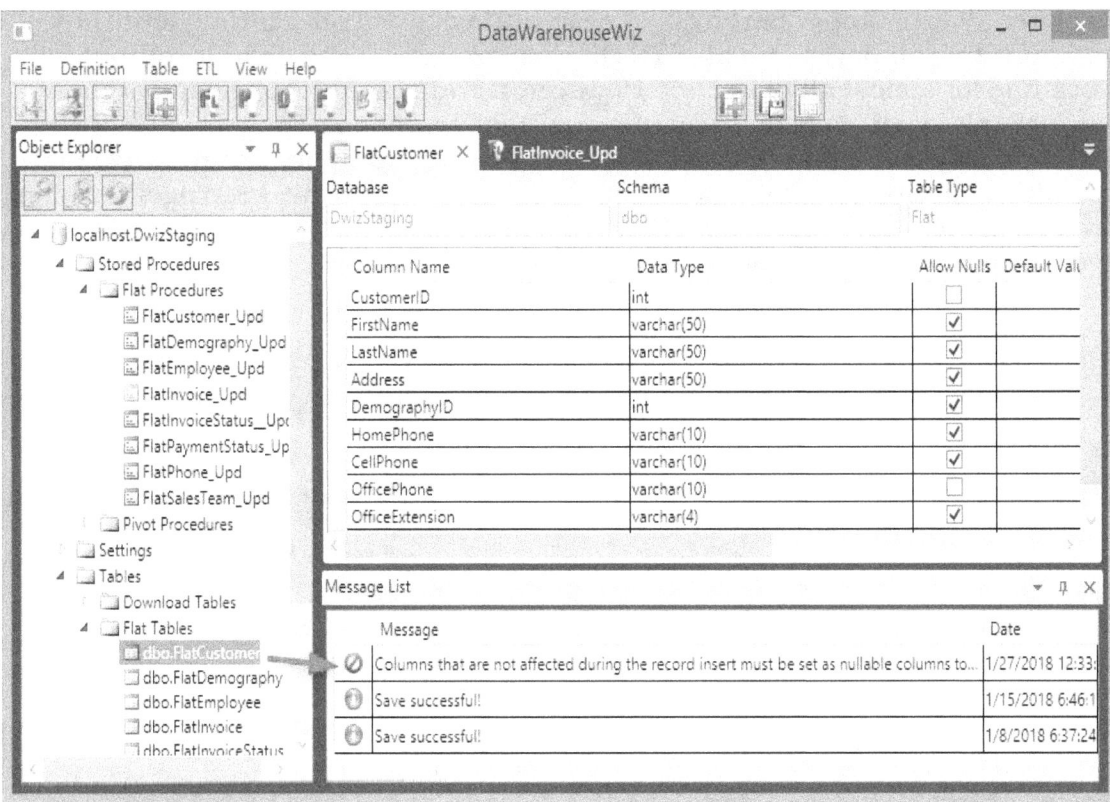

Illustration 16: The Message List Shows Warnings, Errors, and Success Messages

Review Global Settings

As shown in the figure, the Global Settings are accessed from the Object Explorer by expanding "Settings". These settings are global throughout the app, affecting all pages and all ETL Groups (projects). The default settings will work fine for almost all projects. However, if you plan to change any of these settings, please do so before creating any "real" warehouse projects. Changing a setting may make it necessary to recompile all existing procedures and re-download all source table data. Changing the settings while keeping an existing project can become laborious. However, in most cases it is safe to quickly skim over the following Global Settings definitions.

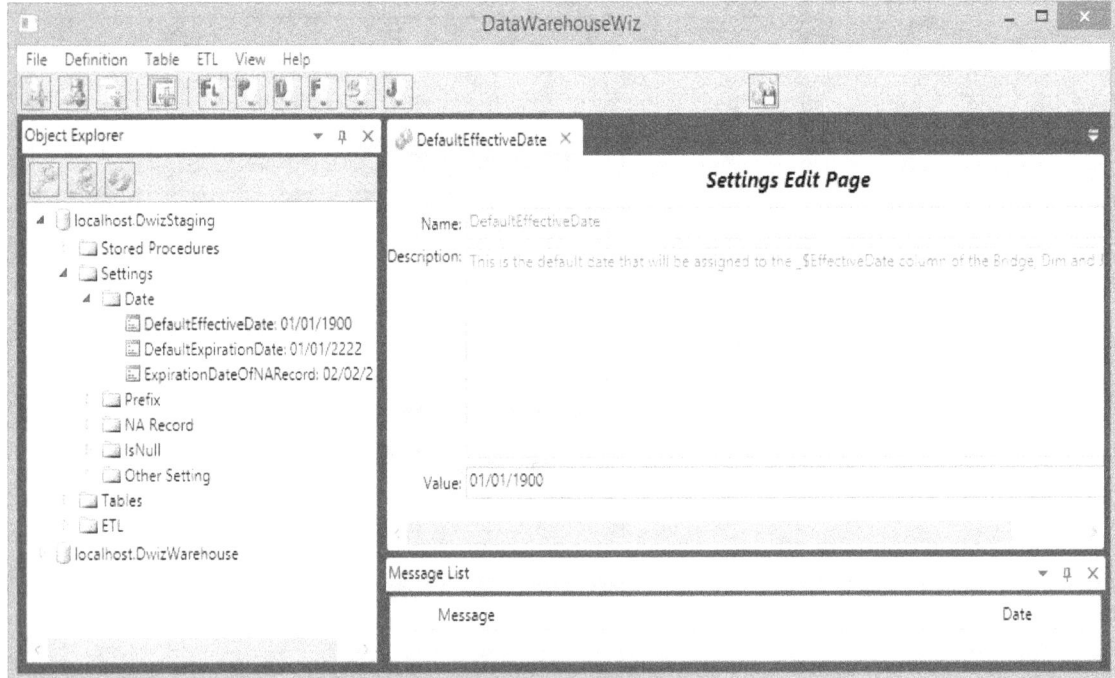

Illustration 17: Editing the Global Settings

The global settings and their values can be viewed in the Object Explorer under "Settings". Any setting can be changed by these steps:

- Open its page from the Object Explorer
- Review the Description to understand the way the setting is used
- Enter your new value of choice in the "Value" box
- Press the Save button in the Tab Bar (floppy-disk icon)

Following is a review of all settings by category.

Date Settings

These settings are used in date columns when the actual date is not available or has not yet occurred.

DefaultEffectiveDate, default 01/01/1900: This is the default date that will be assigned to the _$EffectiveDate column of the Bridge, Dim and Junk tables. It is not advisable to change this if your table already has data.

DefaultExpirationDate, default 01/01/2222: This is the default date that will be assigned to the _$ExpirationDate column of the Bridge, Dim and Junk tables. It is not advisable to change this if your table already has data.

ExpirationDateOfNARecord, default 02/02/2222: This is the date that will be assigned to the _$ExpirationDate column of the Unknown or NA (Not Available) record of the Bridge, Dim and Junk tables. It is not advisable to change this if the Unknown record already exists on your tables.

SnapshotDateTableName, default 'SnapshotDate': Name given to the Snapshot Date Table.

IsNull Settings

These are settings that replace a null value under certain circumstances.

IsnullValueForBit, default 0: This is the value assigned when an "isnull" function is used on a bit field. If this is changed, you will need to re-save and recompile ALL existing stored procedures.

IsnullValueForBitComparison, default -1: When comparing two columns, it is often necessary to use an "isnull" function before the comparison is performed. This is the value compared when an "isnull" function is used within a bit comparison. If this is changed, you will need to re-save and recompile ALL existing stored procedures.

IsnullValueForDate, default 01/01/1900: This is the value assigned when an "isnull" function is used on a date, smalldate, datetime, or datetime2 field. If this is changed, you will need to re-save and recompile ALL existing stored procedures.

IsnullValueForDateComparison, default 01/01/1901: When comparing two columns, it is often necessary to use an "isnull" function before the comparison is performed. This is the value compared when an "isnull" function is used within a date, smalldate, datetime, or datetime2 comparison. If this is changed, you will need to re-save and recompile ALL existing stored procedures.

IsnullValueForInt, default 0: This is the value assigned when an "isnull" function is used on a bigint, int, or smallint field. If this is changed, you will need to re-save and recompile ALL existing stored procedures.

IsnullValueForIntComparison, default -1: When comparing two columns, it is often necessary to use an "isnull" function before the comparison is performed. This is the value compared when an "isnull" function is used within a bigint, int, or smallint comparison. If this is changed, you will need to re-save and recompile ALL existing stored procedures.

IsnullValueForNumeric, default 0: This is the value assigned when an "isnull" function is used on a money, smallmoney, numeric, or decimal field. If this is changed, you will need to re-save and recompile ALL existing stored procedures.

IsnullValueForNumericComparison, default -0.01: When comparing two columns, it is often necessary to use an "isnull" function before the comparison is performed. This is the value compared when an "isnull" function is used within a money, smallmoney, numeric, or decimal comparison. If this is changed, you will need to re-save and recompile ALL existing stored procedures.

IsnullValueForTime, default 00:00:00: This is the value assigned when an "isnull" function is used on a time field. If this is changed, you will need to re-save and recompile ALL existing stored procedures.

IsnullValueForTimeComparison, default 00:00:01: When comparing two columns, it is often necessary to use an "isnull" function before the comparison is performed. This is the value compared when an "isnull" function is used within a time comparison. If this is changed, you will need to re-save and recompile ALL existing stored procedures.

IsnullValueForTinyint, default 0: This is the value assigned when an "isnull" function is used on a tinyint field. If this is changed, you will need to re-save and recompile ALL existing stored procedures.

IsnullValueForTinyintComparison, default 255: When comparing two columns, it is often necessary to use an "isnull" function before the comparison is performed. This is the value compared when an "isnull" function is used within a tinyint comparison. If this is changed, you will need to re-save and recompile ALL existing stored procedures.

IsnullValueForVarchar, default '': This is the value assigned when an "isnull" function is used on a char, varchar nchar or nvarchar field. If this is changed, you will need to re-save and recompile ALL existing stored procedures.

IsnullValueForVarcharComparison, default '-1': When comparing two columns, it is often necessary to use an "isnull" function before the comparison is performed. This is the value compared when an "isnull" function is used within a char, varchar nchar or nvarchar comparison. If this is changed, you will need to re-save and recompile ALL existing stored procedures.

NA Record Settings

These settings are values that are used when a column value is Not Available.

NAValueForDate, default 01/01/1900: This is the value given to the date, smalldatetime, datetime or datetime2 field of the Unknown or NA (Not Applicable) record of a Junk, Dim or Bridge table. It is not advisable to change this if the Unknown record already exists on your tables.

NAValueForIdentity, default -1: This is the value given to the identity field of the Unknown or NA (Not Applicable) record of a Junk, Dim or Bridge table. It is not advisable to change this if the Unknown record already exists on your tables.

NAValueForInt, default 0: This is the value given to the int, smallint, bigint, tinyint, or bit field of the Unknown or NA (Not Applicable) record of a Junk, Dim or Bridge table. It is not advisable to change this if the Unknown record already exists on your tables.

NAValueForNumeric, default 0: This is the value given to the money, smallmoney, decimal or numeric field of the Unknown or NA (Not Applicable) record of a Junk, Dim or Bridge table. It is not advisable to change this if the Unknown record already exists on your tables.

NAValueForTime, default 00:00:00: This is the value given to the time field of the Unknown or NA (Not Applicable) record of a Junk, Dim or Bridge table. It is not advisable to change this if the Unknown record already exists on your tables.

NAValueForVarchar, default '': This is the value given to the varchar, char, nvarchar, or nchar field of the Unknown or NA (Not Applicable) record of a Junk, Dim or Bridge table. It is not advisable to change this if the Unknown record already exists on your tables.

Prefix Settings

These settings are prefixes and suffixes that are used when auto-generating table and column names.

BridgeIDPrefix, default '': This is the prefix that is added to the root table name when creating the column name of a Bridge ID. It is not advisable to change this if Bridge tables have already been created.

BridgeIDSuffix, default 'ID': This is the suffix that is added to the root table name when creating the column name of a Bridge ID. It is not advisable to change this if Bridge tables have already been created.

BridgeKeyPrefix, default '': This is the prefix that is added to the root table name when creating the key name in a Bridge table. It is not advisable to change this if Bridge tables have already been created.

BridgeKeySuffix, default 'Key': This is the suffix that is added to the root table name when creating the key name in a Bridge table. It is not advisable to change this if Bridge tables have already been created.

BridgePrefix, default 'Bridge': This is the prefix that is added to the root table name when creating the name of a Bridge table. It is not advisable to change this if Bridge tables have already been created.

BridgeSuffix, default '': This is the suffix that is added to the root table name when creating the name of a Bridge table. It is not advisable to change this if Bridge tables have already been created.

DimKeyPrefix, default '': This is the prefix that is added to the root table name when creating the key name in a Dim table. It is not advisable to change this if Dim tables have already been created.

DimKeySuffix, default 'Key': This is the suffix that is added to the root table name when creating the key name in a Dim table. It is not advisable to change this if Dim tables have already been created.

DimPrefix, default 'Dim': This is the prefix that is added to the root table name when creating the name of a Dim table. It is not advisable to change this if Dim tables have already been created.

DimSuffix, default '': This is the suffix that is added to the root table name when creating the name of a Dim table. It is not advisable to change this if Dim tables have already been created.

DownloadPrefix, default 'Download': This is the prefix that is added to the root table name when creating the name of a Download table. It is not advisable to change this if Download tables have already been created.

DownloadSuffix, default '': This is the suffix that is added to the root table name when creating the name of a Download table. It is not advisable to change this if Download tables have already been created.

FactIDPrefix, default '': This is the prefix that is added to the root table name when creating the column name of a Fact ID. It is not advisable to change this if Fact tables have already been created.

FactIDSuffix, default 'ID': This is the suffix that is added to the root table name when creating the column name of a Fact ID. It is not advisable to change this if Fact tables have already been created.

FactPrefix, default 'Fact': This is the prefix that is added to the root table name when creating the name of a Fact table. It is not advisable to change this if Fact tables have already been created.

FactSuffix, default '': This is the suffix that is added to the root table name when creating the name of a Fact table. It is not advisable to change this if Fact tables have already been created.

FlatPrefix, default 'Flat': This is the prefix that is added to the root table name when creating the name of a Flat table. It is not advisable to change this if Flat tables have already been created.

FlatSuffix, default '': This is the suffix that is added to the root table name when creating the name of a Flat table. It is not advisable to change this if Flat tables have already been created.

JunkKeyPrefix, default '': This is the prefix that is added to the root table name when creating the key name in a Junk Dimension table. It is not advisable to change this if Junk tables have already been created.

JunkKeySuffix, default 'Key': This is the suffix that is added to the root table name when creating the key name in a Junk Dimension table. It is not advisable to change this if Junk tables have already been created.

JunkPrefix, default 'JDim': This is the prefix that is added to the root table name when creating the name of a Junk Dimension table. It is not advisable to change this if Junk tables have already been created.

JunkSuffix, default '': This is the suffix that is added to the root table name when creating the name of a Junk Dimension table. It is not advisable to change this if Junk tables have already been created.

PivotPrefix, default 'Pivot': This is the prefix that is added to the root table name when creating the name of a Pivot table. It is not advisable to change this if Pivot tables have already been created.

PivotSuffix, default '': This is the suffix that is added to the root table name when creating the name of a Pivot table. It is not advisable to change this if Pivot tables have already been created.

StoredProcPrefix, default '': This is the prefix that is added to the target table name when creating the name of a stored procedure. It is not advisable to change this if stored procedures have already been created.

StoredProcSuffix, default '_Upd': This is the suffix that is added to the target table name when creating the name of a stored procedure. It is not advisable to change this if stored procedures have already been created.

Other Settings

These are other miscellaneous settings that do not fall within the previous categories.

_$ChangeFlagResetDays, default 0: The _$ChangeFlag contains the insert(2), change(3,4,5), or delete(1) information about a record. The first thing that is done in a Flat stored procedure is to reset the target table's _$ChangeFlag to 0. If this resetting is not desirable, set this $ChangeFlagResetDays to the number of days before the resetting should occur. Note that when a record is to be deleted from the Flat table, that record is first marked as deleted by setting _$ChangeFlag to 1 (soft delete). A soft delete is done so that the delete information can be passed on to other Flat, Dim or Fact tables. The record that has been soft deleted is physically deleted from the table during the next execution of the ETL. If this physical delete is not wanted, set the _$ChangeFlagResetDays to the number of days you want to retain the soft delete. Make sure to recompile the stored procedures after changing this setting.

_$ChangeInfoPersistDays, default 7: If SProc B uses as input the output of

SProc A, then the _$Change information of the output of SProc A will continue to persist until SProc B is executed. If SProc B does not execute, then the _$Change information will continue to persist for the number of days specified in this variable.

IsChangeTrackingUsedInStaging, default N: This Y/N setting indicates whether Change Tracking is used in the staging database. For small data warehouses, the _$ChangeFlag column that is appended to each table is sufficient to handle change management. However, for large data warehouses, it is recommended to use the more robust Change Tracking to monitor record changes within the staging database. Note that all stored procedures must be re-compiled when switching from one change management method to another. Please be aware that both staging and data mart databases MUST be on the same server for Change Tracking to work.

RowCounterName, default 'RowCounter': The name of the column in the fact table that will always have a value of 1. This is a convenience that allows rows to be counted by summing RowCounter.

WeeklySnapshotDay, default 'Sunday': This defines the day when a weekly Snapshot is taken on the Fact table. This variable will only affect the Fact stored procedure that does a Weekly Snapshot. Make sure to re-save and recompile the affected stored procedure after changing this setting.

7. Create an ETL Group

An ETL Group may be thought of as a "project". This group will begin empty, and grow to contain tables and processes related to one manageable portion of the overall ETL (extract, transform, and load) needed to feed our warehouse. In many cases, you will only need one ETL group. However, for warehouses with multiple sources or a large number of tables, it is helpful to be able to divide the action into smaller manageable chunks—and thus multiple ETL Groups. The following diagram shows an example of a warehouse wherein two ETL Groups are created to facilitate easier maintenance of modules.

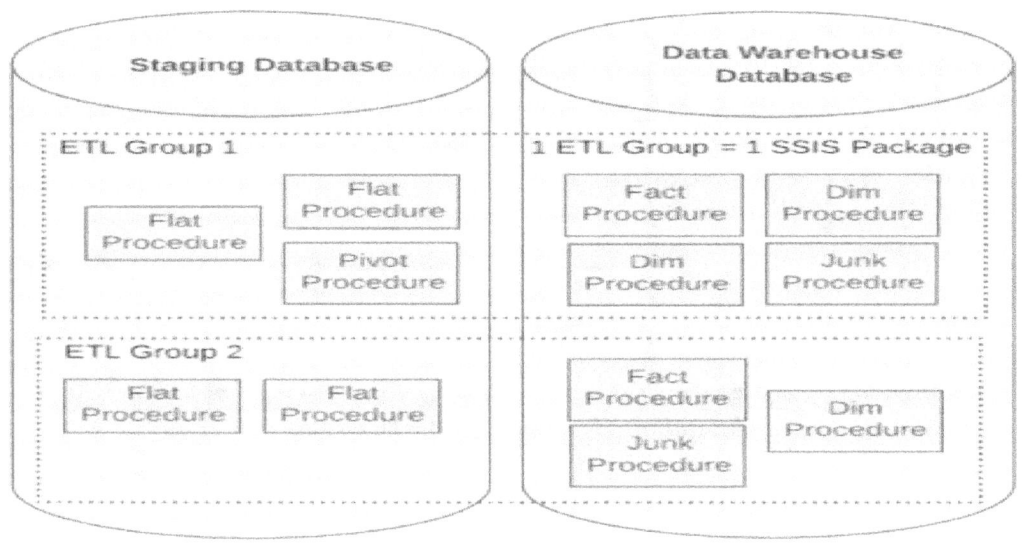

Illustration 18: Example of a Warehouse Using Two ETL Groups

In the DWiz Object Explorer, expand DWizStaging-->ETL-->Groups, and right-click "Groups", then select "New Group":

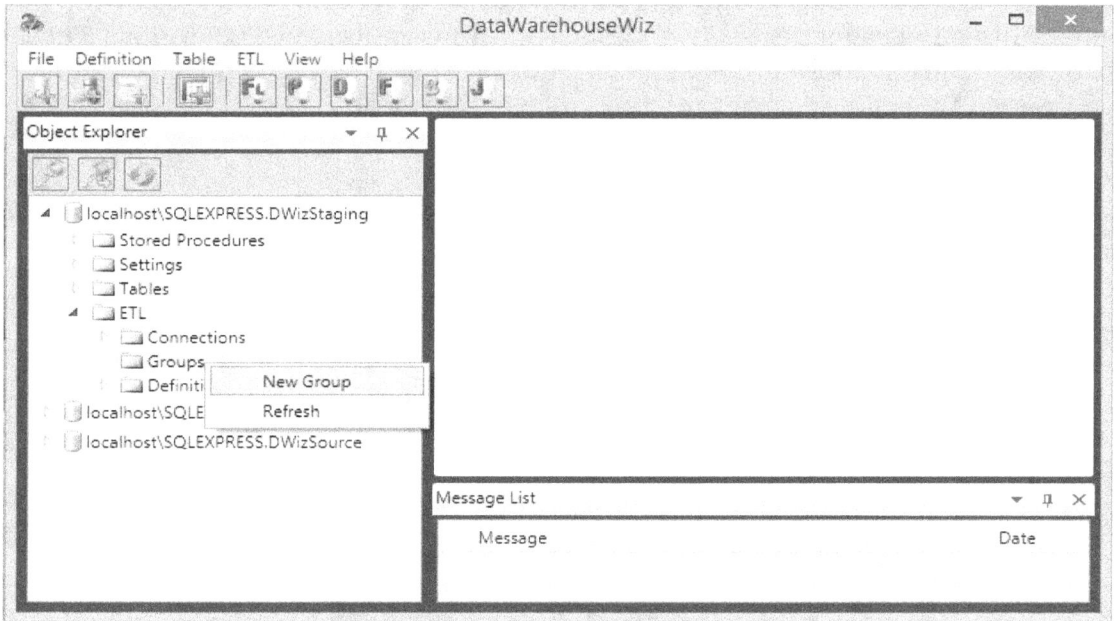

Illustration 19: Creating an ETL Group

Next enter a name ("TutorialGroup" in the example) in the ETL Group Page, and save by using the Floppy-Disk icon on the page. After a successful save, you will see a "Save successful!" message at the bottom:

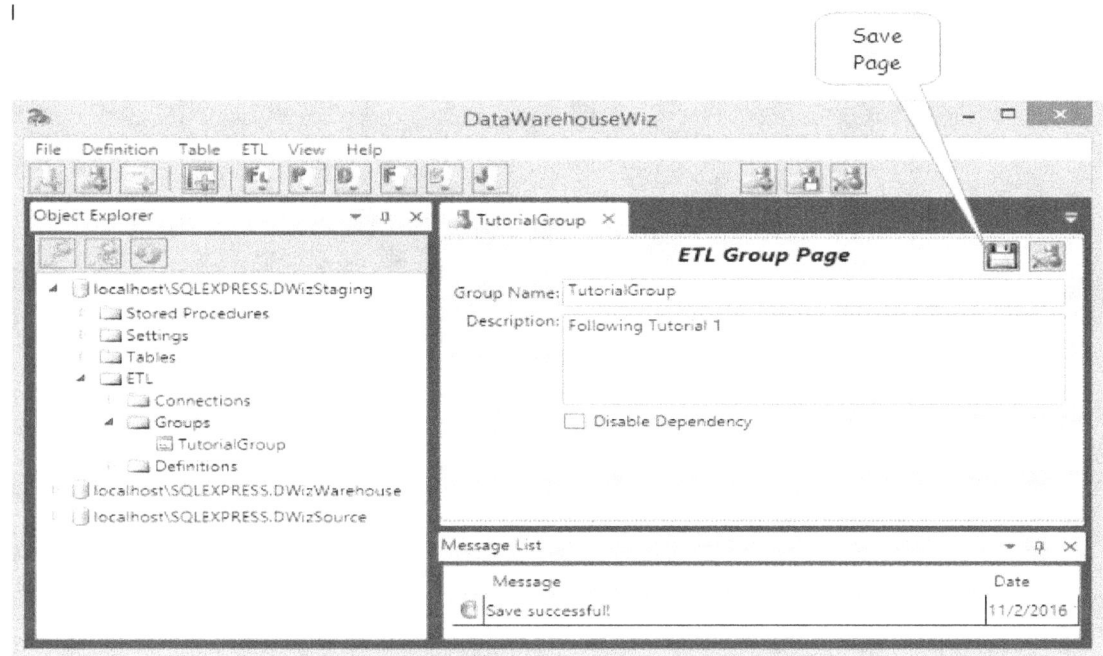

Illustration 20: Save Page (Floppy-Disk Icon Button)

Now that we have our ETL Group, we can define tables and processes to go into it. For the first module of our first data mart, we need to choose an important table in the Source that will feed our first Fact Table. Then we will identify the Dimensions that will relate to this fact table. Let us suppose, for the purposes of the rapid prototype example, that we have made the very common choice of our company's sales invoices for our first Fact table, which we have found in the Source database in a table called "Invoices". Furthermore, we have identified a related dimension of "Customer". In our first little module, we will create a data mart from this one fact table and one dimension table.

8. Design Download Tables

Download tables capture the new data from your source tables. Each download table has a one-to-one relationship with a single table from a Source DB. During the design phase, only the schema of the source table is copied, no data. When the future ETL Group Process is **first** run, the entire data of the source table will be copied to the download table (excepting any columns that are omitted by design). Thereafter, the nightly (or periodic) runs of the ETL will copy only the "delta"--the differences in the source table due to updates and inserts. Optionally, the download table configuration can be set to "Whole Table Download", so that the entire table is copied each night; this is handy for small tables that are frequently rewritten with new primary keys in the source DB. The download tables are truncated in the beginning of each run of their ETL Group Process; so they will only hold the new data downloaded from each run. Typically only the changes in the Source tables are downloaded, depending on the chosen Change Management method. Thus the "*Extract*" part of the ETL Process captures changes in the Source DB and puts them into the Download tables. Download tables form the gateway into the Staging DB; no other type of table is used to extract data from Source DBs.

The Download tables are the destination of the *Extract* portion of the ETL process. In order to make this extraction as efficient as possible—and the least burden on the Sources—there are no *Transforms* performed during the filling of the Download tables. The minor exceptions to this are:

- Some unneeded columns from the Source might be omitted from the Download table, if desired

- Nulls in a Source column may be replaced by a default value, if desired

Design Download Table Example

We will use an example from the Tutorial to demonstrate the design of a Download table. In this example we will create a download table, called DownloadCustomer, in DWizStaging to facilitate the downloading and processing of the "Customer" table data from the Source DB. In Object Explorer, expand DWizSource-->Tables to view the source tables, then right-click the Customer table and select Copy Table:

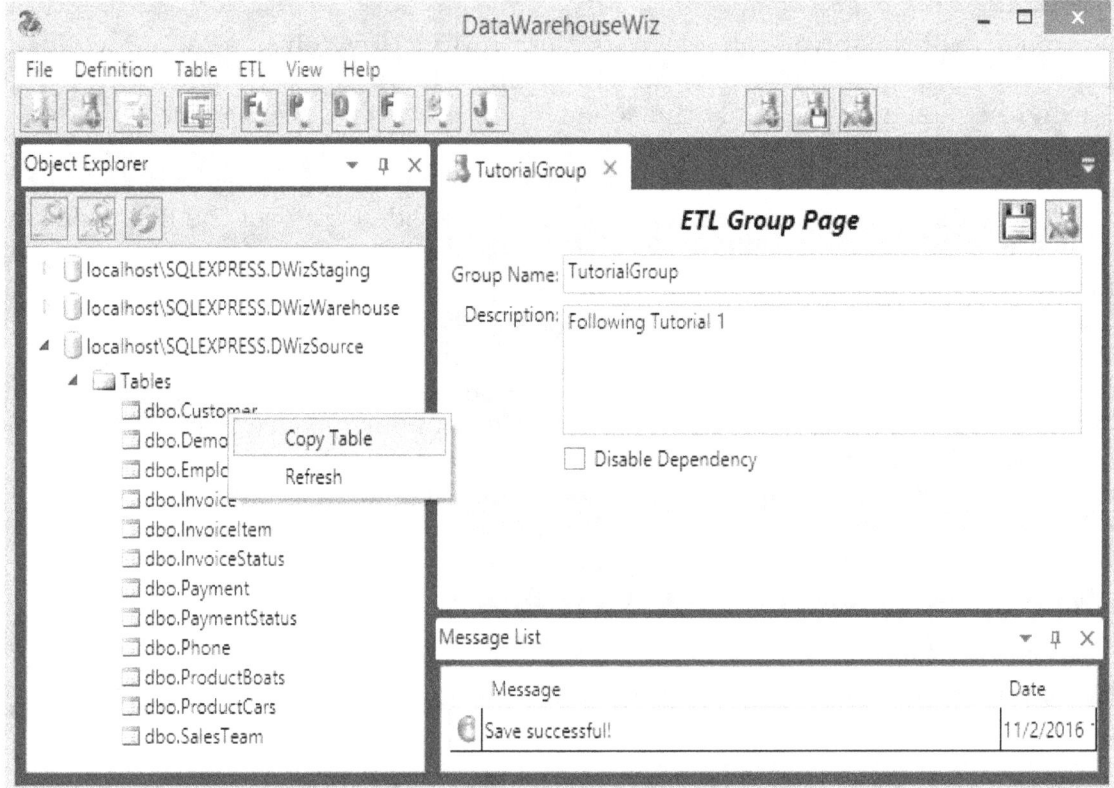

Illustration 21: Copying a Table's Schema

A popup window allows you to choose a name (default is "Download" + source table name) for the new table in Staging. You may also choose a Schema, if you have previously created one other than the default dbo. Press OK:

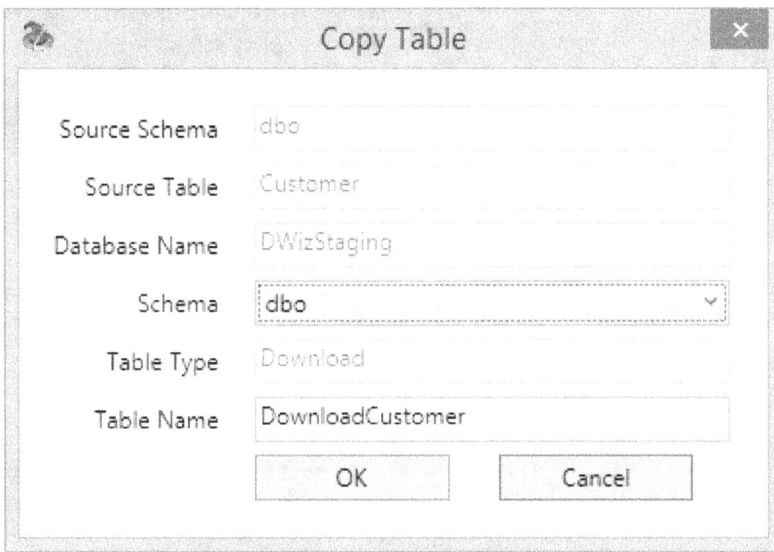

Illustration 22: "Copy Table" Pop-Up

This brings us to the Download Table Definition page, in this example for the new table DownloadCustomer:

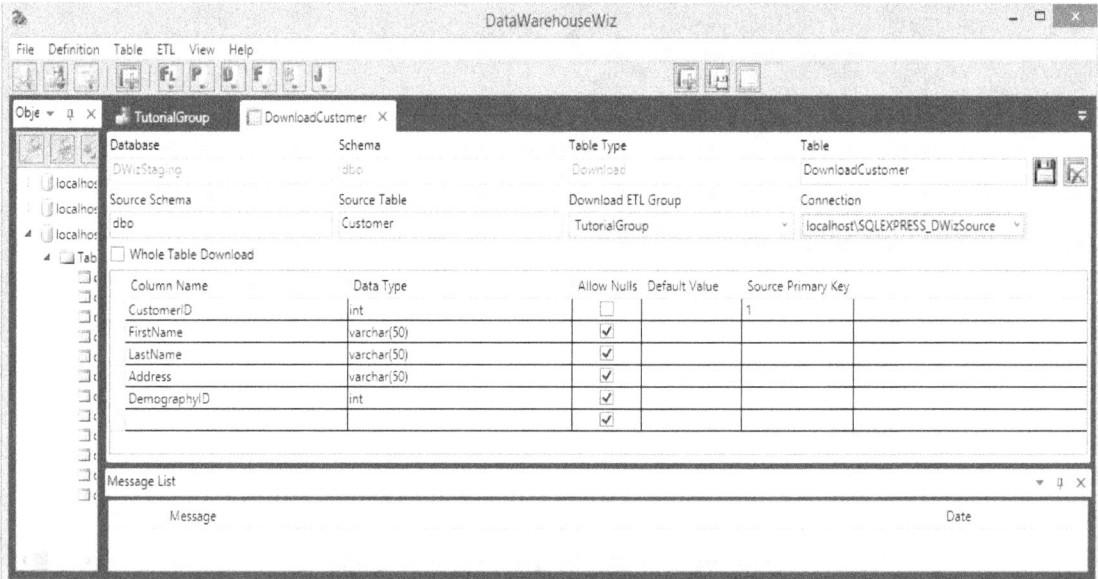

Illustration 23: Download-Table Definition Page

Most of the parameters of this page are conveniently filled with default values by Data Warehouse Wiz, yet you can override any parameter for your own purposes. The first line of the page details the location and type of the new table being designed:

- Database =   DwizStaging <or your Staging DB>

- Schema = dbo <or your pre-existing schema>

- Table Type = Download

- Table = DownloadCustomer <or your chosen name>

The second line details the source:

- Source Schema =   dbo

- Source Table = Customer

- Download ETL Group = <select your ETL group>

- Source DB Connection = <select your connection to the Source DB>

The next field, "Whole Table Download", is normally left un-selected (without a check-mark) except in one specific scenario. The scenario occurs when the source table is a very small table that is periodically truncated and re-written by the SOURCE system. Sometimes a Source system is found to do this, such as for small reference tables which are updated by a complete rebuild. This potentially may cause a problem for your differential-download method (such as Change Tracking or Change Data Capture) by seeming to be deletes and inserts at the source, when in reality the table was simply re-written. To alleviate such problems, in this scenario you can check-mark the Whole Table Download box. This causes DWiz to design code that always downloads the whole source table for this particular download table, regardless of the download method of the overall ETL Group.

The columns of DownloadCustomer default to copies of the source Customer, but may be modified as needed. Also, columns may be added or deleted.

Ensure that the Source Primary Key is indicated properly by a "1". If the source has a multi-part primary key, each part should be indicated sequentially (1,2,...). DWiz usually can detect and set this primary key. DWiz will use this primary key as the primary key of the new Download table in the Staging DB as well, and will thus create an index on it in the Download table. The primary key must be non-nullable.

The app also quietly adds several columns (prefixed by "_$" or "__$") for maintenance purposes. Optionally, you may direct the ETL process to replace nulls in any column with a Default Value (please uncheck the Allow Nulls box when using a Default Value).

When you have completed the page, **save** it with the Floppy-Disk icon. Afterward, it is possible to view the new table within the Staging DB in SSMS. Although the new table is now created in the Staging database, it remains empty for now. Later, when you compile the ETL Group, DWiz will use this Download Table Definition, along with choices from the ETL Definition Page (such as Change Management Method) to design efficient code to extract data from the Source and feed the Download table.

If a table is no longer wanted, it can be deleted with the "Red-X" icon.

Design DownloadInvoice

Now repeat the above step to create a download table called DownloadInvoice, based upon the source DB's Invoice table. Right-click the Invoice table under DWizSource and select Copy Table. Fill in the definition page to create DownloadInvoice, being certain to select the ETL group "TutorialGroup" and to specify the DWizSource Connection. Ensure that the Source Primary Key (InvoiceId) is indicated by a "1". After you press the save icon (Floppy-Disk), it should look like this:

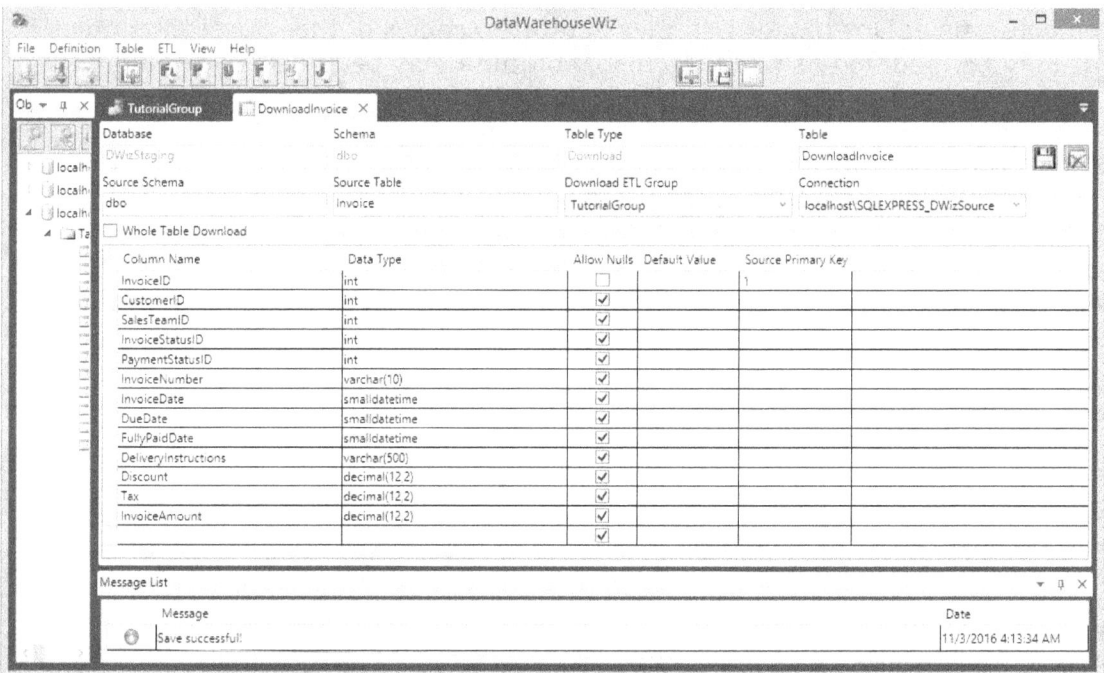

Illustration 24: DownloadInvoice Definition Page

9.   Flat Table Design

Flat tables hold the data staged for updates to the Warehouse tables. The data will be drawn from one or more Download tables, transformed and processed as necessary, and put into Flat tables in a form that facilitates easy updating of the warehouse tables. In many simple cases, a Flat table is used for only one warehouse table, such as a Dimension or Fact. In other cases, a Flat may be used to feed multiple warehouse tables.   A given Flat table, which is in the de-normalized form favored for warehouse tables, may draw and transform data from multiple Download tables. A given warehouse table typically draws only from a single Flat table.

During the design phase, only schema is copied to the Flat tables, no data. In the future Production phase, each run of the future ETL Group Process will use a Flat Procedure to process data from the download tables and update the Flat tables as necessary. Unlike the Download tables, the Flat tables are not truncated during the ETL Process. Before designing a Flat table, you should design the Download table(s) that will source the raw data.

Special Considerations for Flat Tables Built to Feed Fact Tables

A Fact table draws all of its facts from a single Flat table that is built to feed it. Therefore, the design decisions for a Fact table must be anticipated when designing its Flat table. Following are two such considerations that should be implemented in the Flat table to properly format the data in preparation for the Fact table.

⚠ *PITFALL: Defining an inappropriate grain, or implementing inconsistent grains.*

Define the Grain

Decide on the grain, which is the lowest level of detail that will exist in your Fact table. Note that often you will need to join multiple Source tables together to produce one de-normalized Fact table. For example, many company Source transactional DBs have separate tables for SalesInvoices and

SalesInvoiceLineItems. These will be joined together to produce one de-normalized SalesInvoiceFact table, which will have the grain at the lowest detail available: each table row will correspond to a single line-item of an invoice. Your grain is the line-item, not the invoice. Usually, you use the smallest granularity available, with the most detail.

Allocating Facts for which the Source is Less Granular Than the Grain

As most fact tables are formed by joining multiple Source tables, you may find that some facts are not detailed all the way down to the grain. In these cases, decisions must be made as to how to allocate facts according to the grain. This is most easily understood by considering an example. Suppose that, in your Source, you have a sales invoice that has five line-items, for five products sold to one customer in a single transaction. Suppose also, that this sale also has charges for shipping charges and sales taxes, but that these are at the invoice level and not specified at the line-item level. We want the grain to be at the line-item level, yet these extra charges are at the invoice level. Now, we could list the shipping charges and taxes as items 6 and 7, but this poor solution has several major drawbacks, including 1) shipping and taxes are NOT products, and 2) this would not link these extra charges to the actual products sold. A better solution is to allocate the extra charges among the 5 line items, into separate new columns in the fact table. So the shipping charges may be divided among the five line items by: 1) 1/5 of the shipping charge per line item, or 2) [Better] proportional to the item's share of the total cost, or 3) [Even better] Proportional to the line item's share of the total shipping weight, or 4) Some other method that you can implement consistently throughout all your invoices. The allocated shipping cost will be put into a new column (ShippingCosts) in the fact table, and also in the Flat table that feeds it. Likewise, the sales tax can be allocated among line items, and put into new fact table columns like StateSalesTax, LocalSalesTax, LocalAirtimeTax, ExciseTax, etc. Note that there are advantages here: Each type of tax can have its own column. Tax-exempt items can be omitted from the allocations. Specialized taxes that are assessed on special items can be allocated completely among only those items. Round-off errors can be minimized by setting the column precision to at least 5 decimal places.

Second Fact Table Holding Aggregated Grains

Sometimes it is beneficial to create a second fact table that aggregates data from the primary fact table. There are two motivations for this: 1) improve query performance by reducing the number of records to be searched, and 2) decrease storage requirements by keeping the complete history only at the aggregated levels (which has far fewer rows), while retaining only limited running history (e.g., last 90 days) of the detailed level of the original grain. As this second motivation entails the loss of detailed history, it would only be implemented if demanded for the cost savings. Aggregated fact tables may, of necessity, omit some of the original dimensions; however, remaining dimensions should conform to their definitions in the original table. An aggregated fact table requires its own Flat table, as the aggregation itself will be performed in the Flat Procedure.

Special Considerations for Flat Tables Built to Feed Dimension Tables

A Dimension table usually draws all of its data from a single Flat table that is built to feed it. Therefore, the design decisions for a Dimension table must be anticipated when designing its Flat table. As the Flat table is a de-normalized form, it typically has its roots in multiple Source tables that must be joined together. Following are considerations that should be implemented in the Flat table to properly format the data in preparation for the Dimension table.

Uniqueness of Entities within a Dimension

Consider the example of a Customer Dimension. If the customer self-identifies, such as by use of a login or by use of a rewards card, then great. But what about online potential customers browsing without a login? Is every session-cookie a unique "customer"? If, over time, we receive hits from the same IP and the same browser, do we consider these further activity from the same customer? These questions normally have been addressed previously in the design of the company's Sources. The planning and design of a dimension should include these considerations:

- Revisit the definition of uniqueness used within the Sources, and decide whether this same definition is optimal for the DW, or whether changes are desirable

- For each other attribute in the dimension, decide how SCDs (slowly-changing dimensions) should be handled and their type (0, 1, 2, etc).

- Document these decisions about uniqueness and SCDs

- Adhere to these decisions while designing the schema and ETL of the dimension

- This sets the precedent and definitions for conformed dimensions when this dimension is shared with other fact tables or other data marts.

Consider now the example of a Product Dimension. The 64-oz economy-size Shlerp is *not* the same product as the normal 8-oz Shlerp, and is *not* the same as selling quantity 8 of the normal size. For instance, the packaging costs and marketing strategies are very different. So these are two different unique products, with unique records in the Product Dimension. Yet they both source the same Shlerp liquid. Thus, there should be a de-normalized product-line column in the Product dimension table to show that these are both products in the Shlerp product line. Companion columns should show other categorizations that the product belongs to. These categorizations would have usually been separate tables in a normalized Source database, but they are intentionally de-normalized and flattened for use in the DW.

Design Flat Table Example

For our first warehouse module, we anticipate having one fact table (FactInvoice) and one dimension table (DimCustomer). For each of these warehouse tables, we will need to design a Flat table to feed it. When designing a Flat Table, we are designing schema. Later, we will design a Flat Procedure, which has the job of actually processing data and staging it in the Flat table.

We will use an example from the DWiz Tutorial to demonstrate the design of a Flat Table. In this example, we will create a Flat table, called FlatCustomer, in DWizStaging. We will copy the schema of DownloadCustomer to create FlatCustomer, but we will not copy any data yet. In the Object Explorer, expand DWizStaging-->Tables-->Download and right-click on DownloadCustomer, then select Copy Table. In the pop-up window, set the table type to "Flat", and choose a name (Default is "Flat" + source table name). You may also choose an alternate Schema if you have previously created a Schema other than the default dbo. Ensure that the database is set to your staging DB and the table type is **Flat**, then press OK:

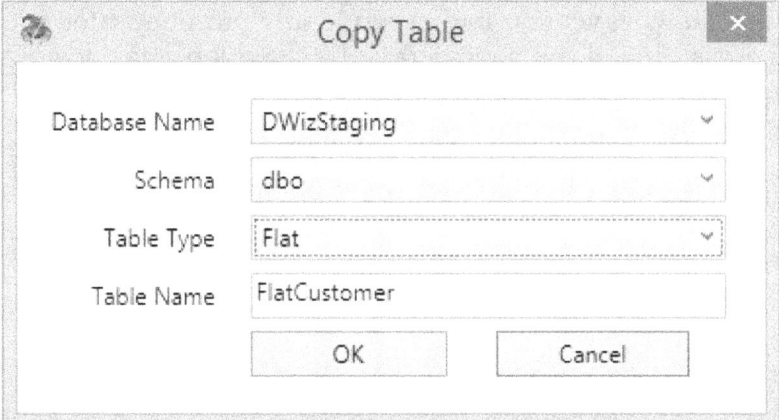

Illustration 25: "Copy Table" Pop-Up for Creating Flat Tables

This brings us to the Flat Table Definition page:

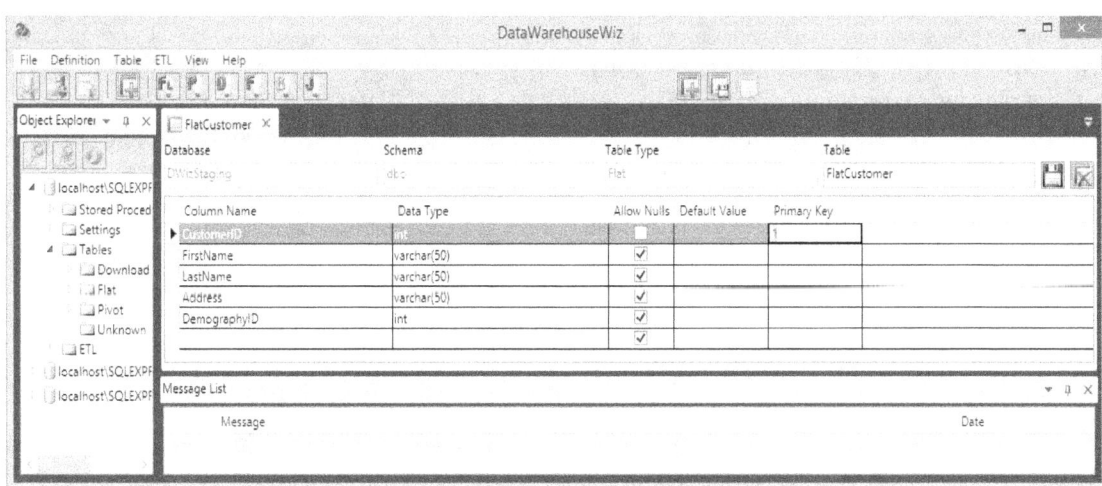

Illustration 26: "Flat Table" Definition Page

Most of the parameters of this page are conveniently filled with default values by Data Warehouse Wiz; yet you can override any parameter for your own purposes. The first line of the page details the location and type of the new table being created:

- Database = DwizStaging <or your Staging DB>
- Schema = dbo <or your pre-existing Schema>
- Table Type = Flat
- Table = FlatCustomer <or your chosen name>

The columns of FlatCustomer default to copies of DownloadCustomer, but may be modified as needed. Also, columns may be added or deleted.

Ensure that the Primary Key is indicated properly by a "1", and is marked as non-nullable. If the table will have a multi-part primary key, each part should be indicated sequentially (1,2,...). DWiz will create a primary key index on this field in the Flat table.

The app also quietly adds several columns (prefixed by "_$" or "__$") for maintenance purposes. Optionally, you may direct the ETL process to replace nulls in any column with a Default Value (uncheck the Allow Nulls box when using a Default Value). When a default value is specified for a character-text field (char, varchar, nchar, nvarchar, etc), this value should be enclosed in single-quotes (').

It is important to note here that a Flat table will typically not have the same data as any single Download table, and in fact can even be designed "from scratch" without using any download table as a template. Using the closest Download table as a template to begin the design of a Flat table is merely a convenience. The goal of the Flat table is to stage denormalized content in a form that can be easily used to load a dimension table (or fact or other warehouse table). So if your goal for a particular Flat table, FlatCustomer, is to hold all the descriptive info about a customer, then you might begin by copying

DownloadCustomer as a template, but also add denormalized columns for address pieces, phone, email, etc--knowing that you will need to draw this data from other Source tables (AddressTable, PhoneTable, etc). In the Flat Table Definition page, we are only concerned with configuring the appropriate columns; filling those columns with processed data is the job of the Flat Procedure, described later.

Another design decision to be considered in the Flat Definition page is that of slowly-changing dimensional attributes (SCDs). Any attributes of Type 2 ("Add Row"), Type 3 ("Add Row + History Column"), Type 6 ("Type 1 over Type 2"), or Type 7 ("Dual Type 1/Type 2") should be indicated as additional columns of the Primary Key in the Flat Definition. For example, suppose our Source customer tables have a single primary key column of "AccountNumber", and we have copied that column to the FlatCustomer definition, where we indicated it with a "1" in the Primary Key field. Yet we also want the customer's address US_State to be a Type 2 SCD ("Add Row") attribute--because our company's Service & Support depends greatly on the US State. So we add the US_State column to the Flat and indicate it with a "2" in the Primary Key column (The "2" here indicates the 2nd part of a multi-part primary key, and is NOT due to the SCD Type 2). This will cause the ETL to generate a new row in the Flat/Dim tables whenever a customer's US State changes--i.e., a Type 2 change. SCDs will be discussed in more detail in a later chapter covering Advanced Flat Procedures.

When you have completed the page, save it with the Floppy-Disk icon. Afterward, it is possible to view the new table within the Staging DB in SSMS. Although the new table is now created in the Staging database, it remains empty for now. The next chapter, "Flat Procedure Design", describes the design of a stored procedure that will feed the new Flat table.

If a Flat table is no longer wanted, it can be deleted with the "Red-X" icon.

Design FlatInvoice

Now repeat the above step to create a flat table called FlatInvoice, based upon the DownloadInvoice table. Right-click the DownloadInvoice table under DWizStaging and select Copy Table. Fill in the definition page to create

FlatInvoice, being certain to specify the primary key(s). After you press the save icon (Floppy-Disk), it should look like this:

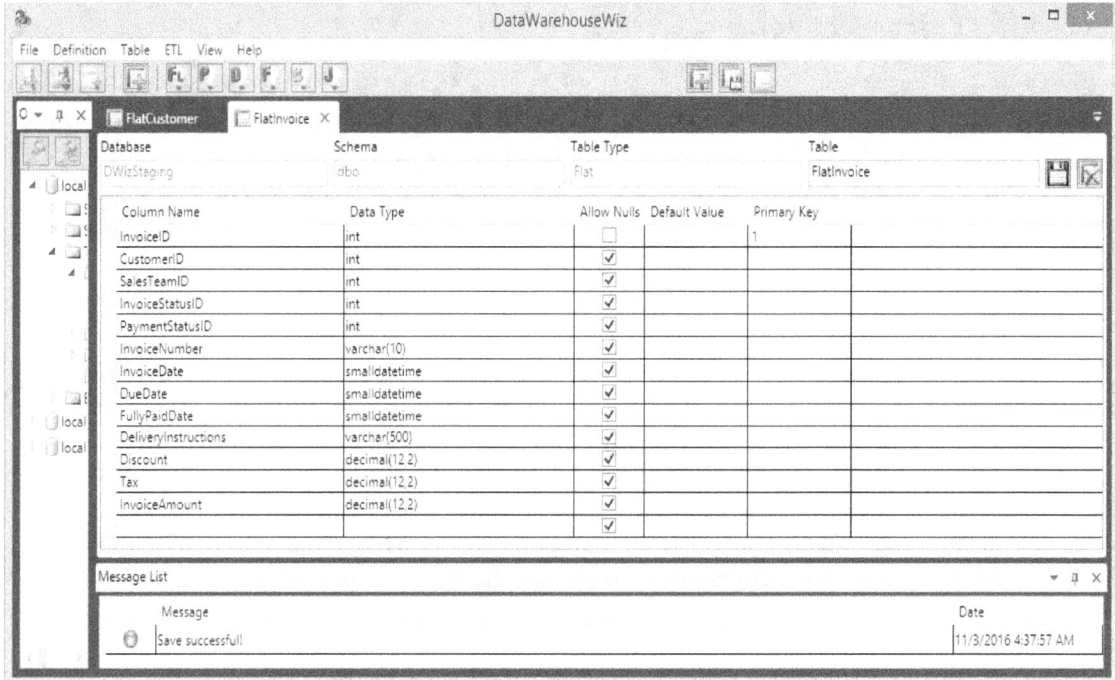

Illustration 27: FlatInvoice Table Definition Page

10. Flat Procedure Design

The Flat Procedure Definition Page defines a Flat Update Stored Procedure to fill and update a Flat Table during the ETL process. This page has powerful options that facilitate any type of transform possible in SQL, including transforms that rely on multiple sources. The following sections describe each input field of the page, and how it affects transforms.

Note: All tables and procedures referenced in the Flat Procedure Definition Page are located in the staging DB. By the time the Flat Procedure runs in the ETL Process, the ETL Process will have already updated Staging's Download tables with the latest data from the original Source DB tables.

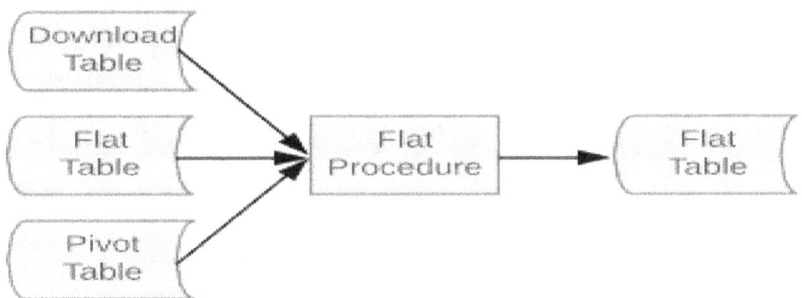

Illustration 28: Flow of a Typical Flat Procedure

Flat Procedure Definition Page

DWiz will write the Flat Procedure for you, based on your inputs to the Flat Procedure Definition Page; however, DWiz will always give you an opportunity to view and modify the code if you wish. The Flat Procedure Definition Page is shown in the following illustration. Each of the fields of this page will be described in detail below. Most of the fields are optional, and not needed for our first rapid prototype, but we will nevertheless describe the full capabilities of this definition page. Afterward, we will use the page to build a Flat Procedure for each of our Flat tables (FlatCustomer and FlatInvoice).

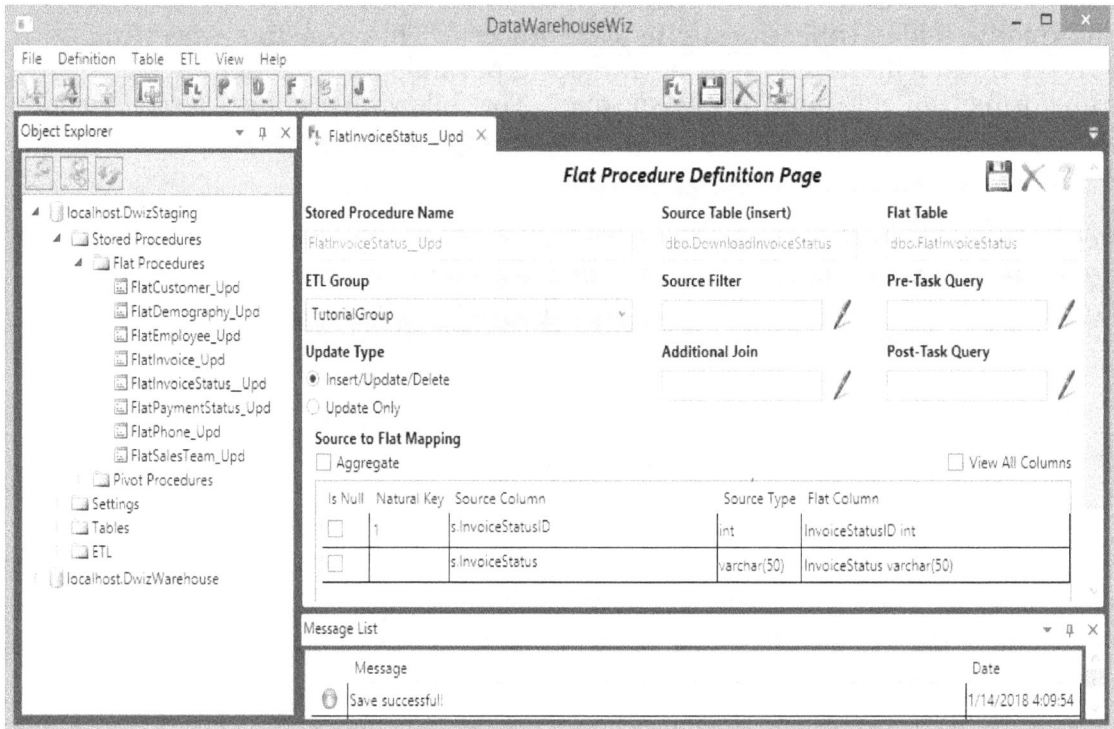

Illustration 29: Flat Procedure Definition Page

Stored Procedure Name

This field contains the exact name of the stored procedure that will be created/altered in the staging DB. The default is `<name of the flat table to be updated>` + `"_upd"`. If desired, these default settings can be changed in the Settings folder under the staging DB of the Object Explorer. You can change any of these global settings for your own purposes, but if you do so, then you must re-compile any stored procedures that made use of the previous setting values.

Source Table (insert)

This field identifies the primary source of data from the Download tables, that will be used for raw data going into the transforms. Within the stored procedure, this table will have the alias "s" (for source). In other input fields below (Source Filter, Source Column), you may reference any primary source column by using the prefix "s." . Other, secondary sources can also be utilized by using one of these fields below: Additional Join, Additional Source, Pre-Task Query, or Post-Task Query. Note that the Source Table is a Download table in the staging DB, **not** the original table of the Source DB. In some cases, such as for Pivot Flat tables, the primary source is a previously-made Flat table; however, the primary source is **never** a table in a Source DB.

Flat Table

This identifies the Flat table, the "target", that will be updated by this stored procedure. Within the stored procedure, this table will have the alias "t" (for target). In other input fields below (Source Filter, Source Column), you may reference any target column by using the prefix "t." .

ETL Group

This field indicates which ETL Group that this stored procedure will be included into. It should be the same ETL Group that includes the primary source table. If the ETL Group is changed in the future, then the primary source table should also be moved to the new group.

Source Filter

This field allows you to specify a filter that will be applied (in a SQL WHERE clause) when the procedure queries the primary source table. Do not include the "WHERE" nor the closing ";". An example is "s.MyFlag = 1", which will then be included in the WHERE clauses, causing all the procedure's queries to be limited to rows where the primary source table has column MyFlag = 1. If your desired source filter has multiple lines, such as a CASE statement, then simply click the InkPen button to the right of the Source Filter input box--this will pop-up a convenient multi-line box for you, as shown in the following illustration.

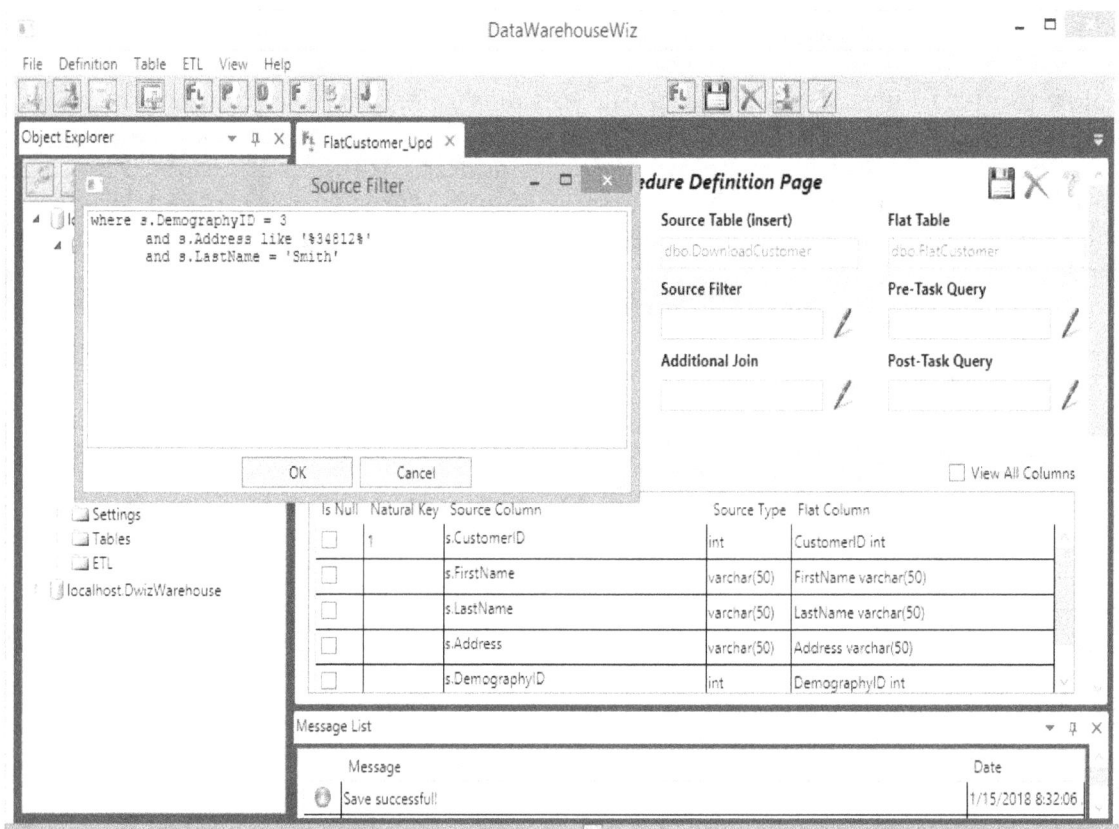

Illustration 30: Creating a Source Filter in a Flat Procedure Definition Page

Pre-Task Query

This field specifies a SQL statement that will be executed immediately *before* the queries of this Flat Stored Procedure run in the ETL process. It is a catch-all to allow you to do any kind of processing that you cannot easily implement through the other fields. An example is "exec MySpecialPreProcessor_SP", where MySpecialPreProcessor_SP is a stored procedure that you have written from scratch and placed into the staging DB. We recommend that this be used only as a last resort, after use of the other input fields has proved insufficient;

using the other powerful input fields is easier, more readable, and more maintainable. To enter a multi-line query, press the InkPen button to the right of the input box, as shown in the following illustration.

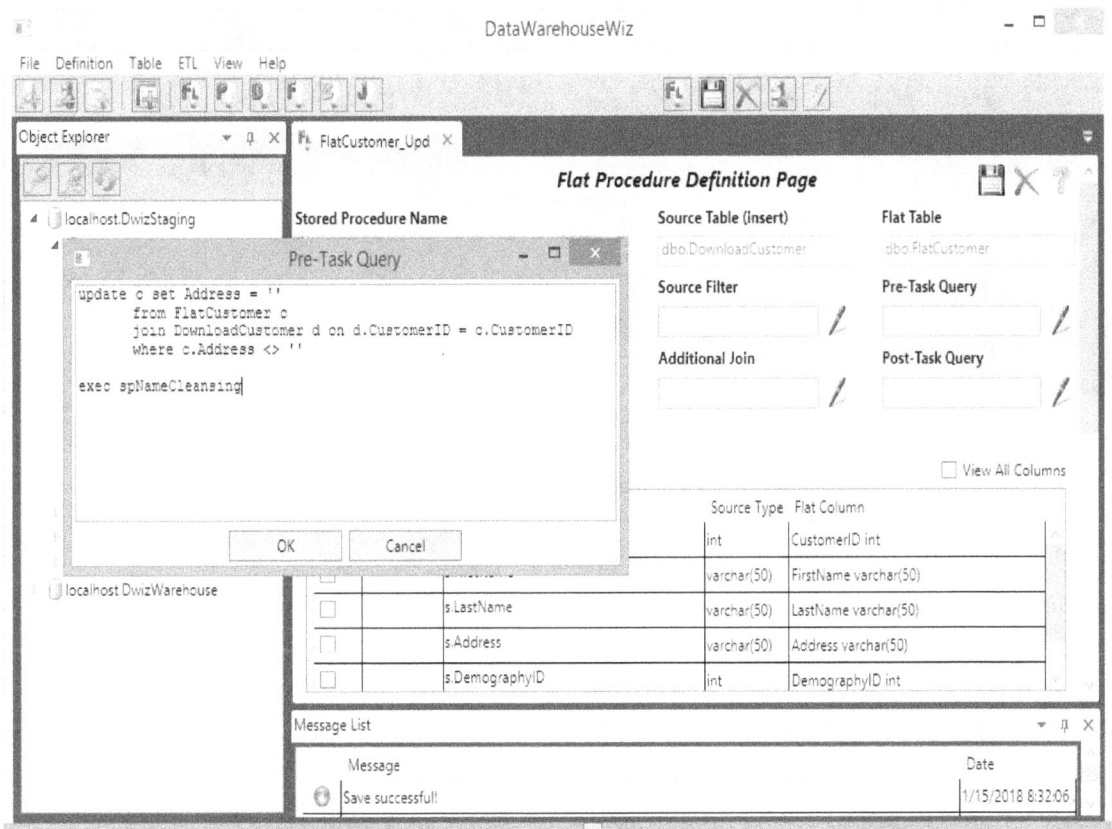

Illustration 31: Adding a Pre-Task Query to a Flat Procedure Definition Page

Update Type

This field has two choices: "Insert/Update/Delete" and "Update Only". The first selection will capture any change in the original source table (in the Source DB)

, including Inserts, Updates, and Deletes. The second choice will capture only Updates. The effects of this Update Type on the procedure code written by DWiz are shown in the following illustration.

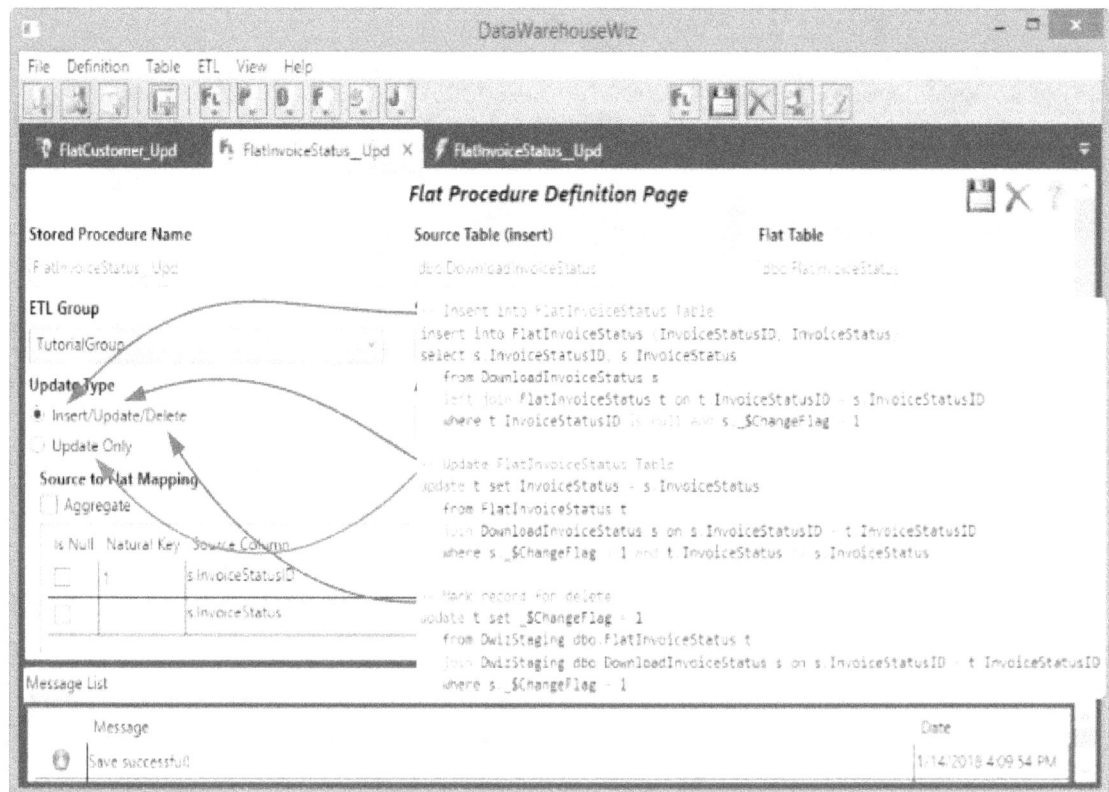

Illustration 32: Effect of the Update Type on a Flat Procedure Definition

Additional Join

This field allows you to specify one or more secondary source tables to be joined in the procedure's queries. Include a unique alias for each table, but not "s" nor "t". An example is "`left join MySecondaryTable s2 on s2.pkid = s.fkMySecondary`", where the new secondary table "s2" will be joined to the primary source table "s" on the indicated columns. For multiple (or multi-line) joins, use the InkPen button to the right of the input box, as shown in the following illustration. We recommend "left" joins unless you specifically want to filter the procedure's queries to rows only existing in the secondary table. Also, if the secondary table has a many-to-one relationship with the primary, you will probably want to use the "Aggregate" operation discussed below.

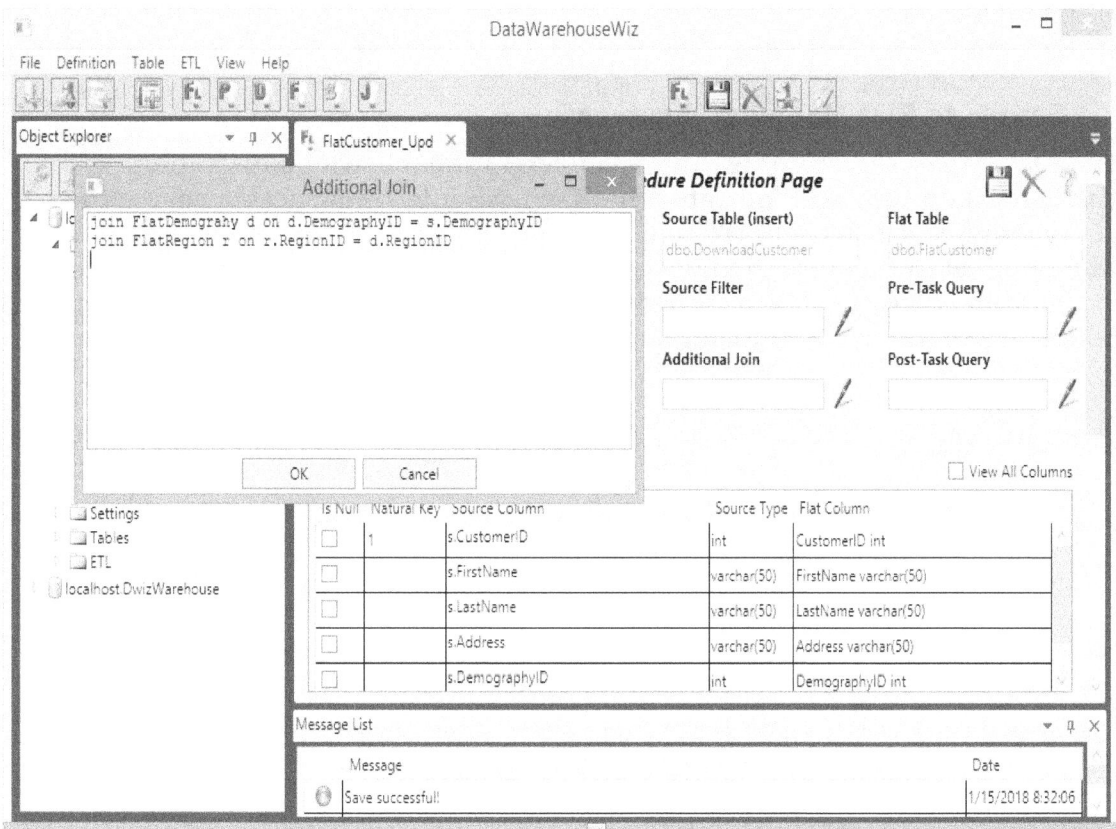

Illustration 33: Adding Addition Joins to a Flat Procedure Definition Page

Post-Task Query

This field specifies a SQL statement that will be executed immediately *after* the queries of this Flat Stored Procedure run in the ETL process. It is a catch-all to allow you to do any kind of processing that you cannot easily implement through the other fields. An example is `"exec MySpecialPostProcessor_SP"`, where MySpecialPostProcessor_SP is a stored procedure that you have written from scratch and placed into the staging DB. We recommend that this be used only as a last resort, after use of the other input fields has proved insufficient; using the other powerful input fields is easier, more readable, and more maintainable. To enter a multi-line query, press the InkPen button to the right of the input box.

Source to Flat Mapping: Aggregate

The use of the "Aggregate" feature is shown in the following illustration. A check-mark in this field indicates that DWiz should construct an aggregation query using SQL's GROUP BY clause. Every Source Column (from the primary source table) that is indicated as a Natural Key part (i.e., has an order number in the Natural Key field) will be included in the GROUP BY clause. All other Source Columns must include an appropriate aggregation function, such as:

- MIN()
- MAX()
- SUM()
- AVG()

Source Columns that are not used must be left blank or explicitly indicated by `"--NotCopied--"`. Remember that, after Saving the page and Creating the stored procedure, DWiz will display the exact SQL programming code for your review before compiling it to the staging server.

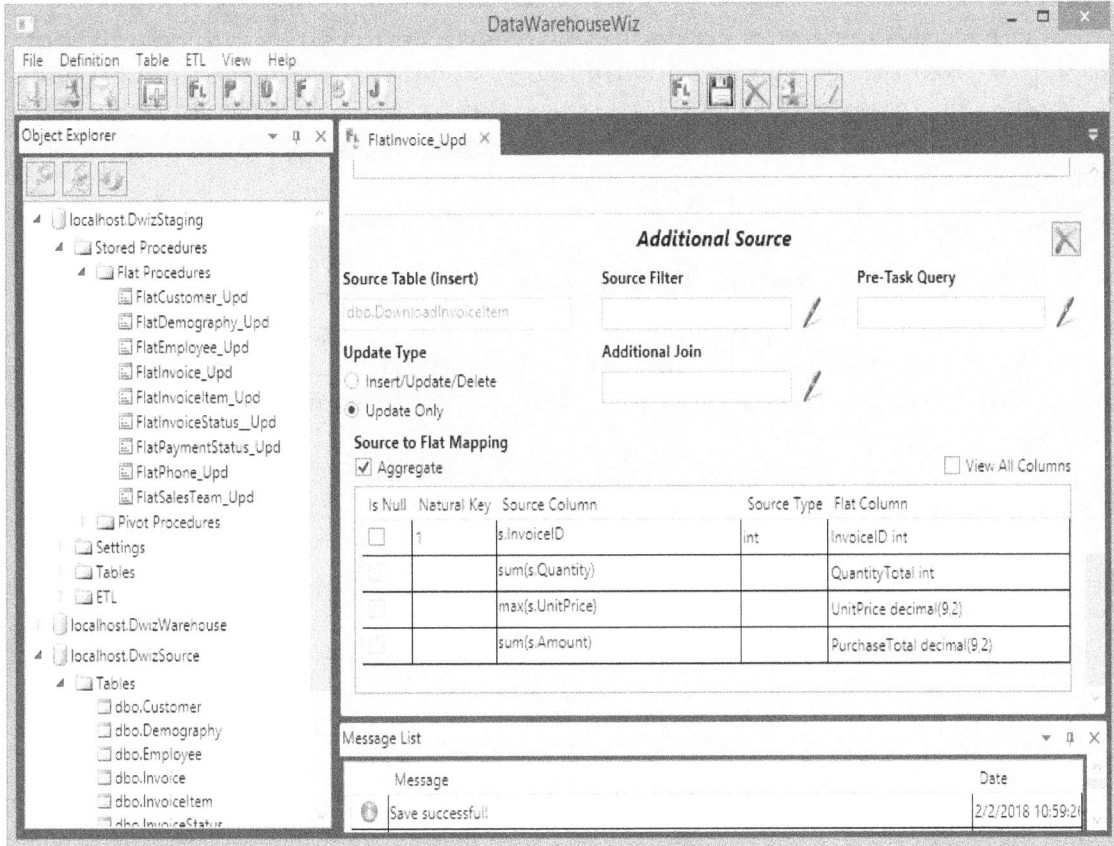

Illustration 34: Using the Aggregate Feature of a Flat Procedure Definition Page

Source to Flat Mapping: View All Columns

Checking this field allows the user to see all columns of the target Flat table schema. When unchecked, after Saving the Definition Page, DWiz will display only the columns being updated by the queries. This field does not affect the actual queries in any way.

Source to Flat Mapping: Is Null

This field is used to generate code that transforms null values into default (Not Applicable) values. Thus, checking this box will convert a Source Column like "s.MyString" to something like "IsNull(s.MyString,'')" In many places in a Kimball type warehouse, nulls are undesirable and therefore replaced by Not Applicable values.

Source to Flat Mapping: Natural Key

This field is used to indicate the Natural Key(s) of the source table. These Natural Keys are generally the primary key(s) of the original table in the Source DB, with a "1" indicating the first part, and a "2" indicating the second part (if existing), etc.

Source to Flat Mapping: Source Column

This field holds the transform for the data to be loaded into the Flat Table Column, as shown in the following illustration. For a simple copy of a source column, it might be similar to "s.Cost". For an aggregation, it might be similar to "SUM(s.Cost)". For a more lengthy transform, click on the Source Column, and then on the InkPen that appears to the right--this will pop-up a multi-line space for you to enter a CASE statement or other lengthy element. The transform may reference any source columns with "s.", any target columns with "t.", and any Additional Join columns with their given aliases.

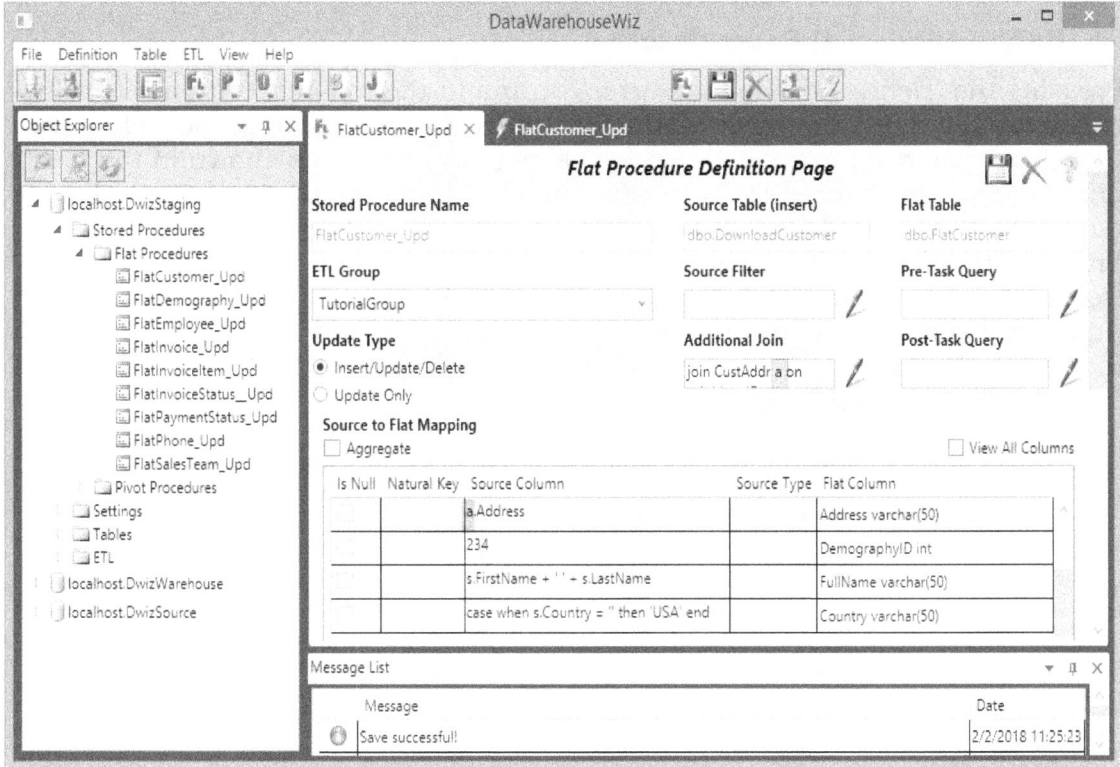

Illustration 35: Using Transforms in the "Source Column" Fields of a Flat Procedure Definition Page

Source to Flat Mapping: Source Type

This field indicates the SQL variable type of the original source column. If the Source Column is changed to a transformation (such as "SUM(s.Cost)"), then DWiz will blank this field.

Source to Flat Mapping: Flat Column

This field indicates the target column into which the transform of Source Column will be loaded.

Define Additional Source section

Pressing the "Define Additional Source" button in the top Tab Button Bar will cause an Additional Source section to be added to the bottom of the Definition Page (you may need to scroll down in the page to view it), as shown in the next illustration. This causes DWiz to generate additional separate queries to load data from this Additional Source. Unlike the Additional Join features of the main page, these Additional Source queries will be separate and independent from the primary source table, not joined to it. All the input fields of the Additional Source section work exactly as in the main page, but of course apply instead to the Additional Source source table, which has the alias "s" in the transforms of this section.

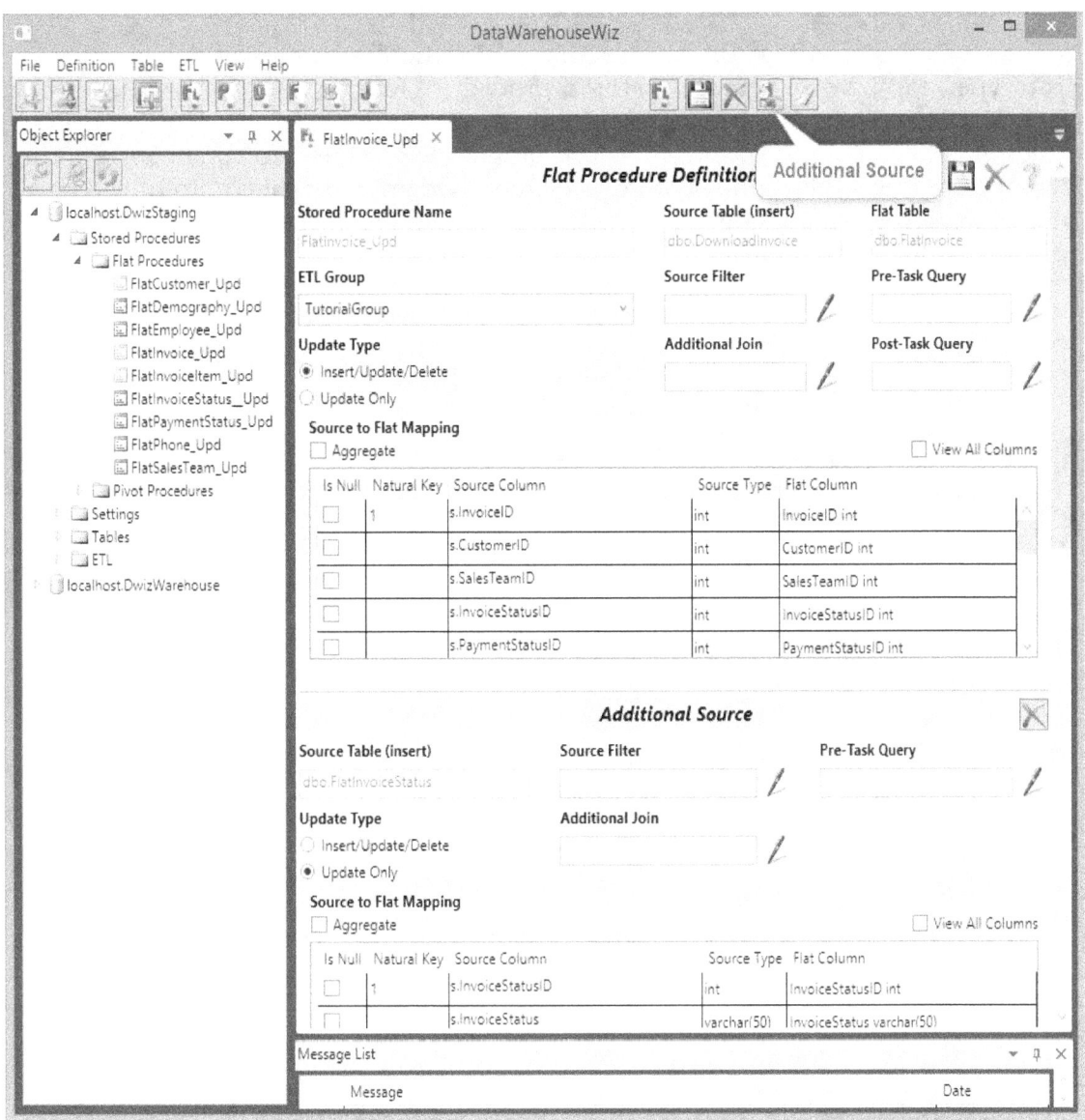

Illustration 36: Adding an Additional Source to a Flat Procedure Definition Page

Example for the Design of a Flat Procedure

Now we will design a Flat Procedure for each of the Flat tables of our rapid prototype. First we will create a stored procedure for the ETL that will feed the table FlatCustomer. We call this a "Flat" procedure because it is loading a Flat table. A "Flat" procedure resides in the Staging DB, where its code controls the ETL of data into a Flat table from one or more Download tables. So in the Object Explorer, we expand DWizStaging-->Stored Procedures-->Flat, right-click on the Flat folder, then select New Flat:

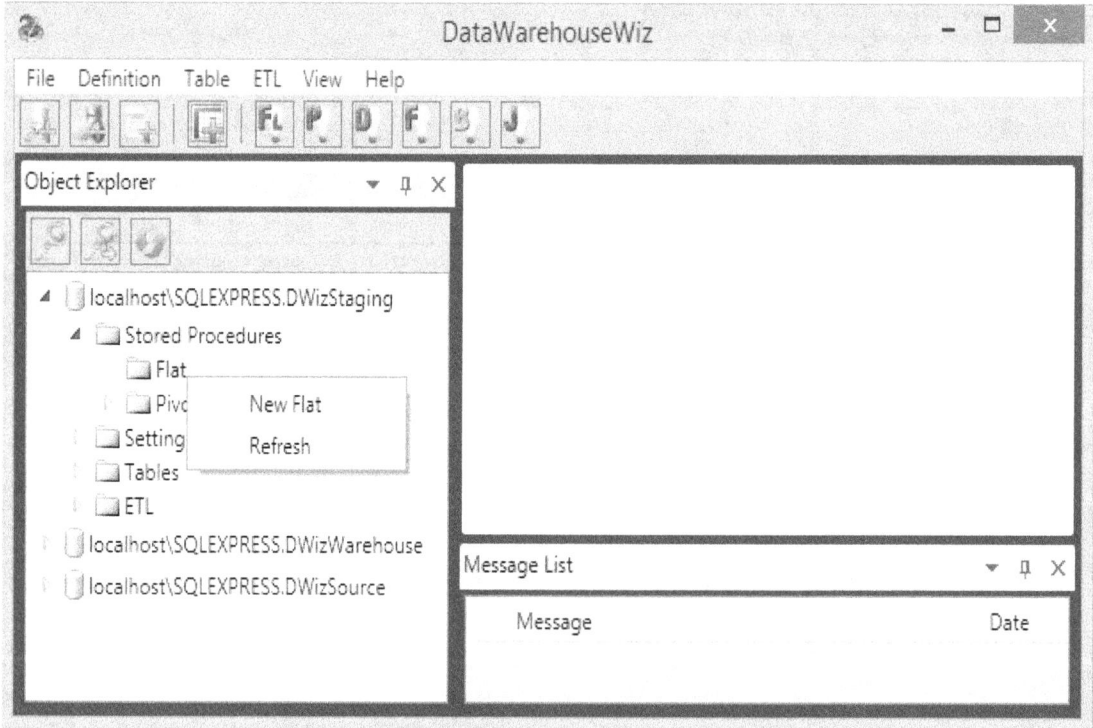

Illustration 37: Creating a Flat-Table Stored Procedure

This gives us a popup window, where we will give the stored procedure a name and indicate the primary source and destination tables:

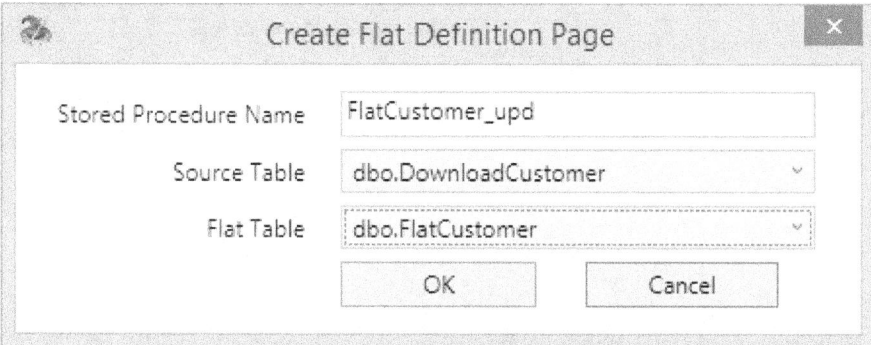

Illustration 38: Pop-Up for Creating a Flat-Table Stored Procedure

We are creating this procedure to load & update FlatCustomer, so a suitable name is "FlatCustomer_upd". The Source Table is DownloadCustomer (note that "Source" here does not refer to the Source DB: all Flat stored procedures draw from tables sourced by the Staging DB). The Flat Table destination is FlatCustomer. When you have completed the form, press OK.

This brings us to the Flat Procedure Definition Page:

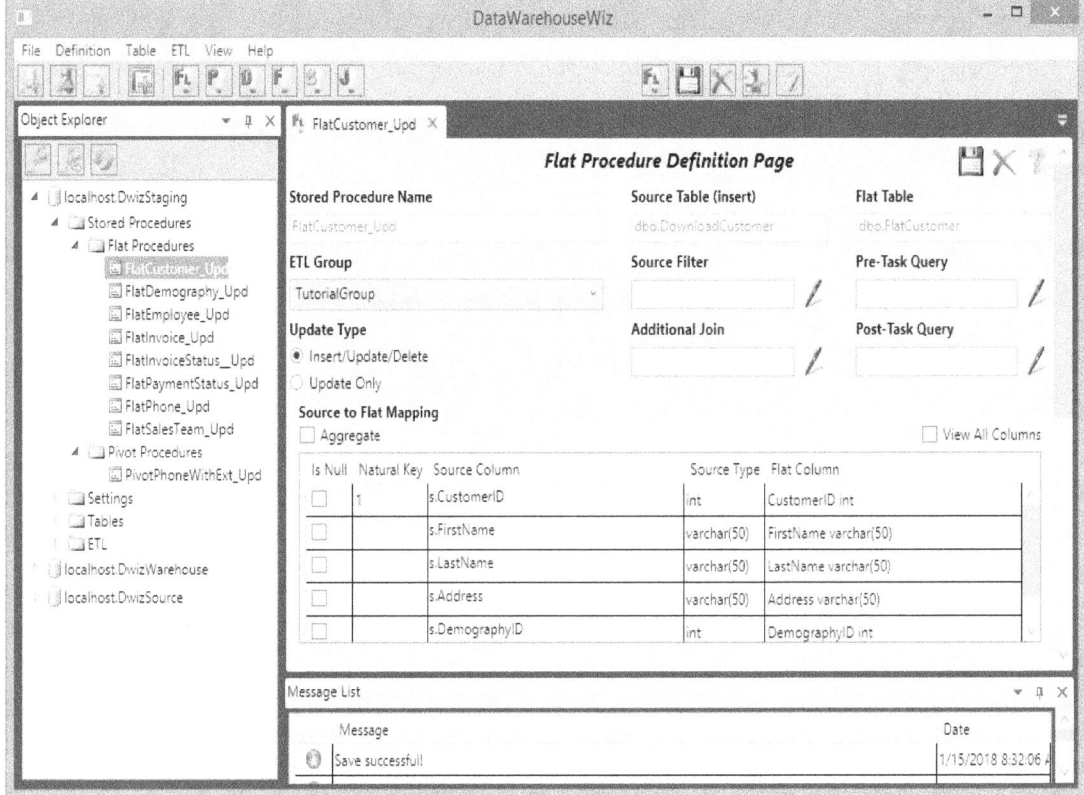

Illustration 39: Flat-Table Stored Procedure Definition Page

On this page, we need to set the appropriate ETL Group, indicate column CustomerID as the Natural Key with a "1", and press the Save button (Floppy-Disk icon). Note that this page provides many other advanced capabilities for transforming the data, as described previously.

After completing the form and pressing Save, we will need to create the stored procedure. We do this by pressing the Create/Alter Procedure button (Lightning/+ icon as shown) below:

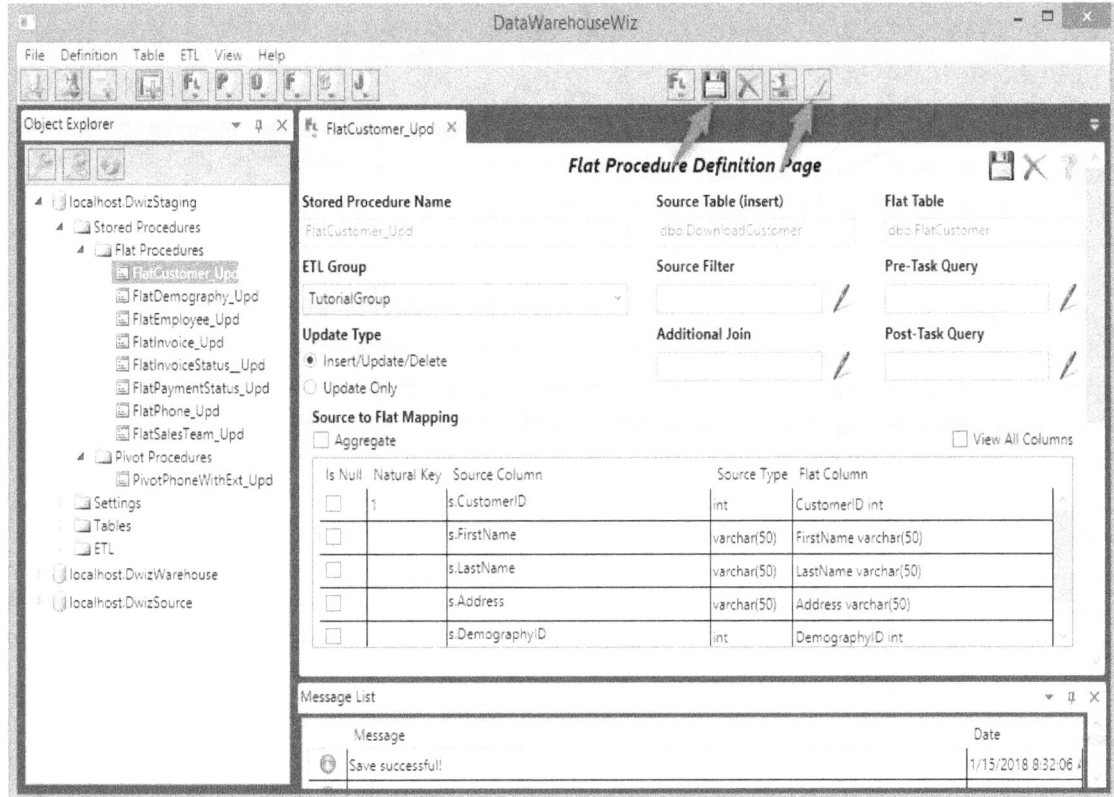

Illustration 40: DWiz Creates a Flat-Table Stored Procedure From Your Form Input

When the above button is pressed, DWiz designs the stored procedure for you!
The actual code is displayed, as shown below, and is complete; however, DWiz
gives you this opportunity to modify the code if desired. After looking at the
code (or not!), press the Save Procedure button as indicated (Lightning over
Floppy-Disk icon):

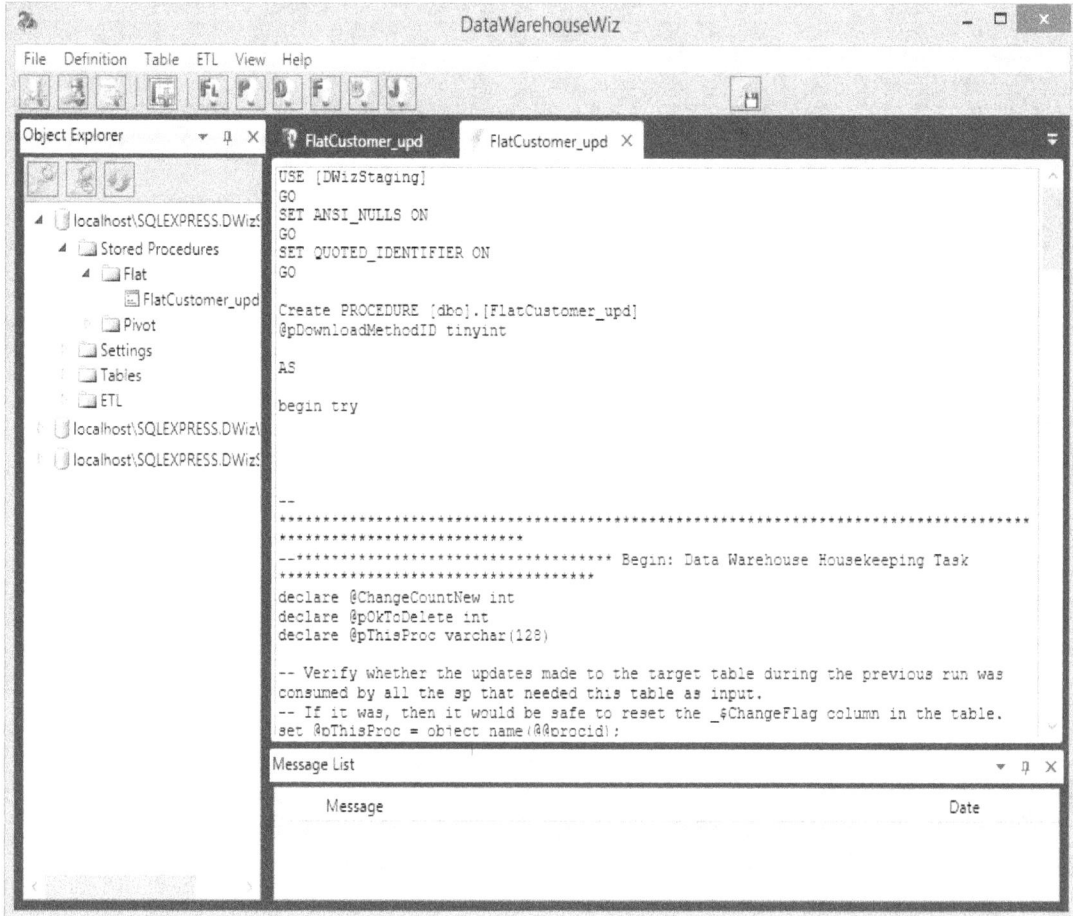

Illustration 41: Reviewing DWiz's Stored Procedure Code Prior to Compiling It

The FlatCustomer_upd stored procedure is now saved into the DWizStaging DB. This Procedure will be executed as part of the ETL Group processing, when the ETL Group is later compiled and run.

Procedure for FlatInvoice

Now you can repeat the above steps to create an ETL stored procedure for FlatInvoice. Perform the following steps:

- Expand DWizStaging-->Stored Procedures-->Flat, right-click the Flat folder, and select New Flat.

- Create Flat Definition Page with Stored Procedure Name = FlatInvoice_upd, Source Table = DownloadInvoice, and Flat Table = FlatInvoice. Then press OK.

- In the Flat Definition Page, select ETL Group = TutorialGroup, enter a "1" in the Natural Key box of column InvoiceID, and then press the Save icon.

- Press the Create/Alter Procedure button (Lightning/+ icon).

- After the code is displayed, press the Save Procedure button (Lightning Over Floppy icon).

11. Dimension Table Design

In the star-schema warehouse, Fact tables hold "the numbers", mostly additive facts about transactions, and foreign keys to various dimensions. In contrast, the **Dimension** tables hold all the other descriptive info about a particular dimension. So if you had a large stack of sales invoices, and wanted to make a warehouse, you would probably create the following warehouse tables:

- Customer Dimension table, holding customer name, address, phone, etc.

- Product Dimension, holding product name, description, specs, etc.

- Salesperson Dimension holding employee name, etc.

- Date Dimension, holding the dates of sales with datepart fields (month, year, etc.)

- Invoice Fact table, holding rows with foreign keys pointing to the above tables for each line item, along with the sales price paid, cost-of-goods (for accounting) and any discount amounts.

Since the Fact table will need to include foreign keys based on the dimension-table primary keys, you should first design the Dimension tables *before* creating your fact table. However, before designing a Dimension table, you should have already designed:

- A Flat table that stages data in the same format as the new Dimension table

- One or more Download tables that extract the required data from Sources

- A Flat Procedure that transforms the raw data from the Downloads and feeds the Flat table

Note that all of the above tables and procedures must be defined within the same ETL Group as the new Dimension table. That is, the same ETL Group must be selected within each of their definition pages.

The Dimension Table's relationship with other warehouse tables is shown in the following illustration:

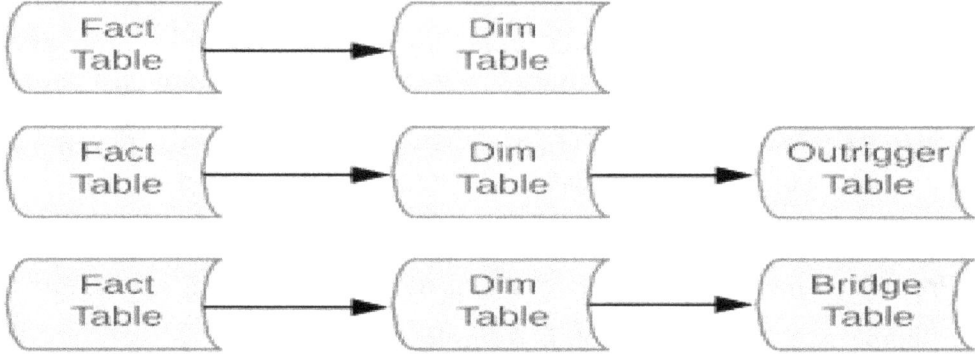

Illustration 42: Relationship of Dimension Table to Other Warehouse Tables

Special Considerations for Design of Dimension Tables

Following are special considerations in the design of Dimension tables. As these must be implemented in the design of the Flat table that feeds the Dimension, they were fully discussed in Chapter 9 Flat Table Design, and will only be listed here.

Uniqueness of Entities within a Dimension

Consideration in establishing the uniqueness of entities in a dimension, in specifying the slowly-changing dimension type of attributes, and of conforming dimensions when they are shared with other fact tables or other data marts.

Example of the Design of a Dimension Table

For our first rapid prototype module, we need to design a Dimension table for the "Customer" dimension. Flat tables should be previously designed so that each Dimension table draws data directly from one Flat table, although it might not use all the columns of that Flat table. In this example, we will create a Dimension table called DimCustomer, in our warehouse DWizWarehouse.

Unlike the intermediate Download and Flat tables, this Dim table will reside in the end-user warehouse. Although we will copy the schema of FlatCustomer to use as a basis for DimCustomer, we will not copy any data yet...that will happen when we run our future ETL Process. In Object Explorer, expand DWizStaging-->Tables-->Flat to view the Flat tables, then right-click the FlatCustomer table and select Copy Table. In the pop-up window, change the database to your warehouse database, and the table type to "Dim". You may also choose an alternative Schema, if you have previously created a Schema other than the default dbo. Choose a table name (default is "Dim" + the original source table name), and press OK:

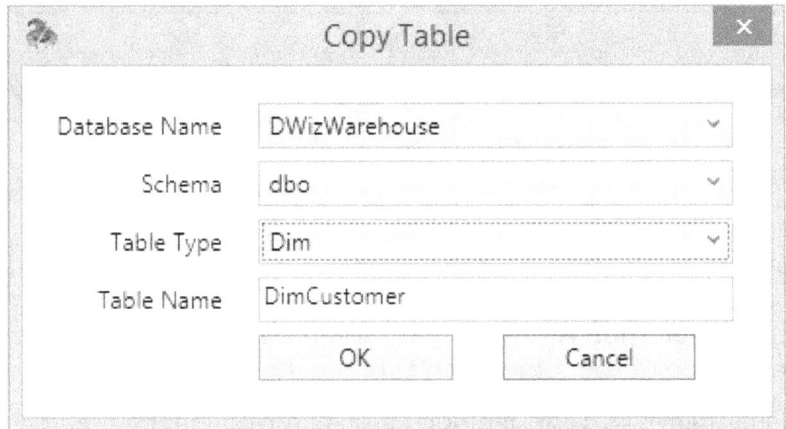

Illustration 43: "Copy Table" Pop-Up for Dimension Tables

This brings us to the Dim Definition page:

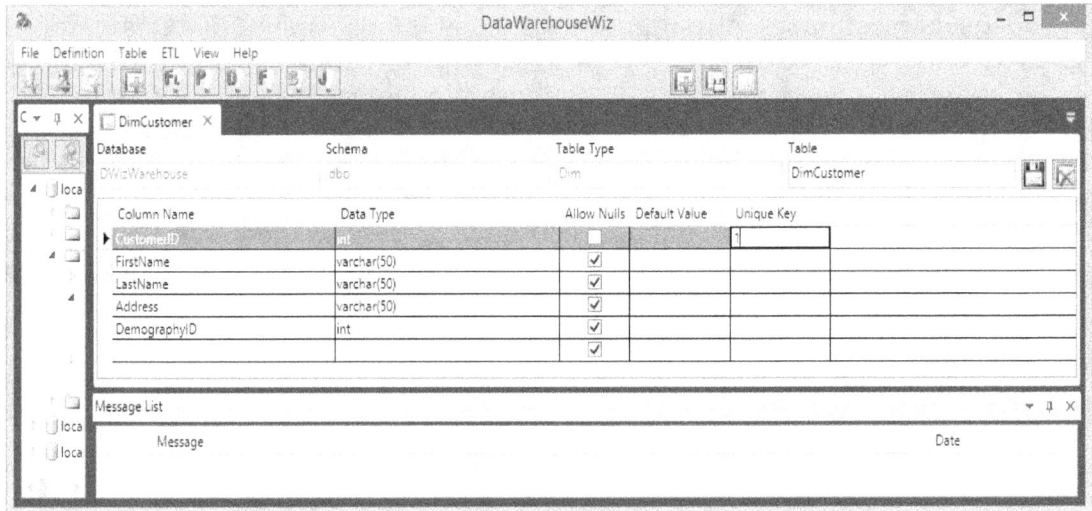

Illustration 44: "Dimension Table" Definition Page

As with the other table definition pages, most of the parameters of this page are conveniently filled with default values by Data Warehouse Wiz; yet you can override any parameter for your own purposes. The first line of the page details the location and type of the dimension table being created:

- Database = DwizWarehouse <or your warehouse DB>

- Schema = dbo <or your pre-existing alternate Schema>

- Table Type = Dim

- Table = DimCustomer <or your chosen table name>

The columns of DimCustomer default to copies of FlatCustomer, but may be modified as needed. Also, columns may be added or deleted. The "Natural Key" corresponds to the primary key(s) of FlatCustomer, but will not be used as a primary key for DimCustomer. The app will quietly add a new surrogate primary key "DimCustomerKey" when the definition page is saved. In keeping with best practices, each warehouse dimension table will use a surrogate primary key (e.g., DimCustomerKey) which is unrelated to the primary key(s) of the source(s). The surrogate primary key will always be of type int.

Ensure that the Natural Key is indicated properly by a "1". If it is multi-part, then each part should be indicated sequentially (1,2,...). The definition page should look like this before you save it:

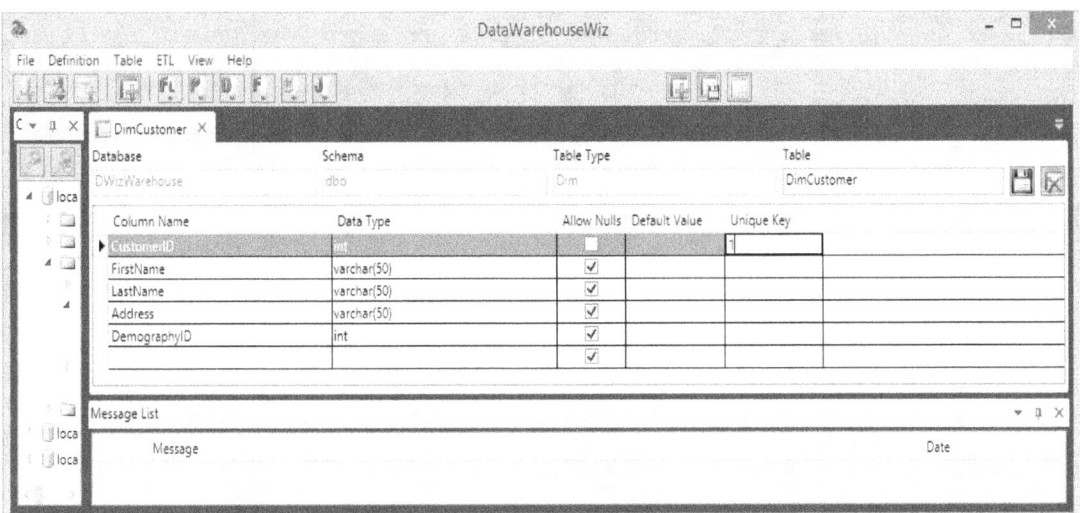

Illustration 45: Completing a Dimension-Table Definition Page Form

When you have completed the page, save it with the Floppy-Disk icon. Afterward, the DimCustomer definition page will show the DimCustomerKey that was quietly added. This DimCustomerKey is the new surrogate primary key:

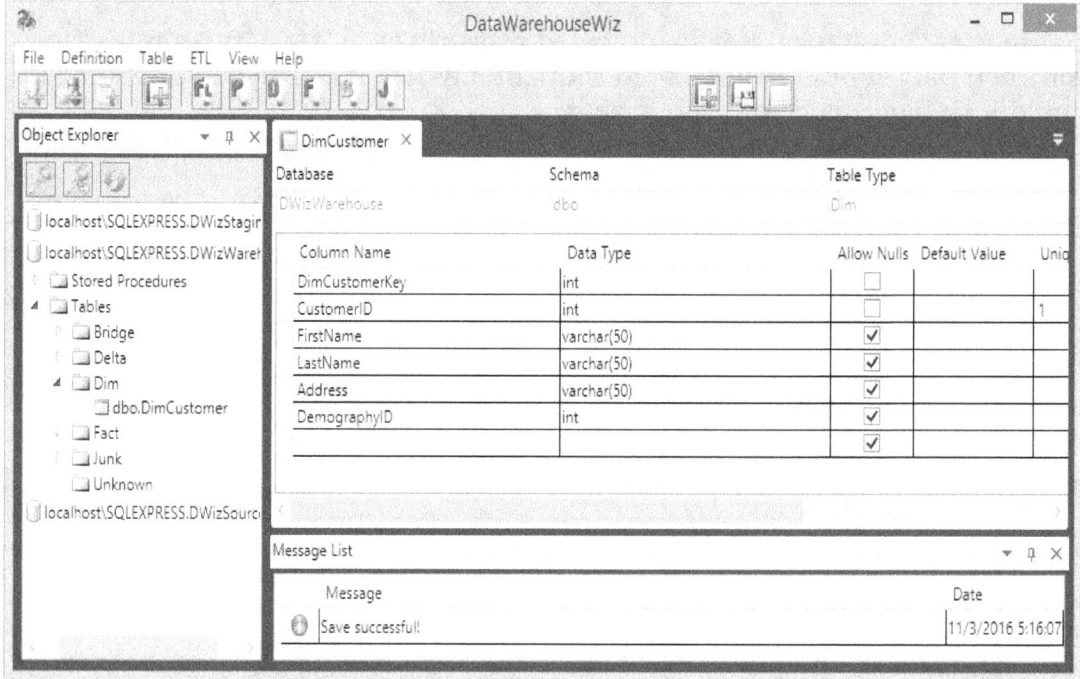

Illustration 46: DWiz Automatically Creates a Surrogate Key

You can review the DimCustomer definition page at any time by expanding DWizWarehouse-->Tables-->Dim and clicking on DimCustomer. Of course, it is also possible to view the new table within the DWizWarehouse DB in SSMS. Although the data has not been copied yet, DWiz has put one special record in the new dim table: the Not Applicable (or "Unknown") record, with DimCustomerKey = -1. This value (-1) of the dimension table primary key will be referenced in the future fact table where-ever the customer table would otherwise not have an entry (hence, Not Applicable or Unknown).   This satisfies the Foreign Key-Primary Key relationship between the tables. To see what values DWiz uses for columns in the Not Applicable records, go to the Object Explorer and expand   Staging-->Settings-->NA Record. Also expand Settings-->IsNull to see the values substituted for nulls where necessary. You can change any of these global settings for your own purposes, but if you do so, then you must re-compile any stored procedures that made use of the previous setting values.

If a table is no longer wanted, it can be deleted with the "Red-X" icon.

12. Dimension Procedure Design

For each Dimension Table, you will need to design a Dimension Procedure to feed it. DWiz makes this very easy with the Dimension Procedure Definition page. Since the Dimension table resides in the warehouse database, its Dimension Procedure resides there also. This stored procedure typically will draw data from a single Flat table that has already formatted the data in the same way as the Dimension table. As shown in the following illustration, a Dimension Procedure may draw from a Pivot Table, which is a special type of Flat table that pivots certain source row data into Flat column data.

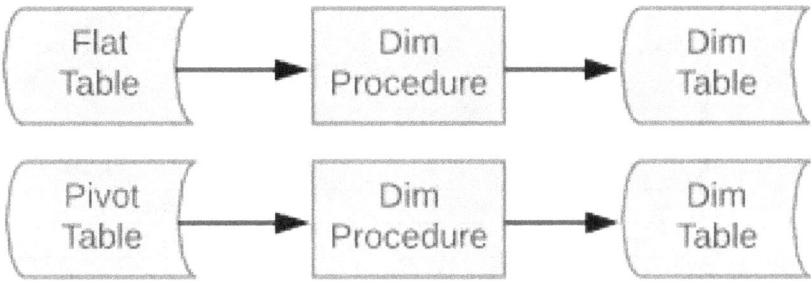

Illustration 47: A Dimension Procedure Feeds a Dimension Table

Dimension Procedure Definition Page

DWiz will write the Dimension Procedure for you, based on your inputs to the Dimension Procedure Definition Page; however, DWiz will always give you an opportunity to view and modify the code if you wish. A Dimension Procedure Definition Page is shown in the following illustration. Each of the fields will be described in detail.

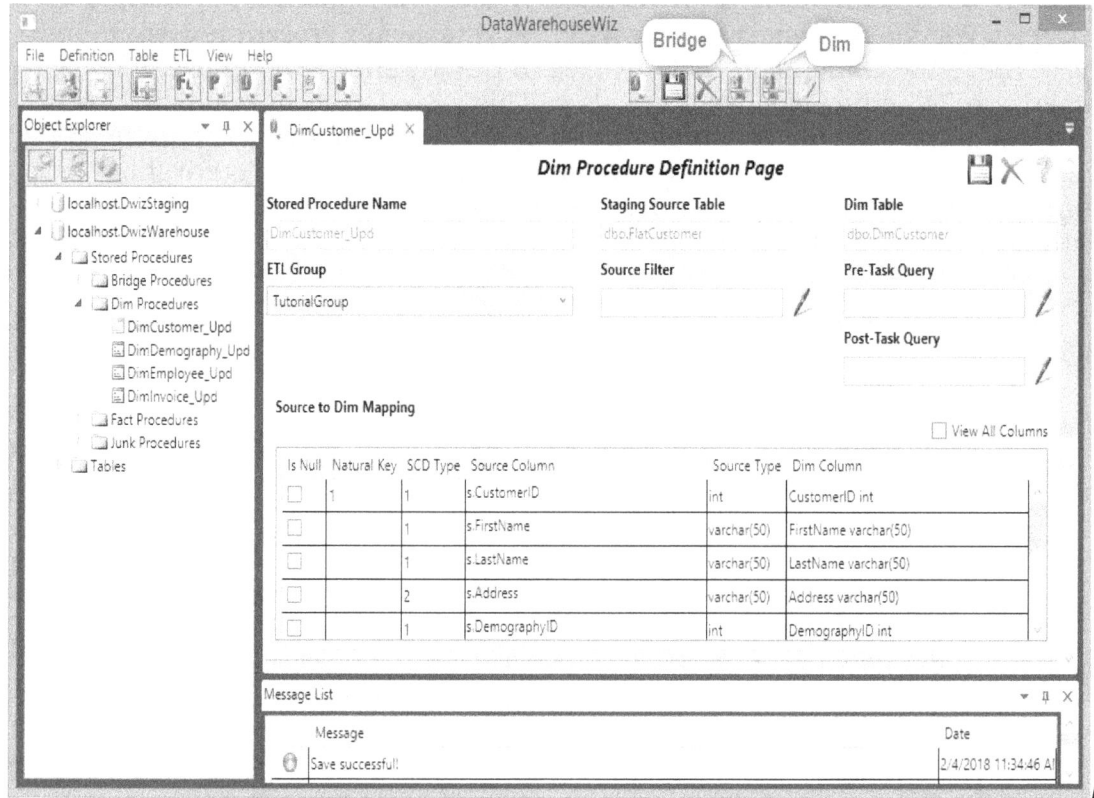

Ilustration 48: The Dimension Procedure Definition Page

Stored Procedure Name

This field contains the exact name of the stored procedure that will be created/altered in the staging DB. The default is `<name of the flat table to be updated>` + `"_upd"`. If desired, these default settings can be changed in the Settings folder under the staging DB of the Object Explorer. You can change any of these global settings for your own purposes, but if you do so, then you must re-compile any stored procedures that made use of the previous setting values.

Staging Source Table

This field identifies the primary source of data from the Flat tables, that will be used for raw data going into the transforms. Within the stored procedure, this table will have the alias "s" (for source). In other input fields below (Source Filter, Source Column), you may reference any primary source column by using the prefix "s.". Note that the Source Table is a Flat table in the staging DB, **not** the original table of the Source DB. The following illustration shows the relationship and mapping of the Source and Target tables.

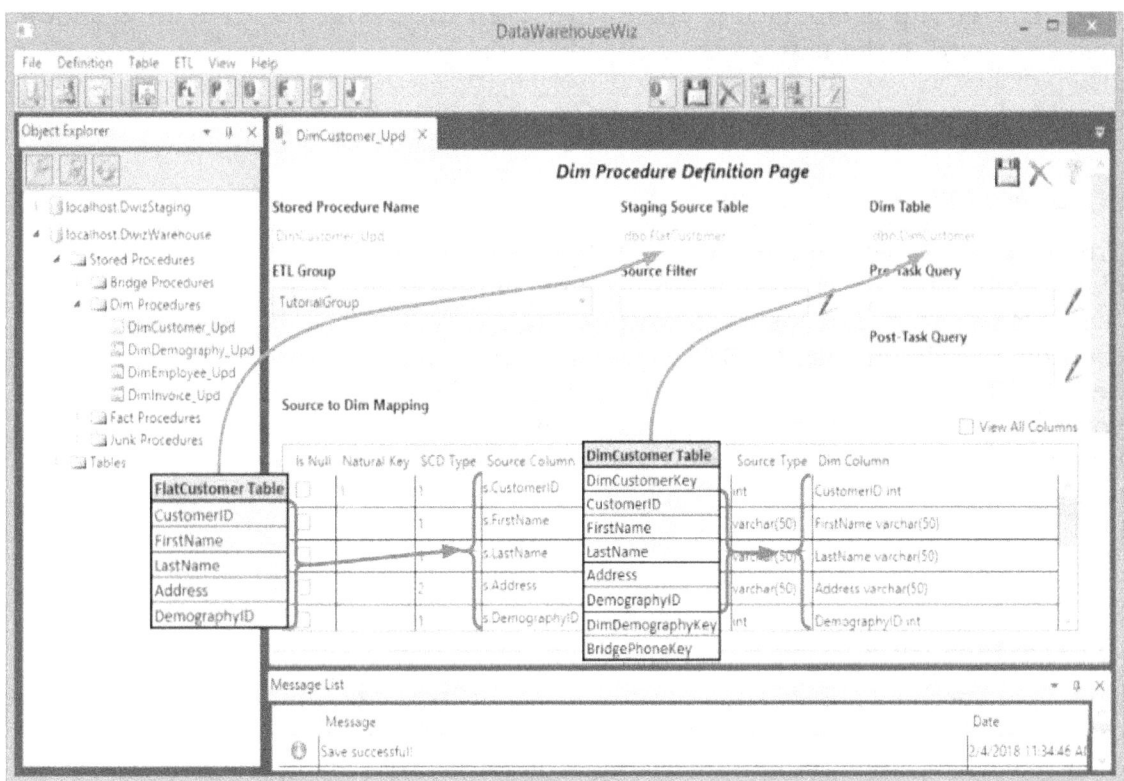

Illustration 49: The Source and Target Tables of the Dim Procedure Definition Page

Dim Table

This identifies the Fact table, the "target", that will be updated by this stored procedure. Within the stored procedure, this table will have the alias "t" (for target). In other input fields below (Source Filter, Source Column), you may reference any target column by using the prefix "t." .

ETL Group

This field indicates which ETL Group that this stored procedure will be included into. It should be the same ETL Group that includes the primary source table. If the ETL Group is changed in the future, then the primary source table should also be moved to the new group.

Source Filter

This field allows you to specify a filter that will be applied (in a SQL WHERE clause) when the procedure queries the primary source table. Do not include the "WHERE" nor the closing ";". An example is "s.MyFlag = 1", which will then be included in the WHERE clauses, causing all the procedure's queries to be limited to rows where the primary source table has column MyFlag = 1. If your desired source filter has multiple lines, such as a CASE statement, then simply click the InkPen button to the right of the Source Filter input box--this will pop-up a convenient multi-line box for you.

Pre-Task Query

This field specifies a SQL statement that will be executed immediately *before* the queries of this Flat Stored Procedure run in the ETL process. It is a catch-all to allow you to do any kind of processing that you cannot easily implement through the other fields. An example is "exec MySpecialPreProcessor_SP", where MySpecialPreProcessor_SP is a stored procedure that you have written from scratch and placed into the staging DB. We recommend that this be used only as a last resort, after use of the other input fields has proved insufficient; using the other powerful input fields is easier, more readable, and more maintainable. To enter a multi-line query, press the InkPen button to the right of the input box.

Post-Task Query

This field specifies a SQL statement that will be executed immediately *after* the queries of this Flat Stored Procedure run in the ETL process. It is a catch-all to allow you to do any kind of processing that you cannot easily implement through the other fields. An example is "exec MySpecialPostProcessor_SP", where MySpecialPostProcessor_SP is a stored procedure that you have written from scratch and placed into the staging DB. We recommend that this be used only as a last resort, after use of the other input fields has proved insufficient; using the other powerful input fields is easier, more readable, and more maintainable. To enter a multi-line query, press the InkPen button to the right of the input box.

Source to Dim Mapping: View All Columns

Checking this field allows the user to see all columns of the target Flat table schema. When unchecked, after Saving the Definition Page, DWiz will display only the columns being updated by the queries. This field does not affect the actual queries in any way.

Source to Dim Mapping: Is Null

This field is used to generate code that transforms null values into default (Not Applicable) values. Thus, checking this box will convert a Source Column like "s.MyString" to something like "IsNull(s.MyString,'')" In many places in a Kimball type warehouse, nulls are undesirable and therefore replaced by Not Applicable values.

Source to Dim Mapping: Natural Key

This field is used to indicate the Natural Key(s) of the source table. These Natural Keys are generally the primary key(s) of the original table in the Source DB, with a "1" indicating the first part, and a "2" indicating the second part (if existing), etc.

Source to Dim Mapping: SCD Type

The "SCD Type" indicates the desired type of slowly-changing dimension handling, as defined by Kimball et al[2]. DWiz directly supports SCD Types 1 and 2, by selecting the type in this SCD Type column.

SCD 1 is "Overwrite". If a non-key attribute of a Dimension changes, then the new value overwrites the previous value in the Dimension table, with no change to the primary key.

SCD 2 is "New Record". If a non-key attribute of a Dimension changes, this causes a new record to be created in the Dimension table, with a new value of the primary key. However, a maximum of one new record per day will be created for a given Dimension entry. Any further changes to the same entry within the same day are handled as SCD 1 Overwrites. This is the behavior that most warehouse designers want for Type 2 dimensions, as it captures slowly changing dimensions without accumulating trash from transient changes within a day.

Source to Dim Mapping: Source Column

This field holds the transform for the data to be loaded into the Fact Table Column, as shown in the following illustration. For a simple copy of a source column, it might be similar to "s.Cost". For an aggregation, it might be similar to "SUM(s.Cost)". For a more lengthy transform, click on the Source Column, and then on the InkPen that appears to the right--this will pop-up a multi-line space for you to enter a CASE statement or other lengthy element. The transform may reference any source columns with "s.", any target columns with "t.".

Source to Dim Mapping: Source Type

This field indicates the SQL variable type of the original source column. If the Source Column is changed to a transformation (such as `"SUM(s.Cost)"`), then DWiz will blank this field.

Source to Dim Mapping: Dim Column

This field indicates the target column into which the transform of Source Column will be loaded.

The Add Outrigger section

Pressing the "Add Outrigger button in the top Tab Button Bar will cause a pop-up menu that asks which Outrigger table should be added. Then a Dim-To-Outrigger section is added to the bottom of the Definition Page (you may need to scroll down in the page to view it), as shown in the next illustration. This provides the information needed for DWiz to add a foreign-key link to an Outrigger table. The first field of this section, Outrigger Table, displays the name of the Outrigger table to be linked (DimDemography, in this illustration). The next area shows the "Dim-to-Outrigger Surrogate Key Relationship". In these dropdowns, select the correct foreign-key column in the Dim table, and the surrogate primary key of the Outrigger table (both are "DimDemographyKey" in this illustration). Finally, in the area called "Dim to Outrigger Natural Key Mapping", select the Natural Key field of the Dimension, as well as the Natural Key field of the Outrigger table itself. For more details about Outrigger Design, see the Chapter "Outrigger Dimension Design".

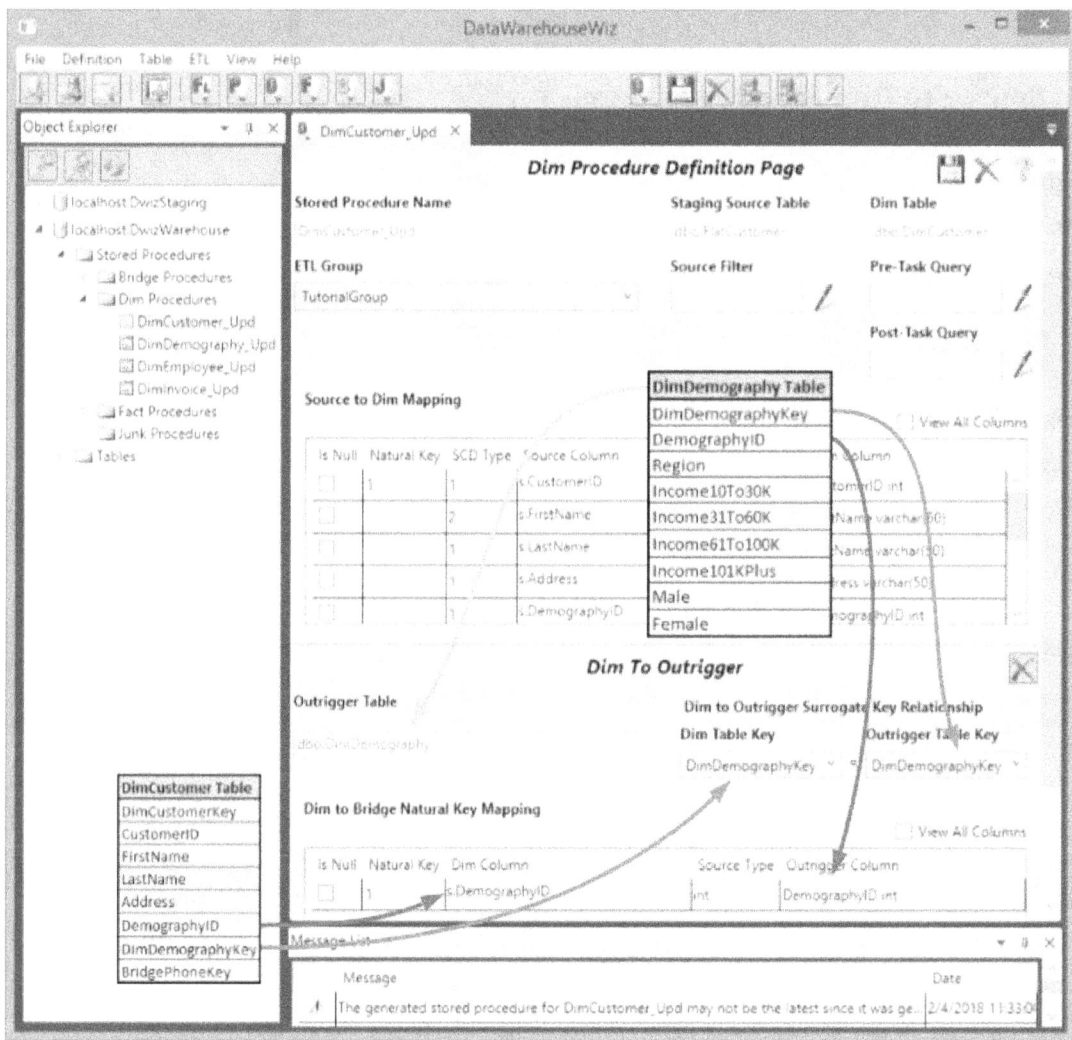

Illustration 50: Adding an Outrigger Mapping to a Dim Procedure Definition Page

The Add Bridge section

DWiz provides two different ways to craft a Bridge Subsystem, by attaching the

Bridge to a Fact table or to a Dimension table. To use a Bridge through the Fact table, see the chapter "Bridge Dimension Design". The use of a Bridge through a Dimension table is described here.

Pressing the "Add Bridge button in the top Tab Button Bar will cause a pop-up menu that asks which Bridge table should be added. Then a Dim-To-Bridge section is added to the bottom of the Definition Page (you may need to scroll down in the page to view it), as shown in the next illustration. This provides the information needed for DWiz to add a foreign-key link to an Bridge table. The first field of this section, Bridge Table, displays the name of the Bridge table to be linked (BridgePhone, in this illustration). The next area shows the "Dim-to-Bridge Surrogate Key Relationship". In these dropdowns, select the correct foreign-key column in the Dim table, and the surrogate primary key of the Bridge table (both are "BridgePhoneKey" in this illustration). Finally, in the area called "Dim to Bridge Natural Key Mapping", select the Natural Key field of the Dimension, as well as the Natural Key field of the Bridge table itself. For more details about Bridge Design, see the Chapter "Bridge Dimension Design".

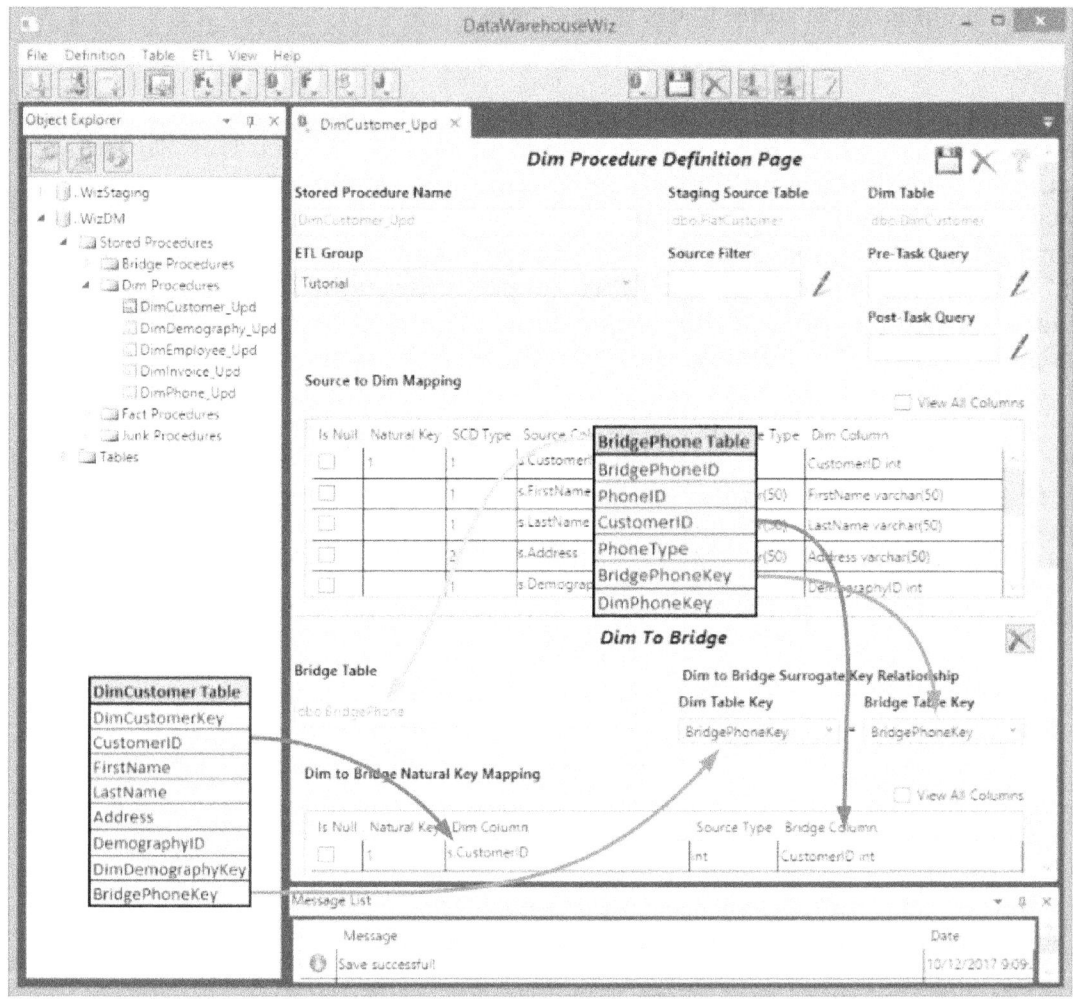

Illustration 51: Adding a Bridge Mapping to a Dim Procedure Definition Page

Example for the Design of a Dimension Procedure

For our rapid prototype, we need to design a Dimension Procedure to feed our dimension table. In this example, we will create the Procedure for DimCustomer. Perform the following steps:

- Expand **DWizWarehouse**-->Stored Procedures-->Dim, right-click the Dim folder, and select New Dim.

- Create Dim Procedure Definition Page with Stored Procedure Name = DimCustomer_upd, Source Table = FlatCustomer, and Dim Table = DimCustomer. Then press OK.

- In the Dim Procedure Definition Page, select the appropriate ETL Group, enter a "1" in the Natural Key box of column CustomerID, and then press the Save icon. Note that the Dim's primary key, DimCustomerKey, is *not* the Natural Key.

- Press the Create/Alter Procedure button (Lightning/+ icon).

- After the code is displayed, press the Save Procedure button (Lightning Over Floppy icon).

The following illustration shows the conceptual function of the Dimension Procedure of this example, feeding the Dimension Table.

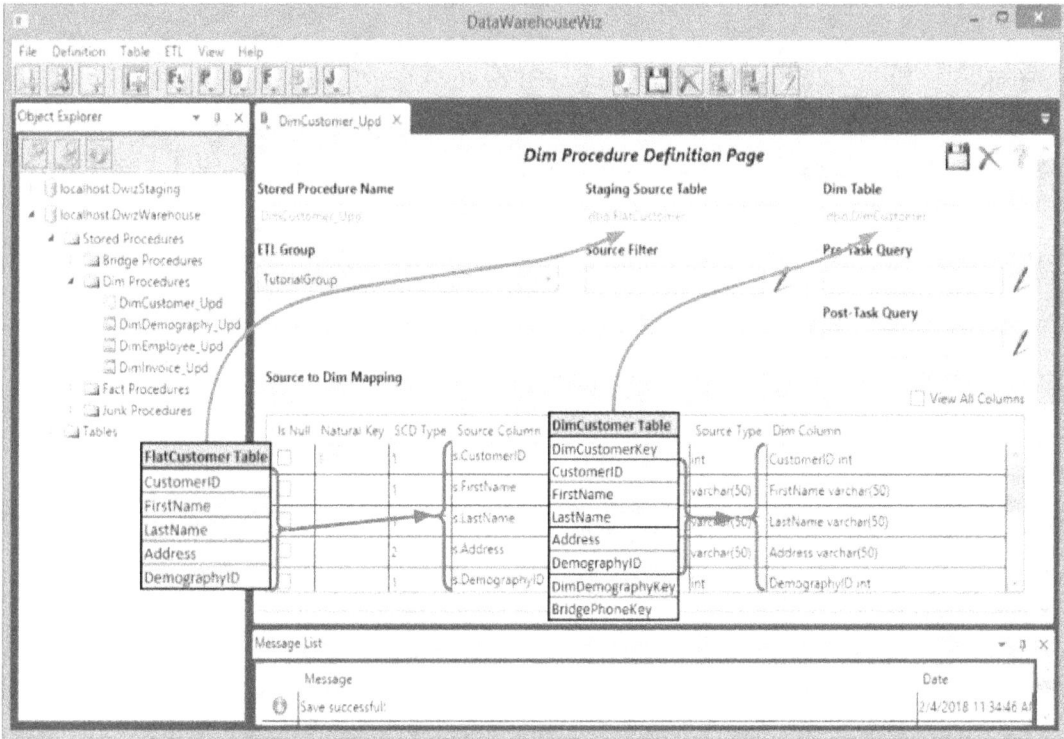

Illustration 52: Conceptual Function of the Dimension Procedure

13. Fact Table Design

Fact tables hold "the numbers", mostly additive facts, about transactions, some non-additive facts such as datetimes, and foreign keys to various dimensions. A Fact table is the center point of the star in your star-schema warehouse.

Fact tables tend to be "tall and thin", meaning they have many rows (often millions, billions, or more), but each row uses as few bytes as possible. This is accomplished by restricting the Fact table to only two types of data:

- facts (Especially additive measures, such as counts, costs, prices. Sometimes dates.)
- foreign-key-pointers to the other tables (mainly Dimensions).

Flat tables should be previously designed so that each Fact table draws data directly from one Flat table, although it might not use all the columns of that Flat table. Also, you should design your related Dimension tables before tackling the Fact table, because the Fact table needs to include foreign-key pointers to the Dim tables.

Altogether, you should have the following in place before designing a Fact table:

- A Flat table that stages data in the same format as the new Fact table
- One or more Download tables that extract the required data from Sources
- A Flat Procedure that transforms the raw data from the Downloads and feeds the Flat table
- All Dimension tables that the Fact Table will reference

Note that all of the above tables and procedures must be defined within the same ETL Group as the new Fact table. That is, the same ETL Group must be selected within each of their definition pages.

Special Considerations for the Design of Fact Tables

Following are three special considerations in the design of Fact tables. As these must be implemented in the design of the Flat table that feeds the Fact, they were fully discussed in Chapter 9 Flat Table Design, and will only be listed here.

Define the Grain

Decide on the grain, which is the lowest level of detail that will exist in your Fact table.

Allocating Facts for which the Source is Less Granular Than the Grain

As most fact tables are formed by joining multiple Source tables, you may find that some facts are not detailed all the way down to the grain. In these cases, decisions must be made as to how to allocate facts according to the grain.

Second Fact Table Holding Aggregated Grains

Sometimes it is beneficial to create a second fact table that aggregates data from the primary fact table.

Example for the Design of a Fact Table

For our first rapid prototype module, we will create a fact table, called FactInvoice. This Fact table will reside in the end-user warehouse. This design phase will copy only schema, and will not copy any data yet...that will happen when we run our future ETL Process. In Object Explorer, expand DWizStaging-->Tables-->Flat to view the flat tables, then right-click the FlatInvoice table and select Copy Table. In the pop-up window, change the database to your warehouse, and the table type to "Fact". You may also choose an alternate Schema if you have previously created a Schema other than the default dbo. Choose a name (default is "Fact" + the original source table name) and press OK:

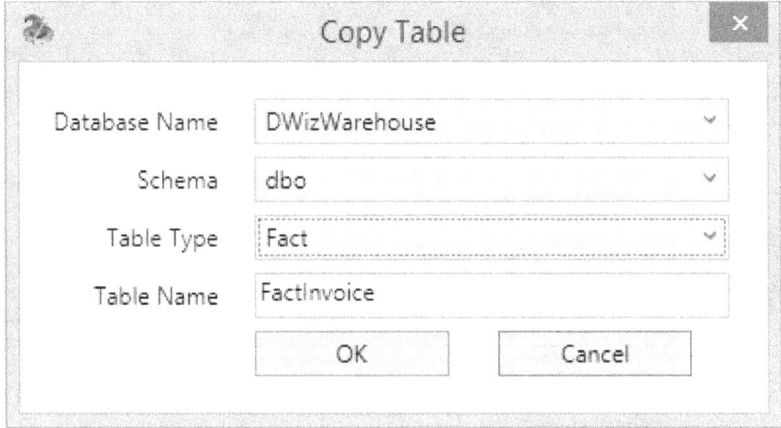

Illustration 53: "Copy Table" Pop-Up for Fact-Tables

This brings us to the FactInvoice definition page. The primary key of the primary source table, in this example InvoiceId, must be included in the new Fact table, as DWiz will use it in the Fact Procedure. This column must be non-nullable, and DWiz will create an index upon it. However, it will not be used as the primary key of the new Fact table. DWiz will quietly create a new surrogate primary key for the Fact table.

You have the option to direct the ETL process to replace nulls in any column with a Default Value (uncheck the Allow Nulls box when using a Default Value). Columns may be deleted by doing a right-click and selecting "Delete". Columns may be added by typing into the blank row at the bottom, or by doing a right-click and selecting "Insert".

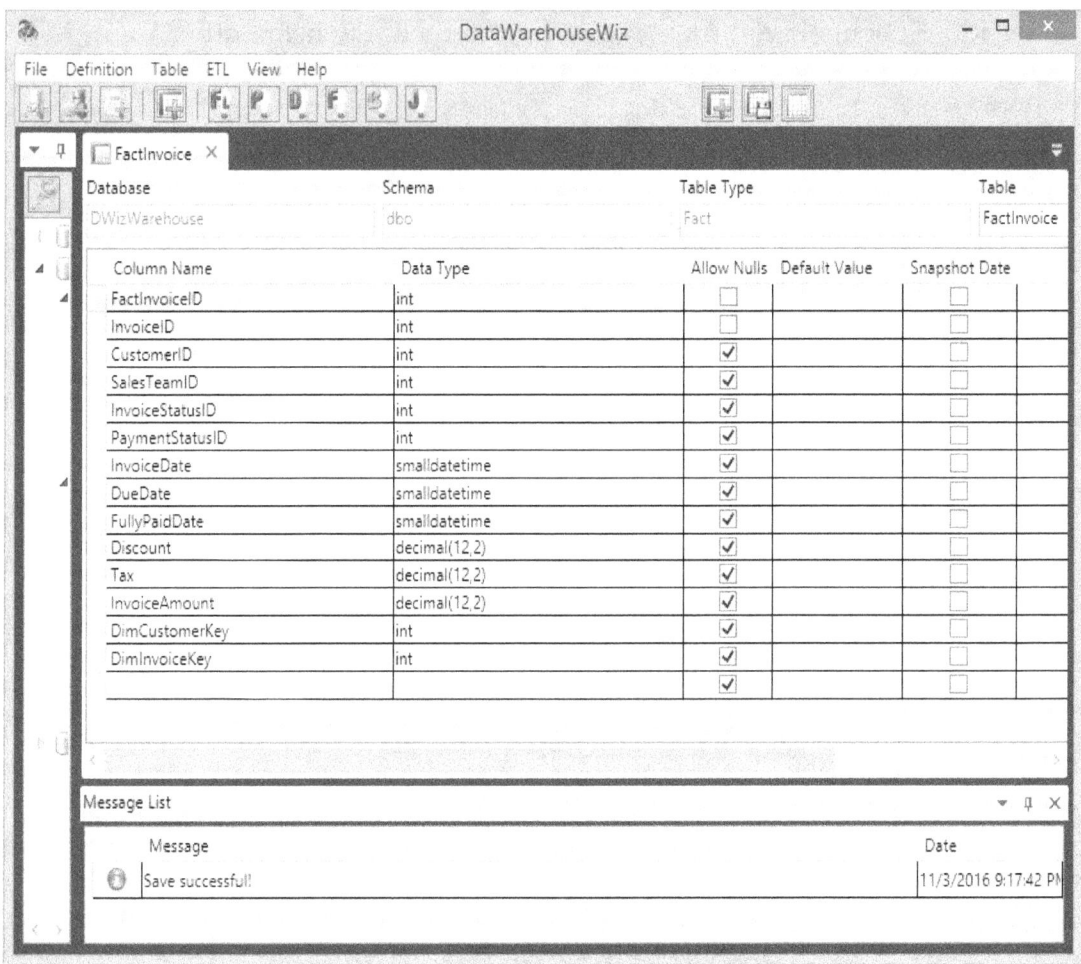

Illustration 54: "Fact Table" Definition Page

You may add, delete, or modify columns as necessary. In this example, we have added two foreign keys, DimCustomerKey & DimInvoiceKey, which we will use to link in the dimension tables. (The actual link mechanism will be coded in the Fact Update Procedure definition page.)

Now press the Save button (Floppy-Disk icon). Notice that DWiz quietly adds a primary key, FactInvoiceID.

If a table is no longer wanted, it can be deleted with the "Red-X" icon.

14. Fact Procedure Design

For each Fact Table, you will need to design a Fact Procedure to feed it. DWiz makes this very easy with the Fact Procedure Definition page. Since the Fact table resides in the warehouse database, its Fact Procedure resides there also. This stored procedure typically will draw data from a single Flat table that has already formatted the data in the same way as the Fact table. As shown in the following illustration, a Fact Procedure may draw from a Pivot Table, which is a special type of Flat table that pivots certain source row data into Flat column data.

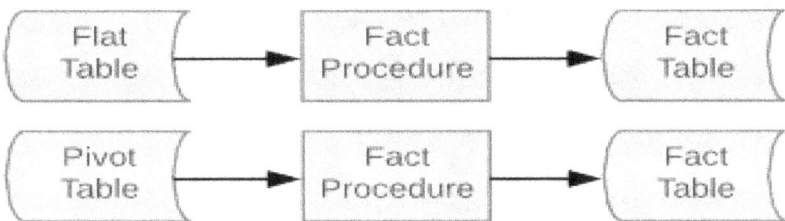

Illustration 55: A Fact Procedure Feeds a Fact Table

The Fact Procedure also needs to link in a foreign key to every related Dimension, Junk, or Bridge. These keys are required because the Fact table is the center of the star in the data mart, as shown in the following illustration.

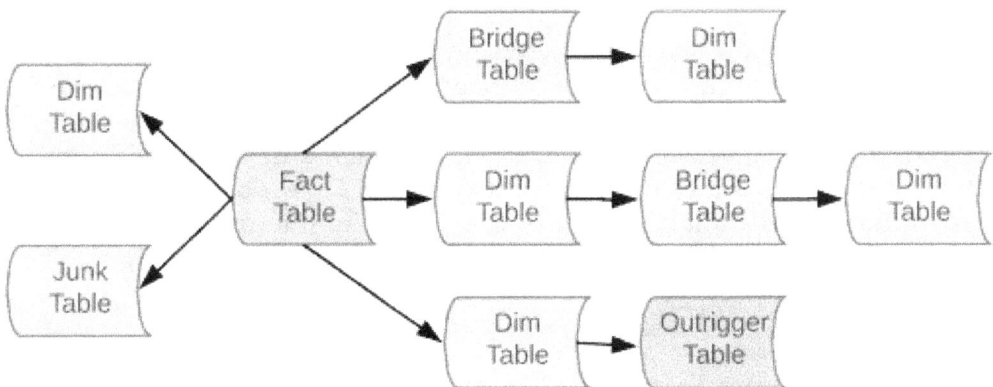

Illustration 56: The Fact Table is the Center of the Star in the Data Mart

Fact Procedure Definition Page

DWiz will write the Fact Procedure for you, based on your inputs to the Fact Procedure Definition Page; however, DWiz will always give you an opportunity to view and modify the code if you wish. The Fact Procedure Definition Page is shown in the following illustration. Each of the fields of this page will be described in detail below, although most of the fields are optional and won't be used for our prototype's FactInvoice Procedure. Afterward, we will use this page to design FactInvoice.

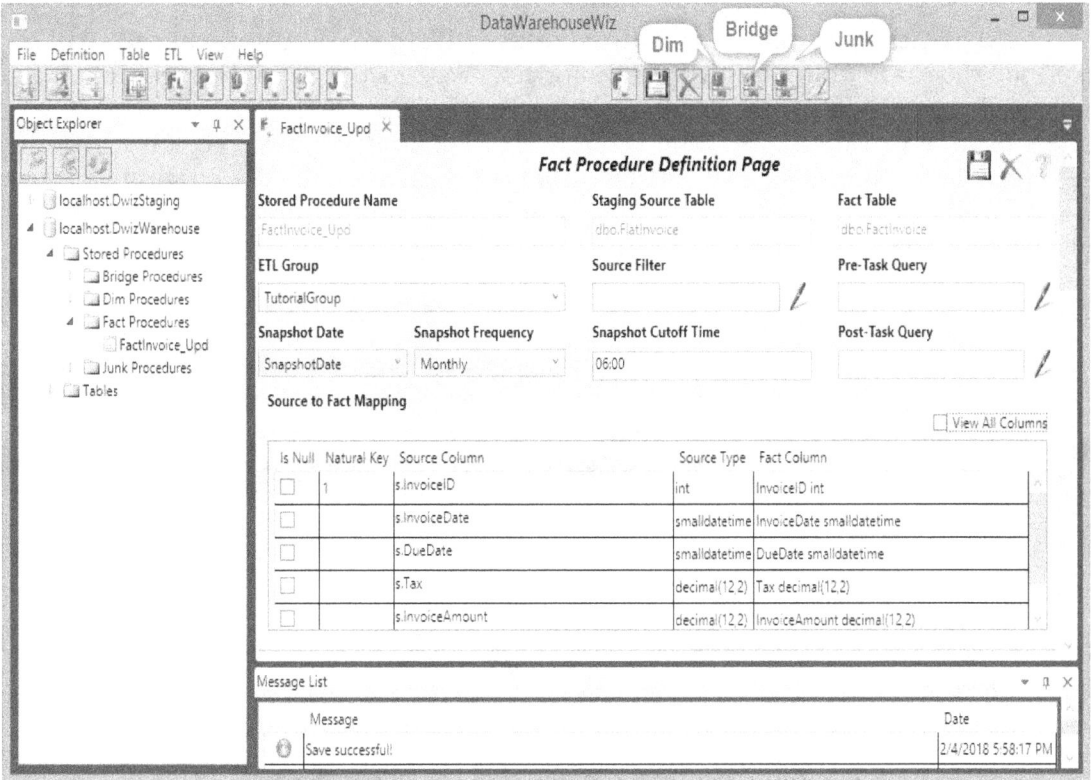

Illustration 57: Fact Procedure Definition Page

Stored Procedure Name

This field contains the exact name of the stored procedure that will be created/altered in the staging DB. The default is `<name of the flat table to be updated>` + `"_upd"`. If desired, these default settings can be changed in the Settings folder under the staging DB of the Object Explorer. You can change any of these global settings for your own purposes, but if you do so, then you must re-compile any stored procedures that made use of the previous setting values.

Staging Source Table

This field identifies the primary source of data from the Flat tables, that will be used for raw data going into the transforms. Within the stored procedure, this table will have the alias "s" (for source). In other input fields below (Source Filter, Source Column), you may reference any primary source column by using the prefix "s.". Note that the Source Table is a Flat table in the staging DB, **not** the original table of the Source DB. The following illustration shows the relationship and mapping of the Source and Target tables.

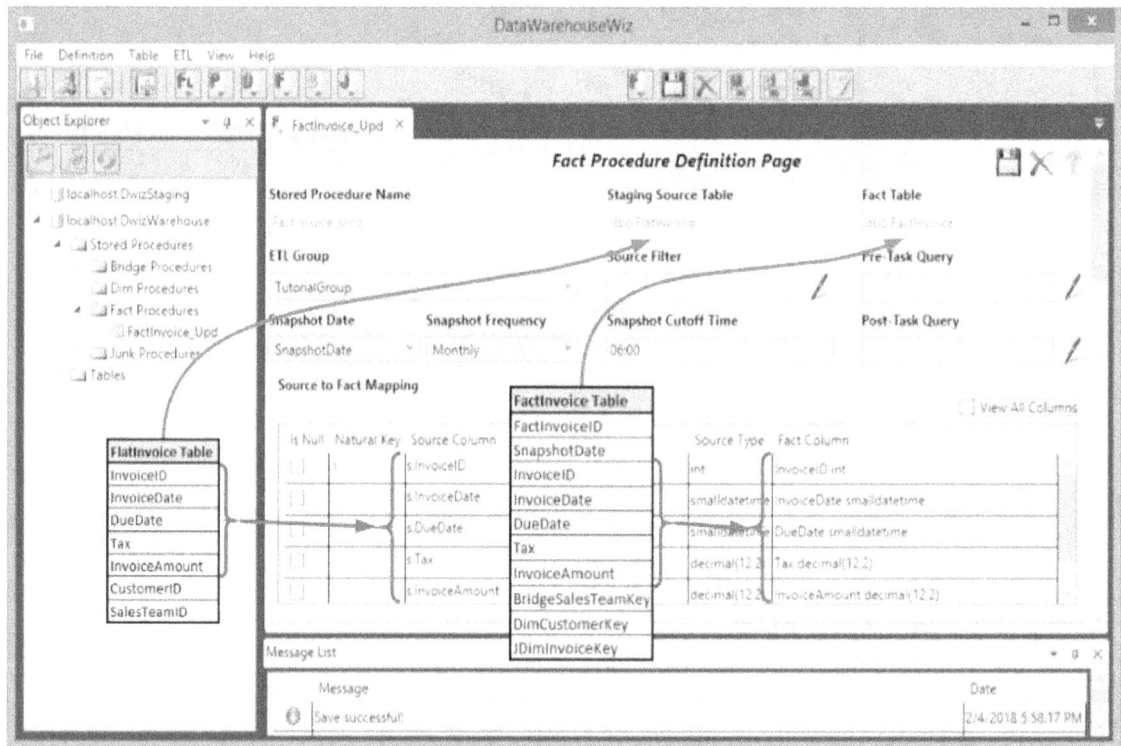

Illustration 58: The Source and Target Tables of the Fact Procedure Definition Page

Fact Table

This identifies the Fact table, the "target", that will be updated by this stored procedure. Within the stored procedure, this table will have the alias "t" (for target). In other input fields below (Source Filter, Source Column), you may reference any target column by using the prefix "t." .

ETL Group

This field indicates which ETL Group that this stored procedure will be included into. It should be the same ETL Group that includes the primary source table. If the ETL Group is changed in the future, then the primary source table should also be moved to the new group.

Source Filter

This field allows you to specify a filter that will be applied (in a SQL WHERE clause) when the procedure queries the primary source table. Do not include the "WHERE" nor the closing ";". An example is "s.MyFlag = 1", which will then be included in the WHERE clauses, causing all the procedure's queries to be limited to rows where the primary source table has column MyFlag = 1. If your desired source filter has multiple lines, such as a CASE statement, then simply click the InkPen button to the right of the Source Filter input box--this will pop-up a convenient multi-line box for you.

Pre-Task Query

This field specifies a SQL statement that will be executed immediately *before* the queries of this Flat Stored Procedure run in the ETL process. It is a catch-all to allow you to do any kind of processing that you cannot easily implement through the other fields. An example is "exec MySpecialPreProcessor_SP", where MySpecialPreProcessor_SP is a stored procedure that you have written from scratch and placed into the staging DB. We recommend that this be used only as a last resort, after use of the other input fields has proved insufficient; using the other powerful input fields is easier, more readable, and more maintainable. To enter a multi-line query, press the InkPen button to the right of the input box.

Snapshot Date

This field specifies which column holds the Snapshot Date. DWiz will use the current date as the snapshot date. If you want to use the previous day ("yesterday") as the snapshot date, then specify a different date in the Snapshot Cutoff Date. If you are not using the snapshot feature, leave this field set to "No Snapshot Date".

Snapshot Frequency

This drop-down field holds the desired frequency of snapshots. The choices are: Daily, Weekly, Monthly, Quarterly, and Yearly. DWiz will save permanently the snapshots at the indicated frequency. Additionally, DWiz will save temporarily some snapshots, typically the last seven days. If the frequency selected is "Weekly", the day of the week will default to Sunday. This can be changed in the Global Settings, under the setting "WeeklySnapshotDay".

Snapshot Cutoff Time

This field sets a cutoff time for the end of the snapshot day, with the default being midnight (00:00). There are scenarios wherein it is desirable to extend this cutoff by a few hours. For example, perhaps you have Monthly snapshots and want to capture a complete end-of-month snapshot on 01/31/2018; however, your system has an Inventory Update job that trues up inventory between 1am and 2am. You want to include this true-up, even though the actual job runs an hour or two after the end of the month. The solution is to set the Snapshot Cutoff Time to 6am (06:00), and to schedule the ETL Process job to run nightly at 4am. Thus the month ends at 1/31/2018 midnight, then your Inventory Update runs at 1am, then the ETL Process runs at 4am 2/1/2018 but dates this snapshot as "1/31/2018" because the cutoff was extended to 6am.

Post-Task Query

This field specifies a SQL statement that will be executed immediately *after* the queries of this Flat Stored Procedure run in the ETL process. It is a catch-all to allow you to do any kind of processing that you cannot easily implement through the other fields. An example is `"exec MySpecialPostProcessor_SP"`, where MySpecialPostProcessor_SP is a stored procedure that you have written from scratch and placed into the staging DB. We recommend that this be used only as a last resort, after use of the other input fields has proved insufficient; using the other powerful input fields is easier, more readable, and more maintainable. To enter a multi-line query, press the InkPen button to the right of the input box.

Source to Fact Mapping: View All Columns

Checking this field allows the user to see all columns of the target Flat table schema. When unchecked, after Saving the Definition Page, DWiz will display only the columns being updated by the queries. This field does not affect the actual queries in any way.

Source to Fact Mapping: Is Null

This field is used to generate code that transforms null values into default (Not Applicable) values. Thus, checking this box will convert a Source Column like `"s.MyString"` to something like `"IsNull(s.MyString,'')"` In many places in a Kimball type warehouse, nulls are undesirable and therefore replaced by Not Applicable values.

Source to Fact Mapping: Natural Key

This field is used to indicate the Natural Key(s) of the source table. These Natural Keys are generally the primary key(s) of the original table in the Source DB, with a "1" indicating the first part, and a "2" indicating the second part (if existing), etc.

Source to Fact Mapping: Source Column

This field holds the transform for the data to be loaded into the Fact Table Column, as shown in the following illustration. For a simple copy of a source column, it might be similar to "s.Cost". For an aggregation, it might be similar to "SUM(s.Cost)". For a more lengthy transform, click on the Source Column, and then on the InkPen that appears to the right--this will pop-up a multi-line space for you to enter a CASE statement or other lengthy element. The transform may reference any source columns with "s.", any target columns with "t.".

Source to Fact Mapping: Source Type

This field indicates the SQL variable type of the original source column. If the Source Column is changed to a transformation (such as "SUM(s.Cost)"), then DWiz will blank this field.

Source to Fact Mapping: Fact Column

This field indicates the target column into which the transform of Source Column will be loaded.

The Add Dim section

Pressing the "Add Dim" button in the top Tab Button Bar will cause a pop-up menu that asks which Dimension table should be added. Then a Fact-To-Dim section is added to the bottom of the Definition Page (you may need to scroll down in the page to view it), as shown in the next illustration. This provides the information needed for DWiz to add a foreign-key link to a Dimension table. The first field of this section, Dim Table, displays the name of the Dimension table to be linked (DimCustomer, in this illustration). The next area shows the "Fact-to-Dim Surrogate Key Relationship". In these dropdowns, select the correct foreign-key column in the Fact table, and the surrogate primary key of the Dimension table (both are "DimCustomerKey" in this illustration). Finally, in the area called "Source to Dim Natural Key Mapping", select the Natural Key field of the dimension in the Flat table that feeds the Fact, as well as the Natural Key field of the Dimension table itself. For more details about Dimension Design, see the Chapters "Dimension Table Design" and "Dimension Procedure Design".

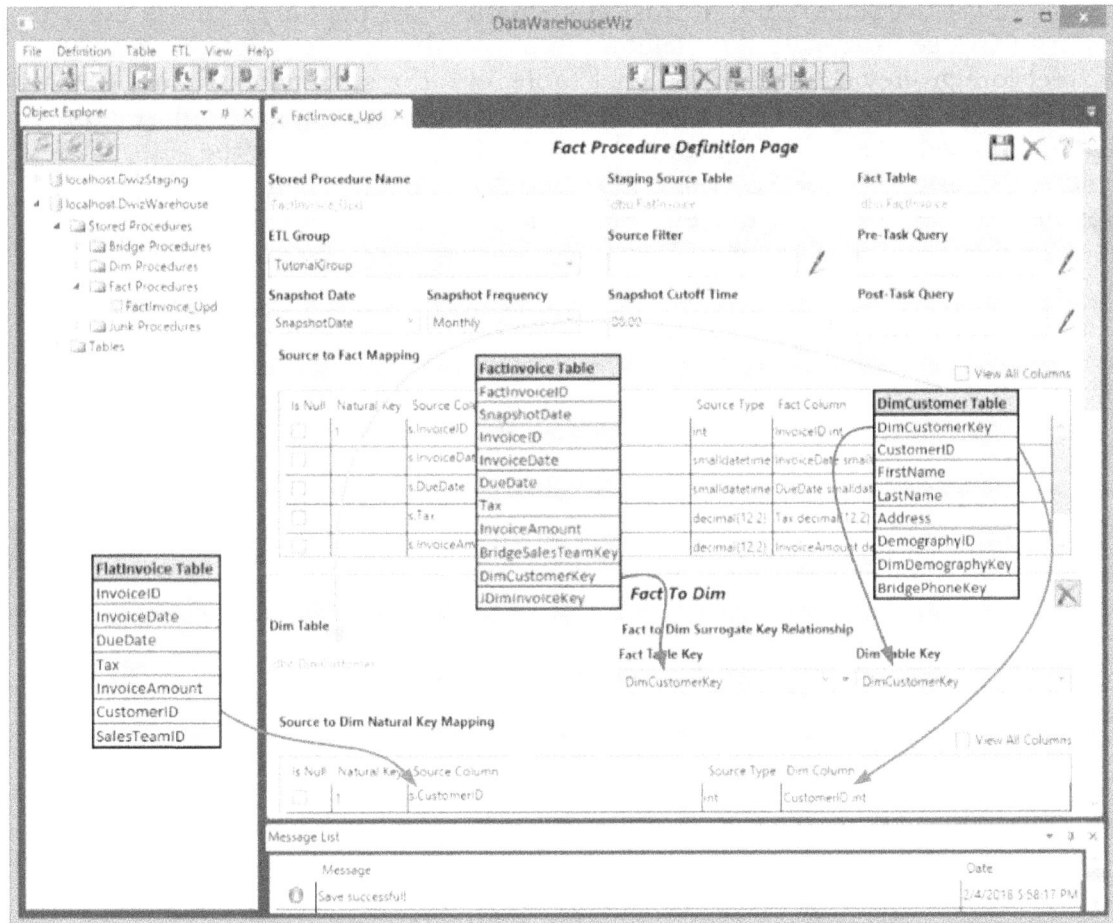

Illustration 59: Adding a Dim Mapping to a Fact Procedure Definition Page

The Add Bridge section

Pressing the "Add Bridge" button in the top Tab Button Bar will cause a pop-up menu that asks which Bridge table should be added. Then a Fact-To-Bridge section is added to the bottom of the Definition Page (you may need to scroll down in the page to view it), as shown in the next illustration. This provides the information needed for DWiz to add a foreign-key link to a Bridge table. The first field of this section, Bridge Table, displays the name of the Bridge table to be linked (BridgeSalesTeam, in this illustration). The next area shows the "Fact-to-Bridge Surrogate Key Relationship". In these dropdowns, select the correct foreign-key column in the Fact table, and the surrogate primary key of the Bridge table (both are "BridgeSalesTeamKey" in this illustration). Finally, in the area called "Source to Bridge Natural Key Mapping", select the Natural Key field of the bridge in the Flat table that feeds the Fact, as well as the Natural Key field of the Bridge table itself. For more details about Bridge Design, see the Chapter "Bridge Dimension Design".

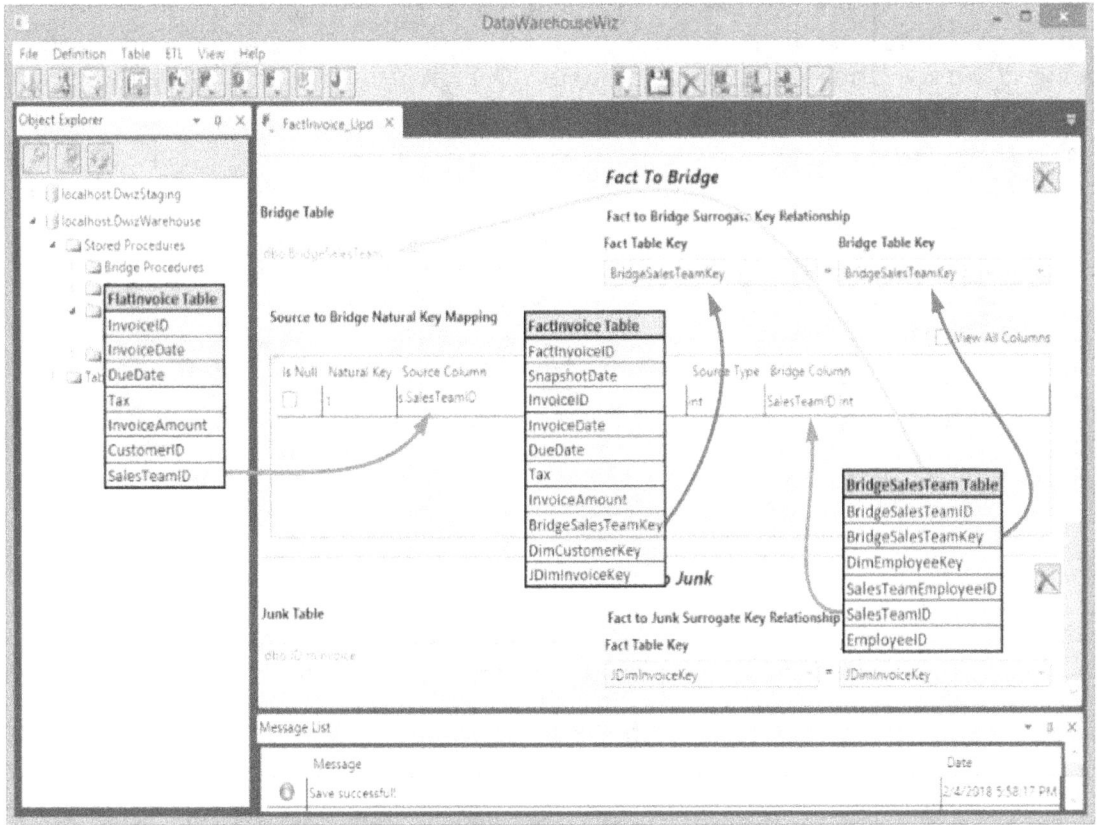

Illustration 60: Adding a Bridge Mapping to a Fact Procedure Definition Page

The Add Junk section

Pressing the "Add Junk" button in the top Tab Button Bar will cause a pop-up menu that asks which Junk table should be added. Then a Fact-To-Junk section is added to the bottom of the Definition Page (you may need to scroll down in the page to view it), as shown in the next illustration. This provides the information needed for DWiz to add a foreign-key link to a Junk table. The first field of this section, Junk Table, displays the name of the Junk table to be linked (JDimInvoice, in this illustration). The next area shows the "Fact-to-

Junk Surrogate Key Relationship". In these dropdowns, select the correct foreign-key column in the Fact table, and the surrogate primary key of the Junk table (both are "JDimInvoiceKey" in this illustration). This section does not need any Natural Key fields for the Junk table. For more details about Junk Design, see the Chapter "Junk Dimension Design".

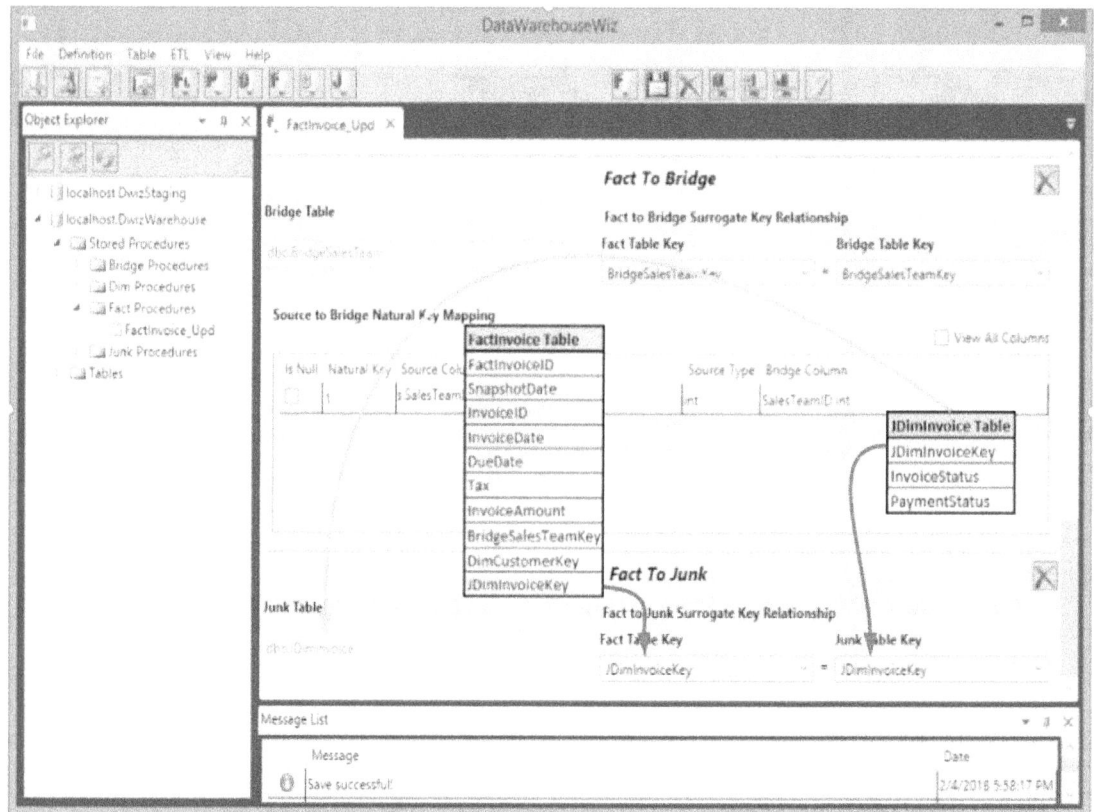

Illustration 61: Adding a Junk Mapping to a Fact Procedure Definition Page

Example for the Design of a Fact Procedure

We will use an example from the Tutorial to demonstrate the design of a Fact Procedure. In this example, we will create the procedure for the Tutorial table FactInvoice. Perform the following steps:

- Expand **DWizWarehouse**-->Stored Procedures-->Fact, right-click the Fact folder, and select New Fact.

- Create Fact Definition Page with Stored Procedure Name = FactInvoice_upd, Source Table = FlatInvoice and Fact Table = FactInvoice. Then press OK.

- In the Fact Definition Page, select ETL Group = TutorialGroup, enter a "1" in the Natural Key box of column InvoiceID, and then press the Save icon.

We saved the Fact Definition page, but we are not finished with it yet, so leave it open please! Now for the new steps. We will define the relationship that the Fact table has with the Dim tables. Press the Add Dim button as shown:

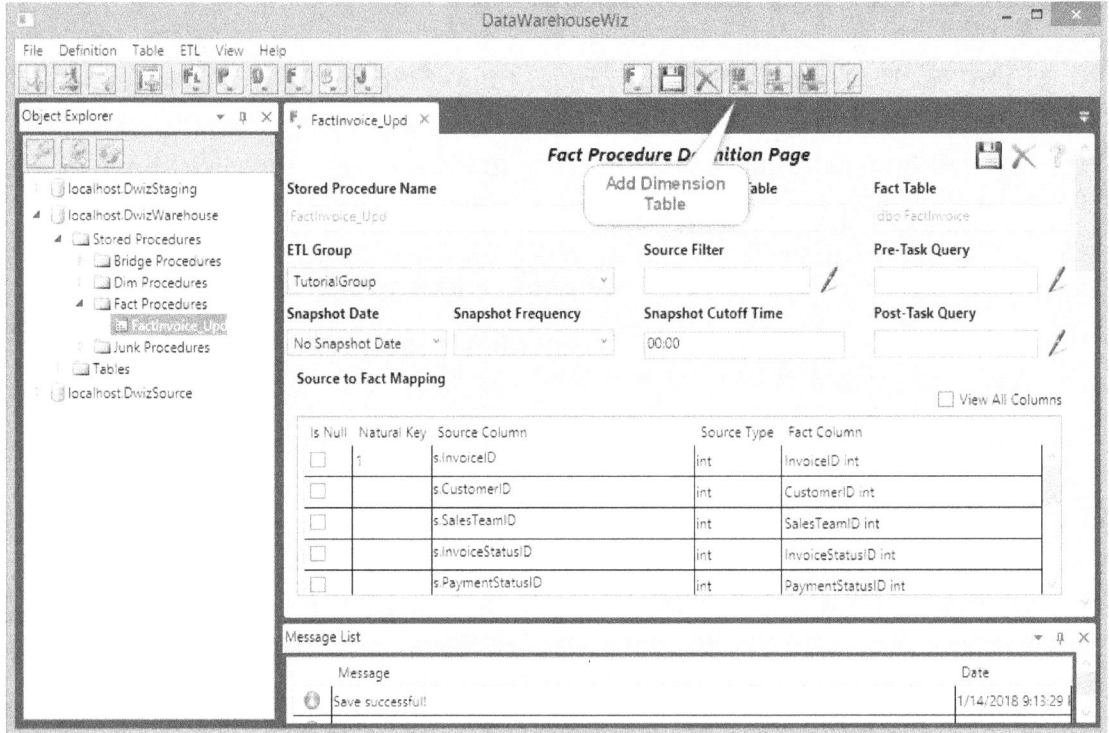

Illustration 62: Adding a Dimension-Table Relationship to a Fact-Table Procedure

In the popup window, select DimCustomer and press OK:

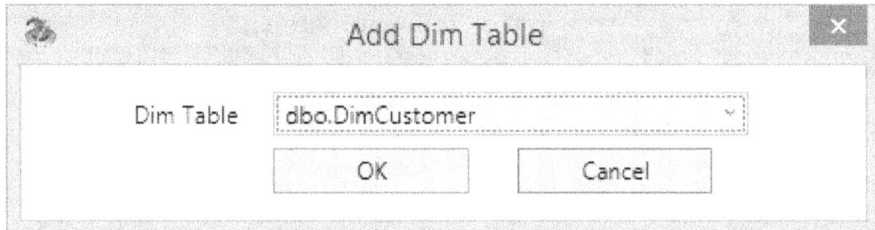

Illustration 63: "Add Dim Table" Pop-Up for Fact-Table Procedure

Now scroll down in the Fact Definition Page to reveal the new Fact To Dim section for the DimCustomer table:

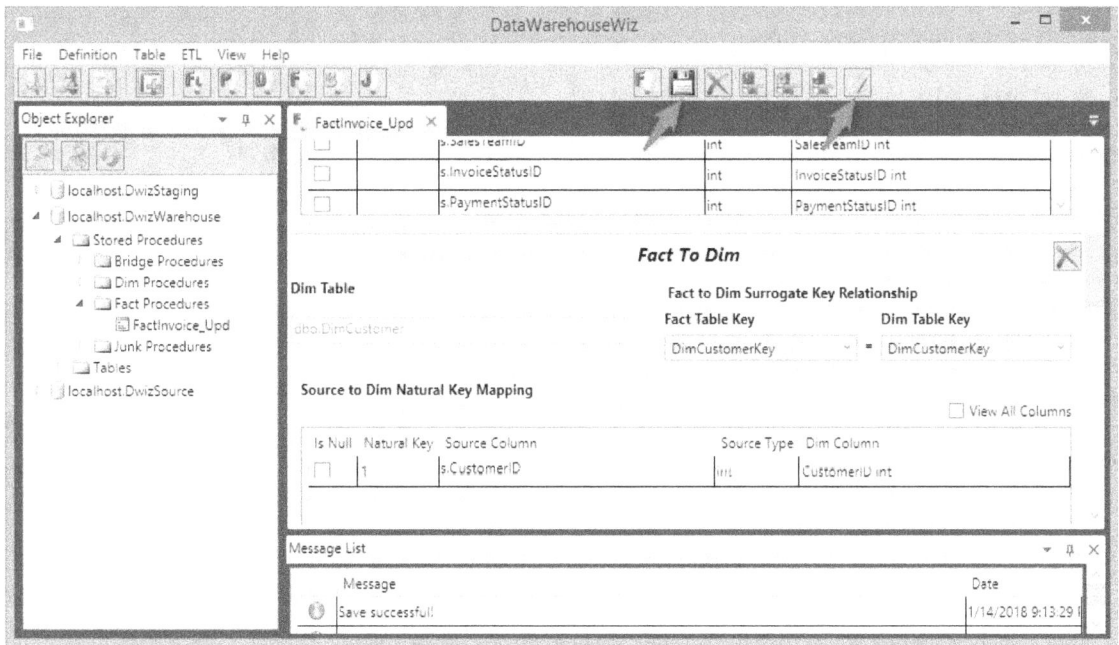

Illustration 64: Scrolling Down in the Fact-Procedure Page to View the Dim Section

This Fact To Dim section defines the relationship of the Fact table to the DimCustomer dimension. Perform the following steps:

- Set Fact Table Key to "DimInvoiceKey"
- Set Dim Table Key to "DimInvoiceKey"
- Indicate InvoiceID as the first (and only) Natural Key with a "1"
- Press the Save button at the top (Floppy-Disk icon indicated in figure above)

Now we will add the DimInvoice relationship in a similar fashion. Perform the following steps:

- Press the Add Dim button
- In the popup, select DimInvoice and press OK
- Scroll down in the Fact Definition page to reveal the new Fact To Dim section for **DimInvoice**
- Set Fact Table Key to "DimInvoiceKey"
- Set Dim Table Key to "DimInvoiceKey"
- Indicate InvoiceID as the first (and only) Natural Key with a "1"
- Press the Save button at the top (Floppy-Disk icon indicated in figure above)
- Press the Create/Alter Procedure button (Lightning/+ icon).
- After the code is displayed, press the Save Procedure button (Lightning Over Floppy icon).

15. Compiling an ETL Group

After all the tables and their procedures have been designed, we will wrap all the ETL processing--including the procedures--into a single package. This package could then be run on a periodic schedule, such as nightly or every 15 minutes, to maintain the warehouse. The advantage of using an ETL Group can be seen now: everything needed for a single ETL Group is wrapped into a single package; additional ETL Groups can be designed and built in a modular fashion without affecting existing groups. After compiling the ETL Group, the design of our first little data mart is complete. The first run of the compiled ETL Process will be longer than normal, as the warehouse begins with empty tables and all of the current data from the Sources must be processed. Subsequent runs of the ETL Process will be much shorter, as they only need to process the data changes in the Sources.

DWiz provides a choice of two ways to build an ETL package:

1. ETL Group Procedure. This is the easier way. One master ETL Group Procedure is created, that calls and orchestrates all the download processing, transform procedures, and Update Procedures, of the ETL group. This ETL Group Procedure can then be scheduled as a SQL Job in SQL Server Agent, or called by a scheduled program.

2. ETL SSIS Package. This way provides superior performance, particularly of benefit when the databases are very big. This method is more complicated to program, as it involves compiling a BIML file in Visual Studio, and building an SSIS package. The SSIS package can then be scheduled in SQL Server Agent.

Before actually compiling the ETL Group, we need to perform two steps of preparation:

- Using the Synchronize Button to check whether all pages are ready, and

- Initializing the Connection Strings which will be used when the ETL package is run

The Synchronize Button

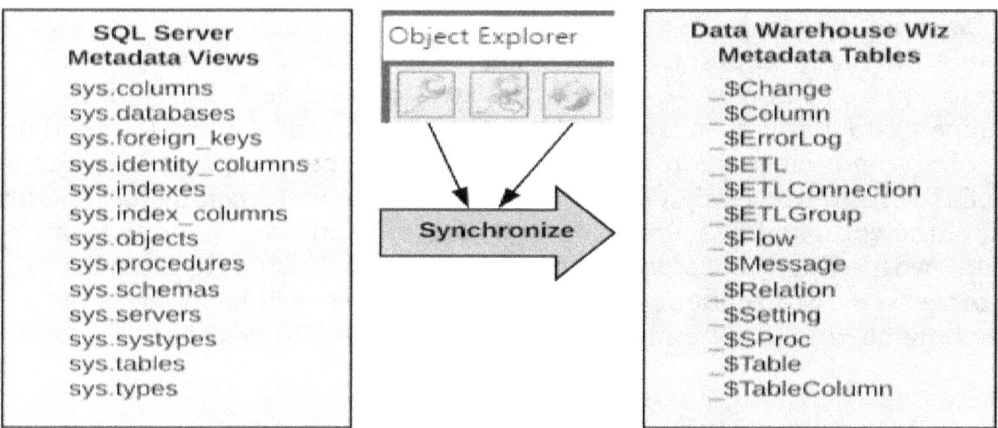

Illustration 65: The Synchronize Button (Blue Arrow Swirls icon)

DWiz needs to know if schema changes occur within the Source DB, or if the Staging or Warehouse table schema is changed outside of DWiz. DWiz keeps track of these schema through metadata tables that it creates in the Staging DB. By pressing the Synchronize button (blue arrow swirls), you can synchronize the schema info into DWiz. If DWiz then determines that the schema changes necessitate that a definition page be re-saved, then it will show that page in yellow in the Object Explorer. Likewise, if a Procedure needs to be re-saved and re-compiled, then it will be shown in yellow. Note that any time a page or procedure is changed within an ETL Group, that Group must be recompiled before the changes become effective in the package. Entities shown in red have an error that must be corrected.

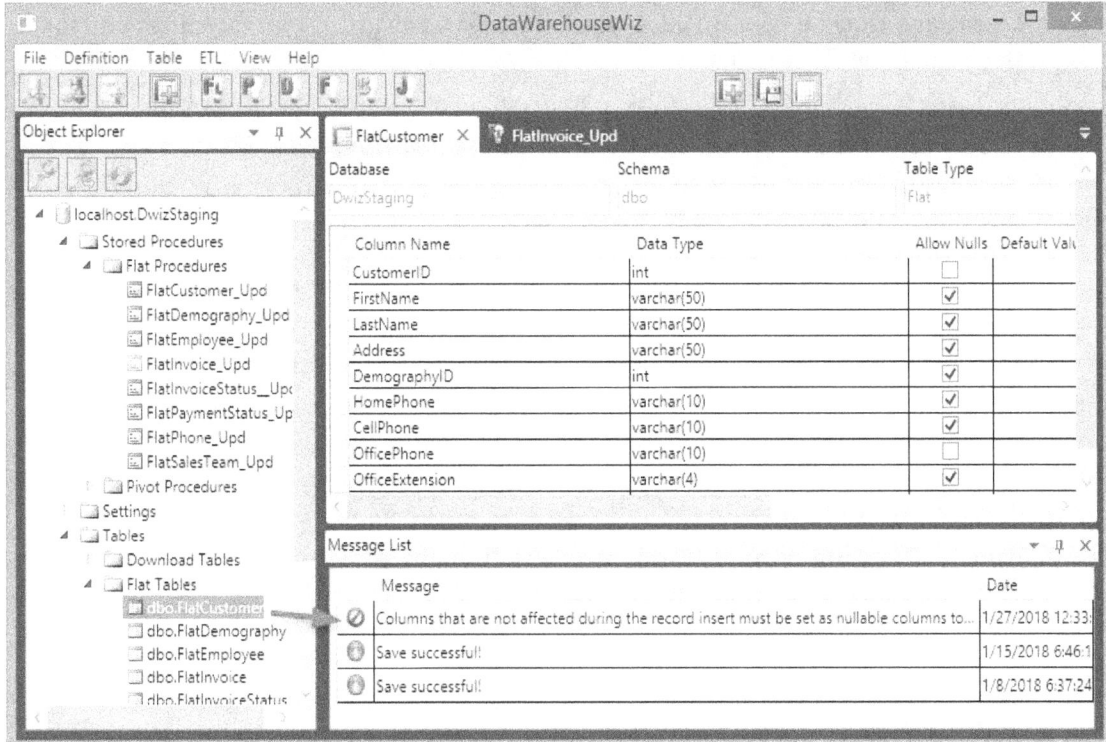

Illustration 66: Entities Shown in Yellow Require Re-Save; Those in Red Have an Error

Connection Strings

Connection Strings contain all the info needed to establish a connection to a database, including user authentication. During the design phase, a connection string is created for each database when the DWiz "Connect to Source" or "Connect to Staging/DW" button is used. There are many situations in which it is desirable to use a different connection string in the "production" environment where your ETL package will be run. Therefore, before the final compile, use DWiz to establish a connection string to your production environment. Note that this capability--of changing the connection strings at the compile time of the ETL process--provides friendly flexibility useful under many circumstances, such as:

- Database access credentials (and therefore, audits) can be different for the run-time ETL processes than what was used during the design phase

- Database access permissions can be lower for the run-time ETL processes than they were during the design phase

- ETL Processes can be deployed to "production" database servers that are different from those used during design or "sandbox" testing

- With care, a "slave" copy of a critical Source database can be used during the design phase and intensive initial loading phase, and afterwards the ETL process can be switched to the "real" master Source database for the less-intensive nightly (or periodic) delta updates

New Connection Strings can be created through the Object Explorer by expanding Staging-->ETL-->Connections and right-clicking on "New Connection". Existing connections can be edited by selecting the appropriate connection, as shown in the illustration.

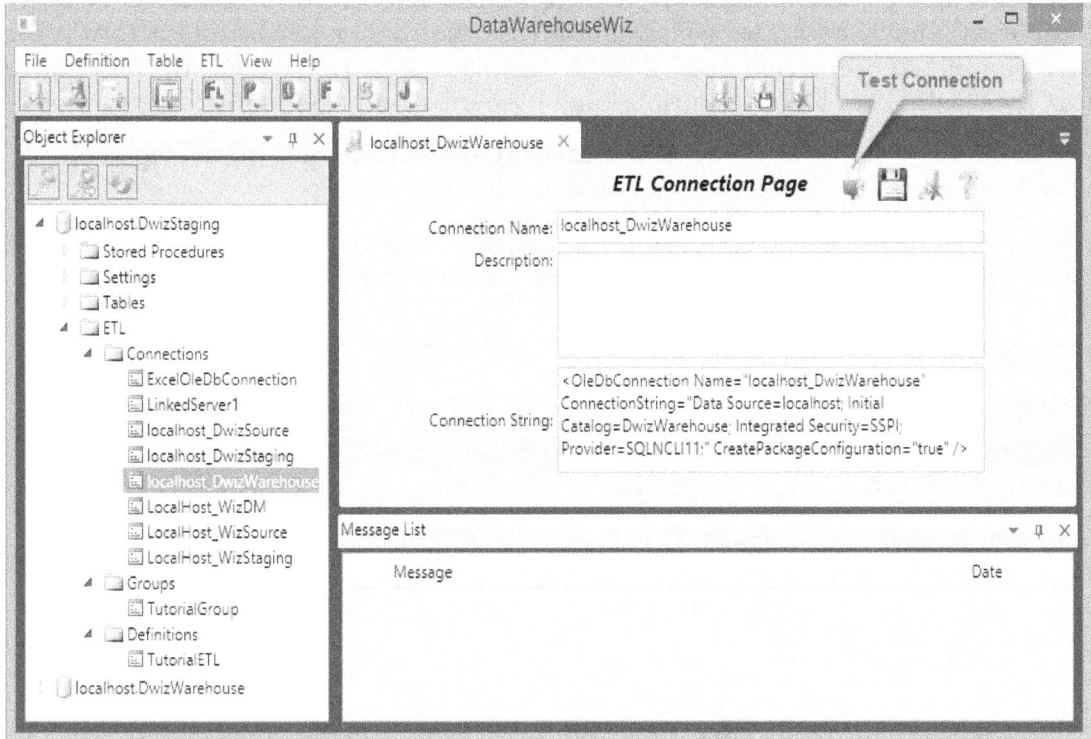

Illustration 67: Establishing a Connection String to the Production Environment

Edit the text in the connection string box, making sure to select your production server/database and to include your production user authentication. Use the convenient Test Connection button to test your connection. Save the final connection string with the (Floppy-Disk) Save button.

ETL Group Procedure

In the example of this section, we will create the ETL Group Procedure. Then, in the next later section, we will demonstrate the higher-performance (but a bit more complicated) method of ETL SSIS Package. For the ETL Group Procedure, start by creating an ETL Definition Page by performing the following steps:

- Expand the Staging Db (e.g., **DWizStaging**)-->ETL-->Definitions, right-click the Definitions folder, and select New Definition.

- In the ETL Definition Page, give the package a name such as TutorialETL, make sure that the ETL Group box is set to the desired ETL Group, check-mark the options "Staging Tasks" and "Data mart Tasks", and select your connections for Staging and DataMart (warehouse).

- Optionally use the Description box to describe your project's purpose.

- Staging Tasks include all ETL within the Staging DB, including downloads, flat updates, and transform processing.

- Datamart Tasks include all ETL within the Warehouse DB, including updates to Dimensions, Facts, and other warehouse tables.

Before pressing Save, the page will look similar to this:

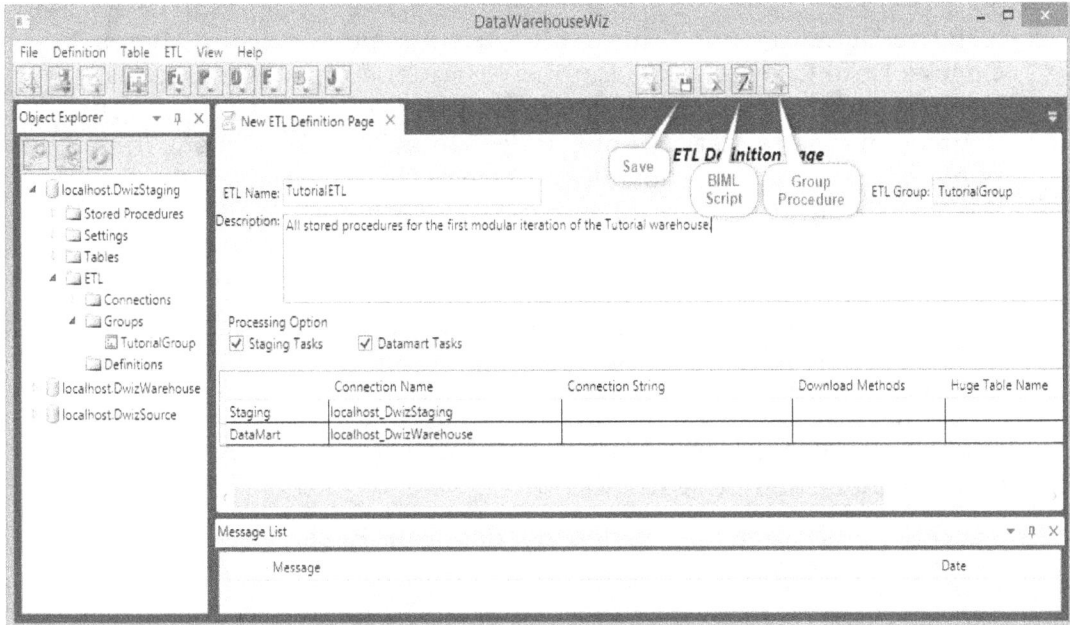

Illustration 68: ETL Definition Page

Now press the Save icon. Notice that DWiz adds a connection for the Source DB, which is DWizSource in this example. In this new Source row, select a Download Method ("Change Tracking" is preferred), and press Save.

1. The available download method choices are:Change Tracking. This is the preferred method, as it is the most efficient. DWiz will use Microsoft Change Tracking in the Source DB to follow and download changes (Updates/Inserts/Deletes). The Source DB must support Change Tracking, and both the DB and the tables to be downloaded must be configured for Change Tracking. In the Staging table "_$Change", DWiz keeps track of the Source database's last Version Number. This is initially set to blank, causing a full download of every Source table on the first run of the ETL Group Procedure. Thereafter, the Source DB's last Version Number will be stored, and each run of the ETL Group Procedure will download only the delta changes (inserts/updates/deletes) of the

Source tables.

2. Change Data Capture. This is an alternate method using Microsoft Change Data Capture. The Source DB must support Change Data Capture. In the Staging table "_$Change", DWiz keeps track of the Source database's last LSN of Change Data Capture. This is initially set to blank, causing a full download of every Source table on the first run of the ETL Group Procedure. Thereafter, the Source DB's LSN will be stored, and each run of the ETL Group Procedure will download only the delta changes (inserts/updates/deletes) of the Source tables.

3. Whole Table. The entire Source table is downloaded on every run. This method is only practical for small source tables.

4. No Download. No data is downloaded from the Source. This method might be used if the data is already being downloaded by a different ETL Group which runs prior to this one.

5. Excel. The Source data is downloaded from Excel spreadsheet files.

Connection Strings:

The connection strings can be viewed by hovering the mouse over their columns. Connection strings can be selected from the drop-down menu. These strings can be created or edited as described in the previous section. If you edit a connection at this point, make sure to re-open the ETL Definition Page and re-save it.

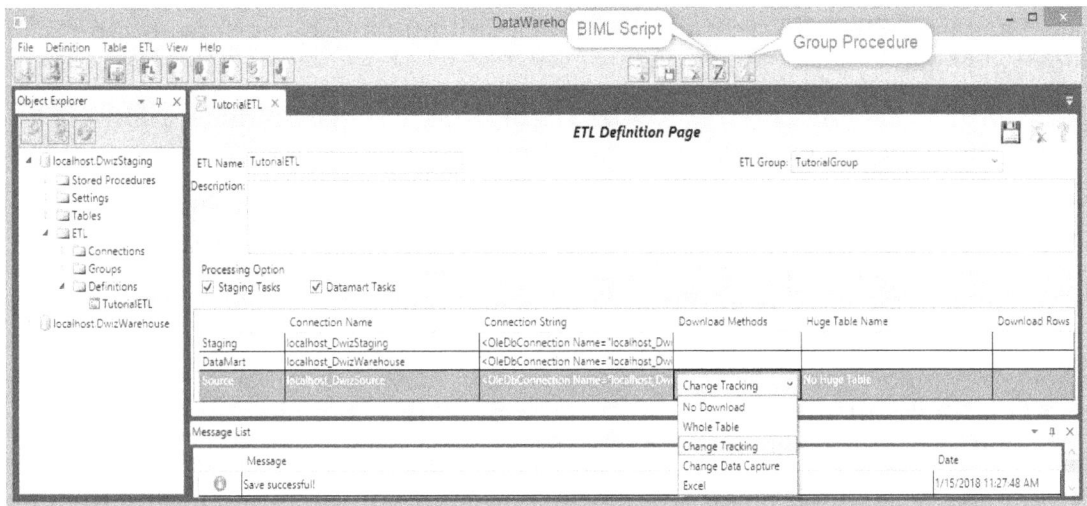

Illustration 69: Choosing a Download Method in the ETL Definition Page

After Saving the ETL Definition Page, press the "Create ETL Group Procedure" button on the Tab Button Bar (icon is lightning bolt with green "plus"). DWiz will write all the code for you and allow you to review it. After reviewing (or not!), press the Save Procedure button (icon is lightning bolt with floppy disk) on the Tab Button Bar, causing DWiz to write the new stored procedure to the staging database. Note that the new procedure created will have the same name as the ETL Name in the definition page. This stored procedure is then all you need to run the ETL. You can skip the next section (ETL SSIS Package) unless you want the better performance of the SSIS package. However, if you are recompiling ETL for an existing warehouse, please read the section "The Queries and Info Button" before running the ETL Group Procedure.

ETL SSIS Package

The ETL SSIS Package is offered as a higher-performance alternative to the ETL Group Procedure. For each ETL Group, you can choose to run an ETL Group

Procedure OR an ETL SSIS Package. In this example, we will create the ETL SSIS Package. Start by creating an ETL Definition Page by performing the following steps:

- Expand the Staging Db (e.g., **DWizStaging**)-->ETL-->Definitions, right-click the Definitions folder, and select New Definition.

- In the ETL Definition Page, give the package a name such as TutorialETL, make sure that the ETL Group box is set to the desired ETL Group, check-mark the options "Staging Tasks" and "Datamart Tasks", and select your connections for Staging and DataMart (warehouse).

- Optionally use the Description box to describe your project's purpose.

- Staging Tasks include all ETL within the Staging DB, including downloads, flat updates, and transform processing.

- Datamart Tasks include all ETL within the Warehouse DB, including updates to Dimensions, Facts, and other warehouse tables.

Before pressing Save, the page will look similar to this:

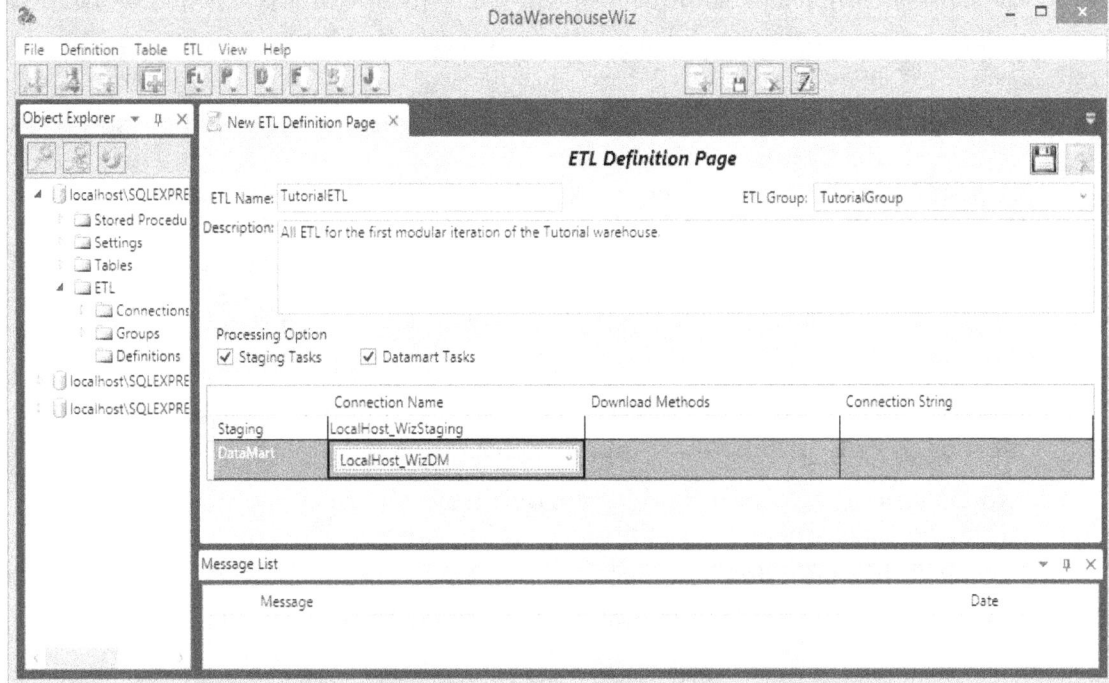

Illustration 70: Selecting Connections in the ETL Definition Page

Now press the Save icon. Notice that DWiz adds a connection for the Source DB, which is DWizSource in this tutorial. In this new Source row, select a Download Method ("Change Tracking" is preferred), and press Save.

1. The available download method choices are:Change Tracking. This is the preferred method, as it is the most efficient. DWiz will use Microsoft Change Tracking in the Source DB to follow and download changes (Updates/Inserts/Deletes). The Source DB must support Change Tracking, and both the DB and the tables to be downloaded must be configured for Change Tracking. In the Staging table "_$Change", DWiz keeps track of the Source database's last Version Number. This is

initially set to blank, causing a full download of every Source table on the first run of the ETL Group Procedure. Thereafter, the Source DB's last Version Number will be stored, and each run of the ETL Group Procedure will download only the delta changes (inserts/updates/deletes) of the Source tables.

2. Change Data Capture. This is an alternate method using Microsoft Change Data Capture. The Source DB must support Change Data Capture. In the Staging table "_$Change", DWiz keeps track of the Source database's last LSN of Change Data Capture. This is initially set to blank, causing a full download of every Source table on the first run of the ETL Group Procedure. Thereafter, the Source DB's LSN will be stored, and each run of the ETL Group Procedure will download only the delta changes (inserts/updates/deletes) of the Source tables.

3. Whole Table. The entire Source table is downloaded on every run. This method is only practical for small source tables.

4. No Download. No data is downloaded from the Source. This method might be used if the data is already being downloaded by a different ETL Group which runs prior.

5. Excel. The Source data is downloaded from Excel spreadsheet files.

Connection Strings:

The connection strings can be viewed by hovering the mouse over their columns. Connection strings can be selected from the drop-down menu. These strings can be created or edited as described in the previous section. If you edit a connection at this point, make sure to re-open the ETL Definition Page and re-save it.

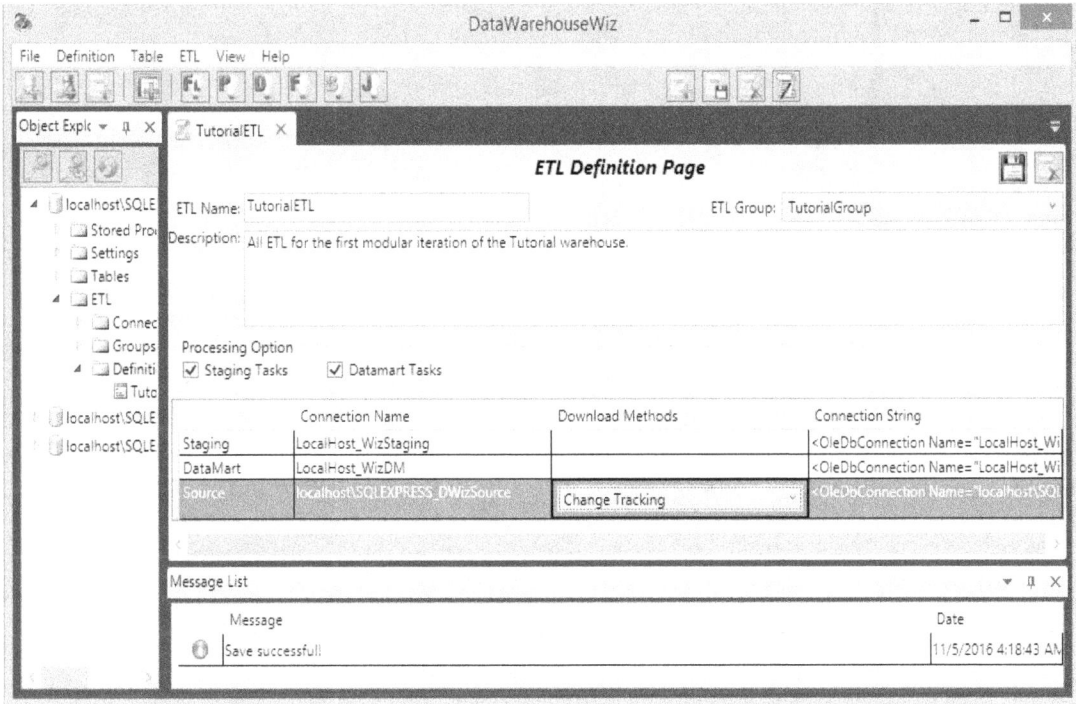

Illustration 71: Re-Save the ETL Definition Page After Changing a Connection

Now press the Create BIML button (Scroll+Pen icon on top right):

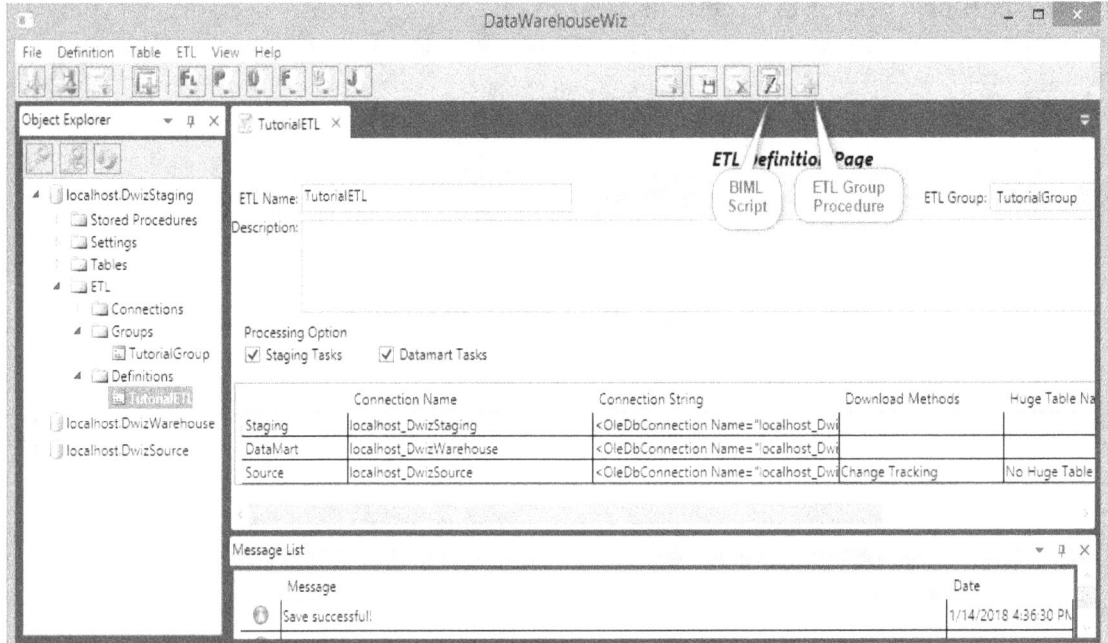

Illustration 72: "Create BIML" Button on the ETL Definition Page

After the BIML button is pressed, DWiz will create the BIML for the entire ETL Process and display:

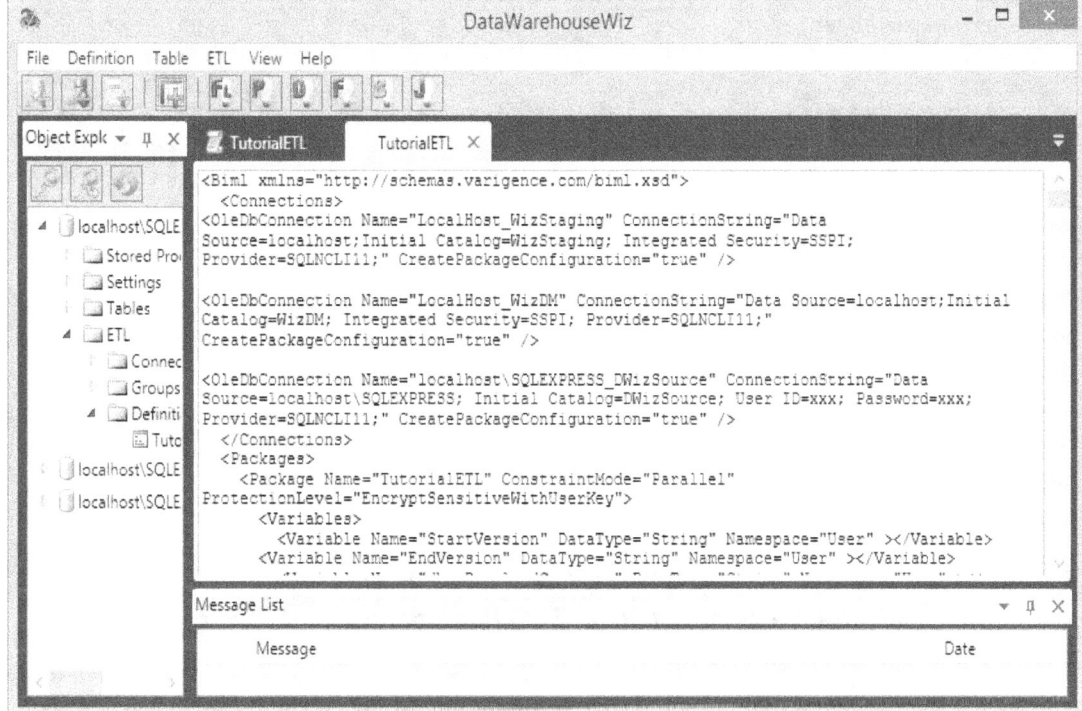

Illustration 73: Reviewing BIML Code Written By DWiz

You will copy this script into the clipboard and paste it into a Visual Studio project. Leave DWiz open, but also open Microsoft® Visual Studio on your PC:

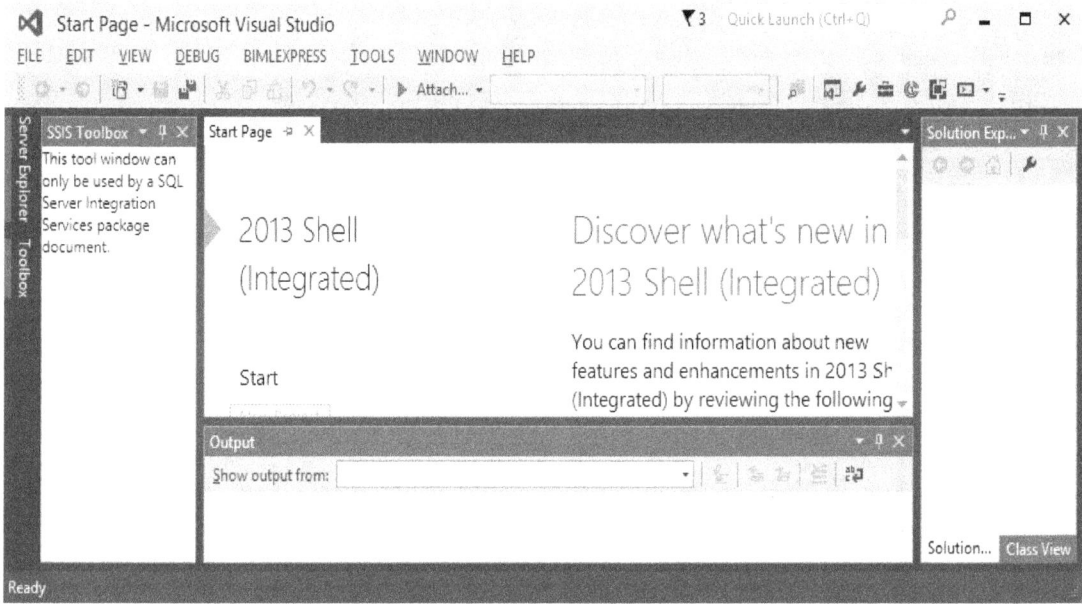

Illustration 74: Creating an SSIS Package in Visual Studio

Your version of Visual Studio should include SQL Data Tools for Visual Studio, and also the Varigence® BIML Express plugin. For full details and installation tips, see the Data Warehouse Wiz Installation Manual.

In Visual Studio, create a new project (click File-->New-->Project) by using the template under Templates-->Business Intelligence-->Integrated Services Project, and name the project "TutorialETL", then press OK:

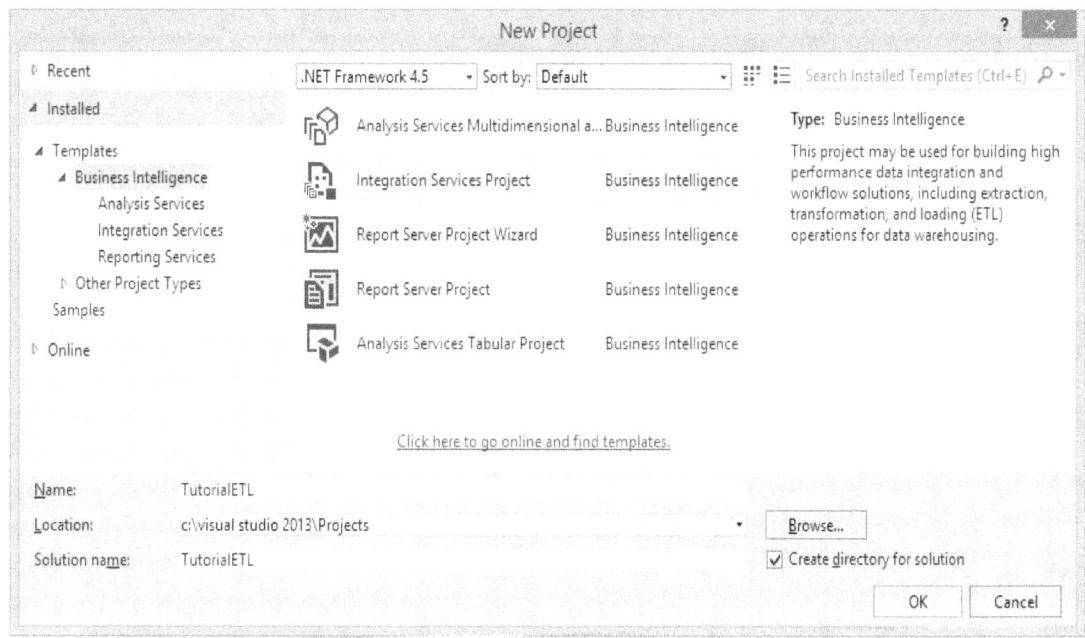

Illustration 75: Creating an Integrated Services Project in Visual Studio

In the Solution Explorer of the new project, right-click Package.dtsx, and select "Add New Biml File":

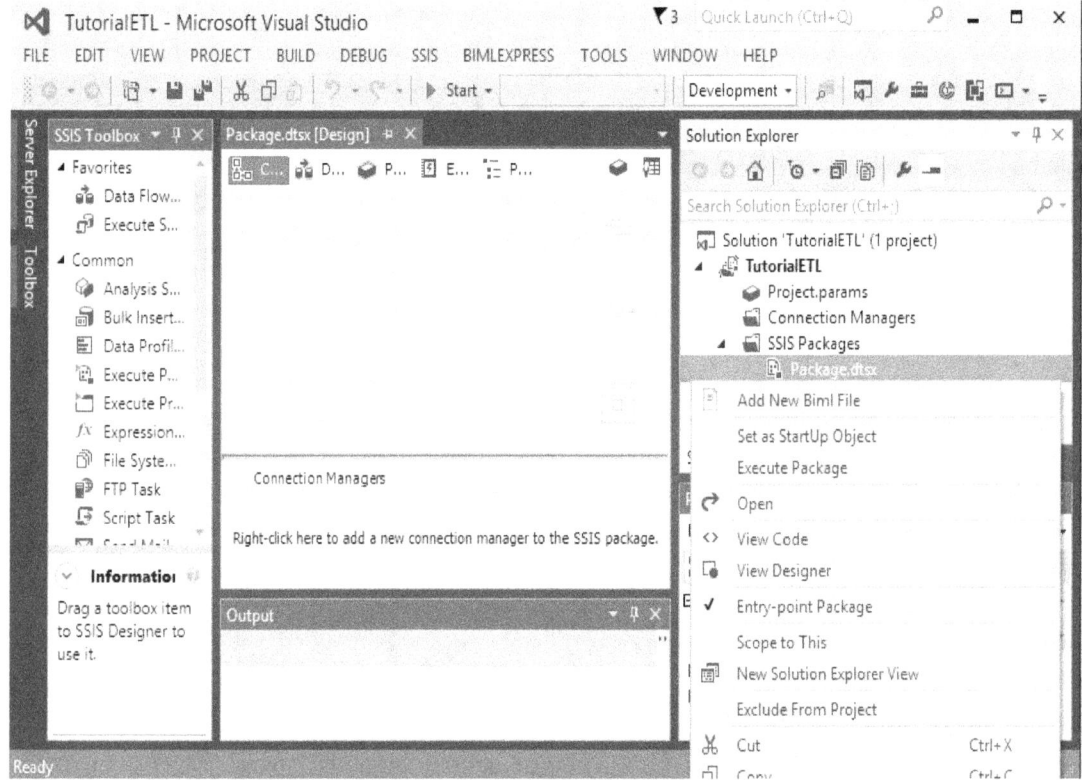

Illustration 76: Adding the BIML to a Visual Studio Project

In the Solution Explorer, now expand the Miscellaneous folder, and double-click on "BimlScript.biml" to open it:

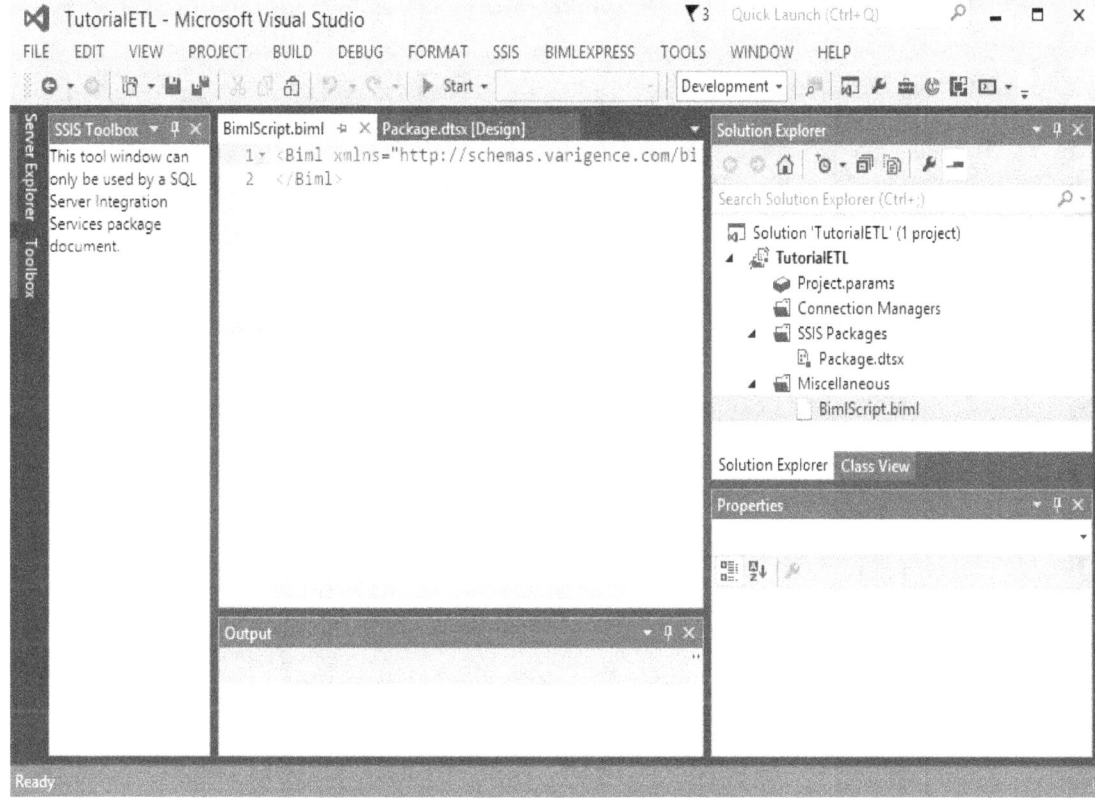

Illustration 77: The default (empty) BIML script

This reveals an "empty" BIML script. Replace this script by cut-and-pasting the script that DWiz generated. Make sure that you overwrite the existing "empty" script completely. Save the file (click File-->Save All). This is what it should look like:

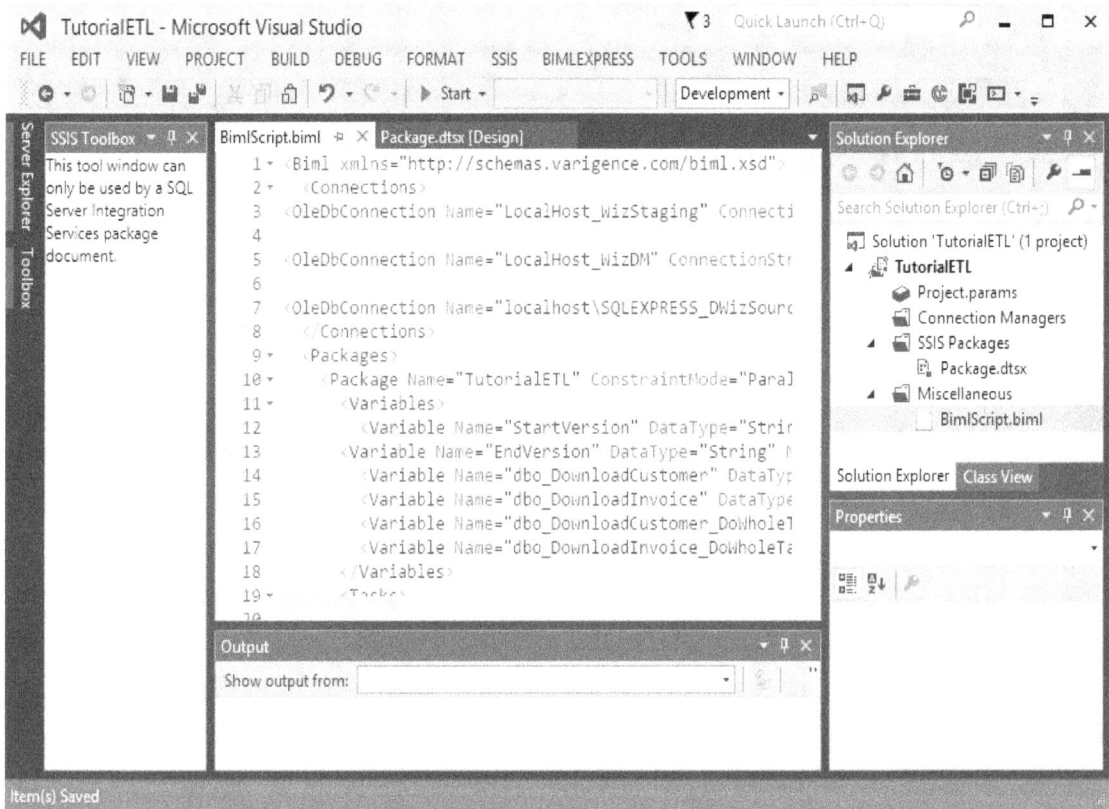

Illustration 78: Saving Your BIML in the Visual Studio Project

Now right-click BimlScript.biml (under Miscellaneous in Solution Explorer) and click "Generate SSIS Packages". This may take a few minutes. Afterward, you may view the data flow by double-clicking on the TutorialETL.dtsx package:

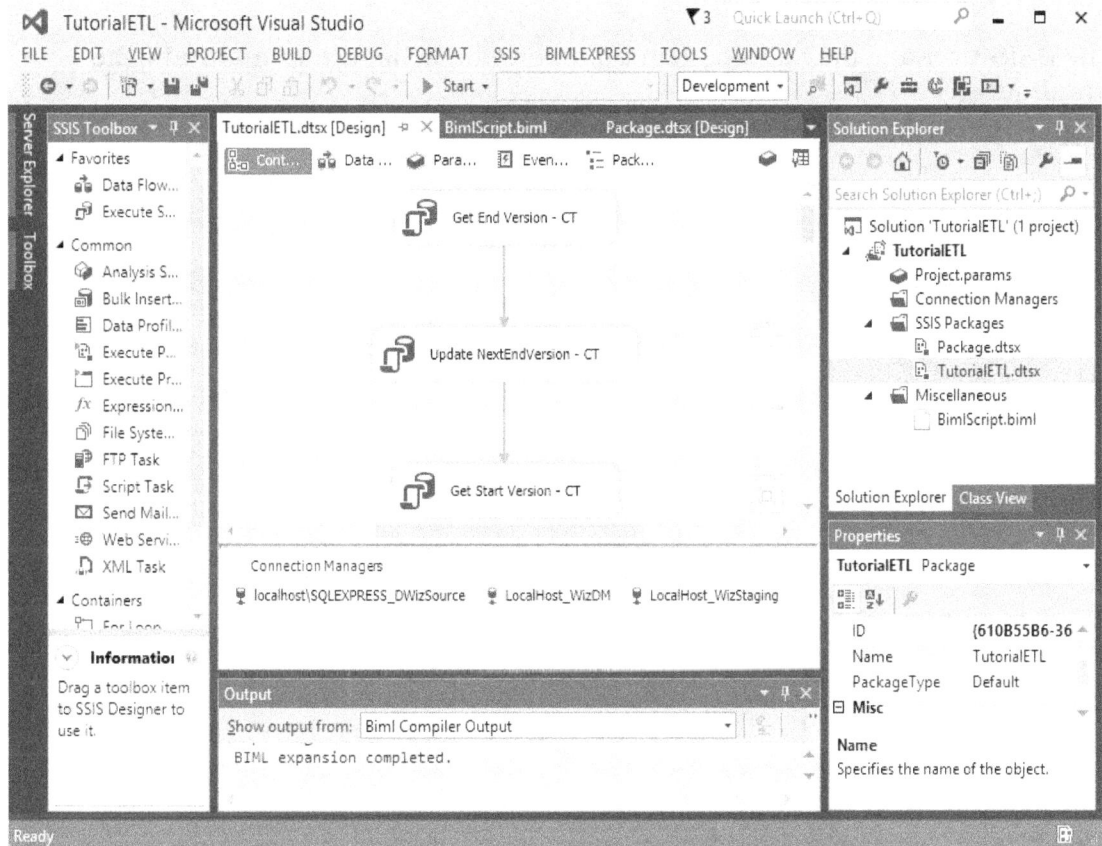

Illustration 79: Generating an SSIS Package

You may run the ETL Package by pressing the Start button on the top menu. Afterward, you can see the filled warehouse tables in SSMS. However, if you are recompiling an ETL Package for an existing warehouse, please read the next section "The Queries and Info Button" before running the ETL package. The ETL Package can be run as a SQL Job like any other SSIS package.

The SSIS package dtsx can be run on a periodic schedule to maintain the warehouse.

16. The "Queries and Info" Section

As shown in the following illustration, the ETL Group Page has a "Queries and Info" button in its top menu bar:

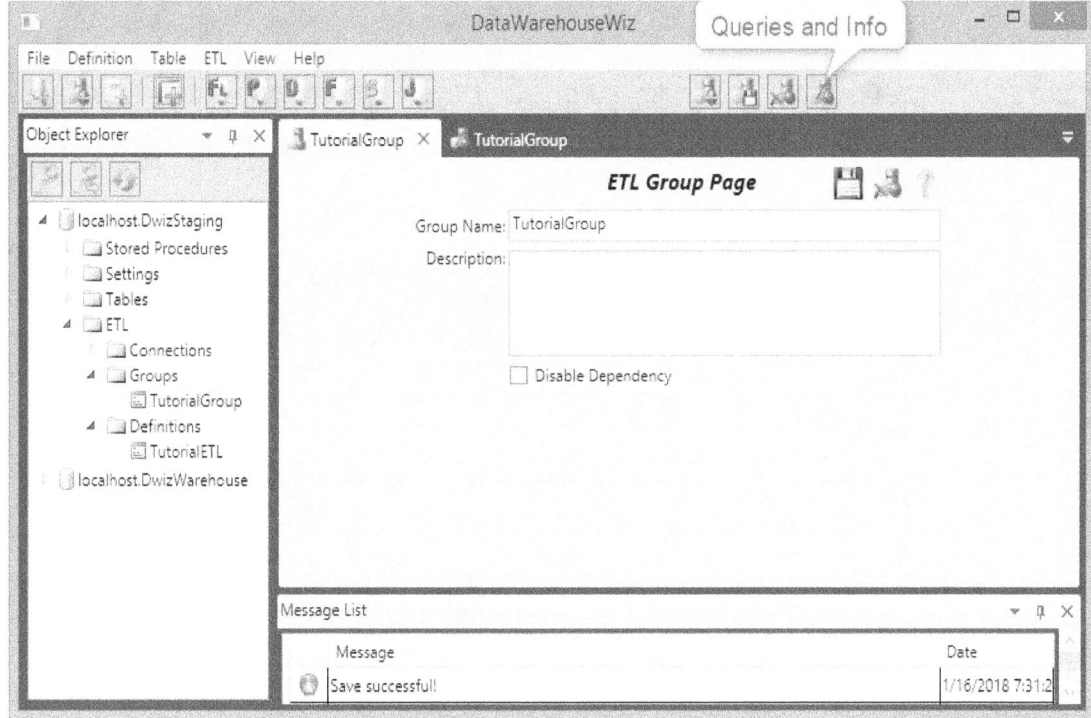

Illustration 80: The "Queries and Info" Button

Pressing this button brings up a helpful page of information and SQL queries that pertain specifically to this particular ETL Group:

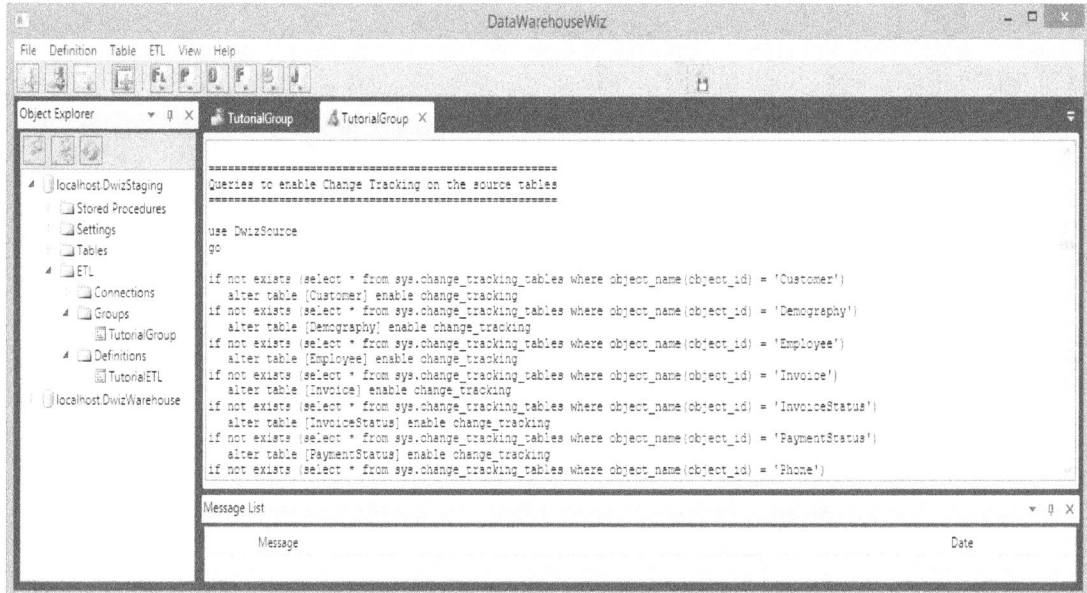

Illustration 81: The "Queries and Info" Page

The SQL queries are provided for your convenience in setting up and maintaining your data warehouse.

Enable Change Tracking

This section of queries enable Change Tracking on the Source tables (of the Source DB) that are downloaded as part of this ETL Group. Change Tracking is the most efficient method for differential download of tables in Microsoft SQL

Server. First, enable Change Tracking on the SQL Server itself. Then, run these queries in the Source DB to enable Change Tracking on the Source tables that you use. Now, you can select the Change Tracking method in the ETL Definition Page (see the Chapter "Compiling An ETL Group") and recompile the ETL Group Procedure or Package.

Enable Change Data Capture

In a very similar way to the previous section, these queries assist in enabling Change Data Capture. Change Data Capture is an alternate change management method, second to the more-preferable Change Tracking.

Add Indexes

These SQL queries add indexes to your warehouse tables. These indexes greatly improve the speed of your reporting queries in the warehouse, and are a definite necessity on any tables with more than 100,000 records. However, after the indexes are added, future inserts/updates/deletes (that occur when the ETL runs) are slower due to the need for the indexes to be maintained. Therefore, the indexes should not be added until the initial run of a new ETL Group is complete, especially if any of the required source tables has over a million records. This is because, even with Change Tracking, the initial run of the ETL will be much larger than normal. So the most efficient way to create your new warehouse is by following steps in this order:

1. Design your warehouse with DWiz all the way to the point where you are ready to compile the ETL Procedure/Package.

2. Set up and test your production Connection Strings.

3. Use the handy queries to enable Change Tracking on your Source tables.

4. Select Change Tracking as the download method in your ETL Definition Page, and compile it.

5. Run your ETL Procedure/Package for the first time. On this first run, it will do a full download of all existing records in your Source tables. For large tables, it is advantageous to not have indexes during this first run. Future runs will be only differential, only downloading the insert/update/deletes that have occurred since the previous run.

6. Finally, use the "Add Indexes" queries to properly index your warehouse tables.

Truncate Flat Tables

If you are recompiling an ETL Group on an existing warehouse, you should consider whether you need to truncate any of your existing Flat or Warehouse tables. If the changes that you are recompiling have modified any existing Flat or warehouse tables (such as by adding a new column), then these tables need to be truncated, and the Change Tracking set back to zero. This guarantees that the tables will be completely reloaded, and the modifications (new columns/etc) will be filled accurately. The "Truncate Tables" SQL queries are designed to help you in this regard.

Referential Integrity Queries

These queries establish formal referential integrity between the tables by explicitly designating foreign keys.

Information Lists

Several lists are included, giving information about the composition of the ETL Group. These include:

- List of Stored Procedures
- List of Download Tables
- Order of Stored Procedure Execution (within the compiled ETL Process)
- Process Flow (input and output tables of each stored procedure)
- Last Run Information (shows error log, and also the start/end times of each procedure)
- Stored Procedure that provides Last Run Information

17. Junk Dimension Design

In the design of your warehouse, you may encounter numerous "facts" that are flags, status indicators, and such low-cardinality fields associated with the transactions in your fact table. These are often Y/N bit fields or other enumerated types with a small range of possible values. Junk Dimension tables are a useful tool for retaining this information without exploding the size of your fact table. Simply put, the idea is to collect up all of this "junk", even if the fields are unrelated, into one Junk Dimension which only requires one foreign key to be added to fact table instead of the many fields that would be necessary if the indicators were added individually.

The following steps are needed to design a Junk Dimension:

1. Identify fields that could be collected together as a Junk Dim. Create the normal staging elements for the source tables of these fields: Download table(s), Flat table(s), Flat Procedure(s) to feed the Flat table(s).

2. Add the new Junk columns to the existing Flat table that feeds the Fact table. Later, Junk data will be drawn from this Flat table, and placed into the Junk table proper, while the Fact table gets only a single foreign key to the Junk Dimension. Modify the Flat Procedure for this Flat table, so that it will fill the new columns. This modification by using the Additional Source feature and drawing from the Flat tables designed in step (1.).

3. Create the new Junk Table proper. This table collects up the miscellaneous junk and groups it under a single surrogate primary key.

4. Create a Junk Procedure to feed the new Junk Table.

5. Add the foreign key (the Junk table's surrogate primary key) to the Fact table. Use the "Add Junk" button to define this relationship in the Fact Procedure Definition page.

6. Recompile the ETL Process.

Junk Dimension Design Example (JDimInvoice)

In the example of this chapter, we begin with an existing fact table from our rapid prototype, FactInvoice, to which we will add a new junk table that holds two status fields. In this example, the "junk" consists of two fields, PaymentStatus and InvoiceStatus, which originate in two separate Source DB tables.

Design Download Tables

We will create download tables, called DownloadInvoiceStatus and DownloadPaymentStatus, in DWizStaging to facilitate the downloading of the "InvoiceStatus" and "PaymentStatus" table data from the Source DB. We will use the same method as for other download tables.

Right-click the InvoiceStatus table under DWizSource and select Copy Table to define the new DownloadInvoiceStatus. Fill in the definition page, being certain to select the ETL group "TutorialGroup" and to specify the DWizSource Connection. Make sure that column InvoiceStatusID is indicated as the Source Primary Key with a "1", then press the Save icon (Floppy-Disk).

Repeat these steps for DownloadPaymentStatus: Right-click the PaymentStatus table under DWizSource and select Copy Table to define the new DownloadPaymentStatus. In the definition page, select the ETL group "TutorialGroup", specify the DWizSource Connection, indicate PaymentStatusID as the Source Primary Key with a "1", and press Save.

Design Flat Tables

We will create Flat tables, called FlatInvoiceStatus and FlatPaymentStatus, in DWizStaging by using the same method as before. Right-click the DownloadInvoiceStatus table under **DWizStaging** and select Copy Table to define the new FlatInvoiceStatus with Table Type = **Flat:**

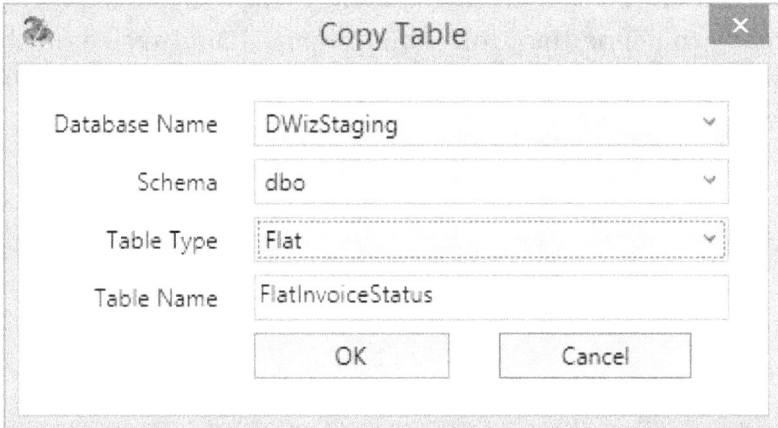

Illustration 82: "Copy Table" Pop-Up for FlatInvoiceStatus

In the definition page, indicate InvoiceStatusID as the Source Primary Key with a "1", and press Save.

Do the same for FlatPaymentStatus: Right-click the DownloadPaymentStatus table under DWizStaging and select Copy Table to define the new FlatPaymentStatus with Table type = Flat. In the definition page, indicate PaymentStatusID as the Source Primary Key with a "1", and press Save.

Add New Junk Columns to Existing Flat

In Object Explorer, double-click FlatInvoice (DWizStaging->Tables->Flat) to open it. In the definition page, append columns InvoiceStatus varchar(50) and PaymentStatus varchar(50); then press Save at the top of the definition page.

Define Junk Table

Now we are ready to define the junk table proper, JDimInvoice, in the Warehouse DB. Right-click the FlatInvoice table under DWizStaging->Tables->Flat, and select Copy Table:

Ilustration 83: "Copy Table" Pop-Up for Defining Junk Tables

Make sure to set:

- Database Name = DwizWarehouse <or your warehouse DB>
- Schema = dbo <or your pre-existing alternate Schema>
- Table Type = Junk
- Table Name = JdimInvoice <or your chosen Junk Dimension Table name>

In the JDimInvoice definition page, delete all the columns (even the keys) except for the two new columns at the bottom, InvoiceStatus and PaymentStatus; then Save:

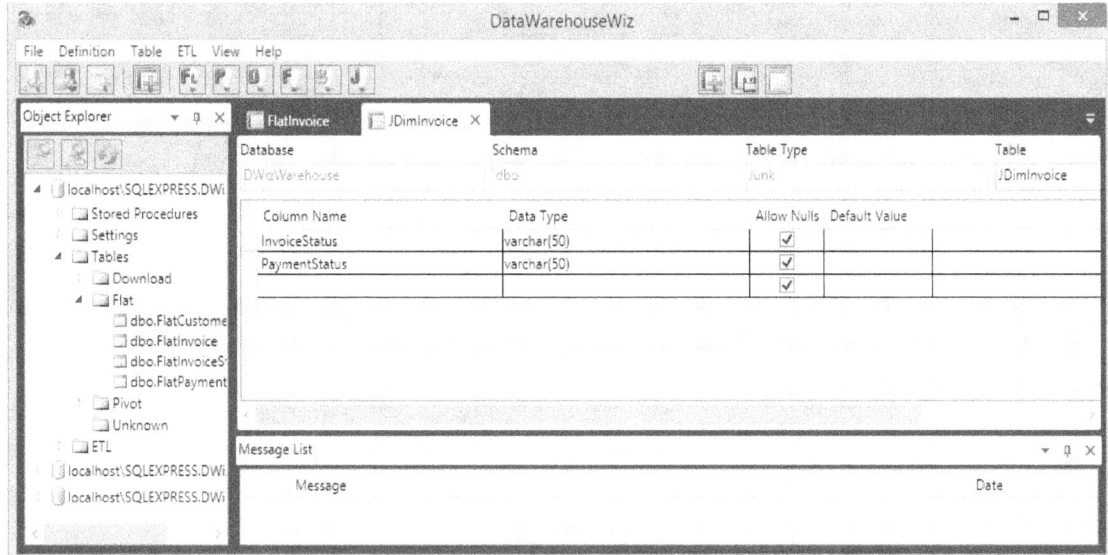

Illustration 84: "Junk Table" Definition Page

Don't forget to Save the definition page! Note that DWiz silently creates the surrogate primary key, JDimInvoiceKey. With the tables all set, we are ready to define the stored procedures to load them.

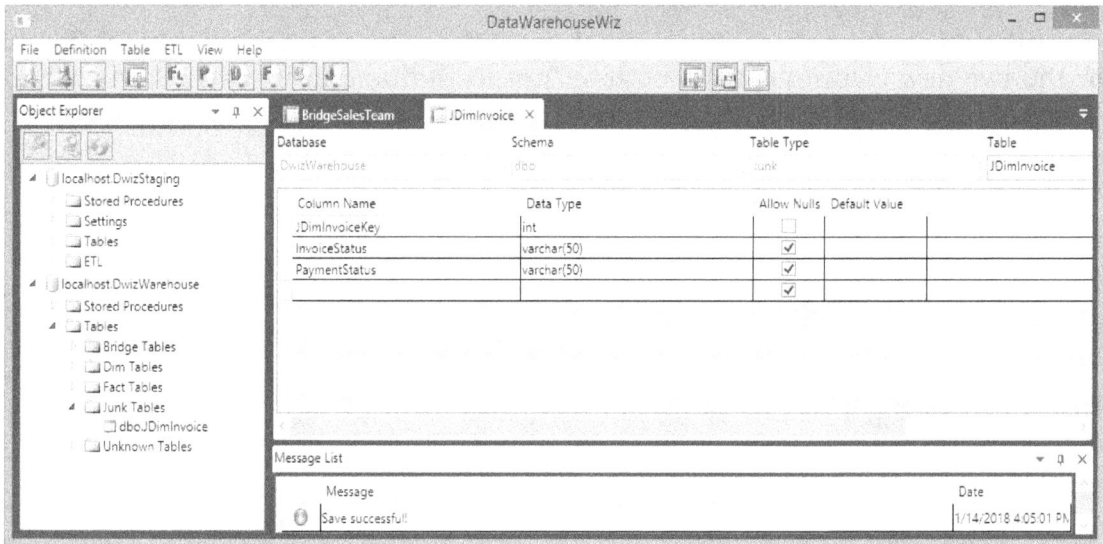

Illustration 85: DWiz Silently Creates a Surrogate Primary Key

Design Procedure for Flat (InvoiceStatus)

Next we will create an ETL stored procedure for FlatInvoiceStatus. Perform the following steps:

- Expand DWizStaging-->Stored Procedures-->Flat, right-click the Flat folder, and select New Flat.

- Create Flat Definition Page with Stored Procedure Name = FlatInvoiceStatus_upd, Source Table = DownloadInvoiceStatus, and Flat Table = FlatInvoiceStatus. Then press OK.

- In the Flat Definition Page, select ETL Group = TutorialGroup, enter a "1" in the Natural Key box of column InvoiceStatusID, and then press the **Save** icon.

- Press the Create/Alter Procedure button (Lightning/+ icon).

- After the code is displayed, press the Save Procedure button (Lightning Over Floppy icon).

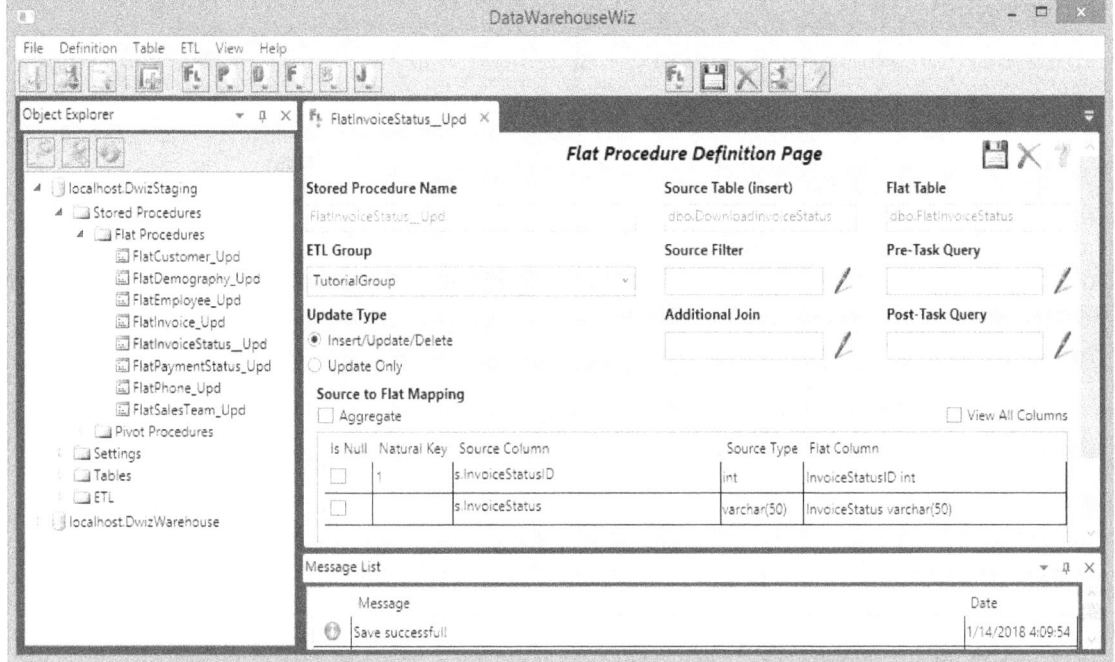

Illustration 86: FlatInvoiceStatus_upd Procedure Definition Page

Design Procedure for Flat (PaymentStatus)

Repeat the steps to create an ETL stored procedure for FlatPaymentStatus:

- Expand DWizStaging-->Stored Procedures-->Flat, right-click the Flat folder, and select New Flat.

- Create Flat Definition Page with Stored Procedure Name = FlatPaymentStatus_upd, Source Table = DownloadPaymentStatus, and Flat Table = FlatPaymentStatus. Then press OK.

- In the Flat Definition Page, select ETL Group = TutorialGroup, enter a "1" in the Natural Key box of column PaymentStatusID, and then press the **Save** icon.

- Press the Create/Alter Procedure button (Lightning/+ icon).

- After the code is displayed, press the Save Procedure button (Lightning Over Floppy icon).

Add New Junk Column ETL to Existing Flat Procedure (FlatInvoice_upd)

In Object Explorer, double-click FlatInvoice_upd (DWizStaging->Stored Procedures->Flat) to open it. In the top Tab Button Bar, press Define Additional Source:

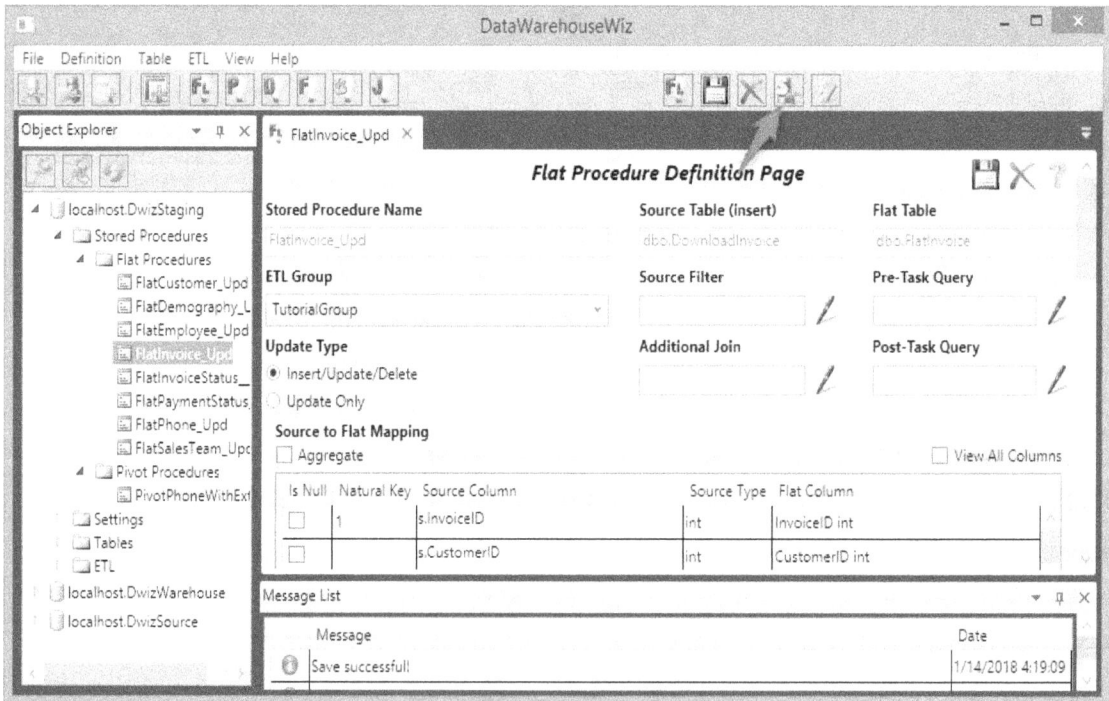

Illustration 87: Revising a Flat Update Stored Procedure

In the resulting pop-up. select FlatInvoiceStatus:

Illustration 88: "Add Addition Source" Pop-Up for a Flat Update Stored Procedure

In the definition page, scroll down to reveal the new section at the bottom, Additional Source. Put a "1" in the Natural Key of column InvoiceStatusID. This Additional Source section should look like the following figure (if the unused columns seem confusing, UN-checkmark "View All Columns"):

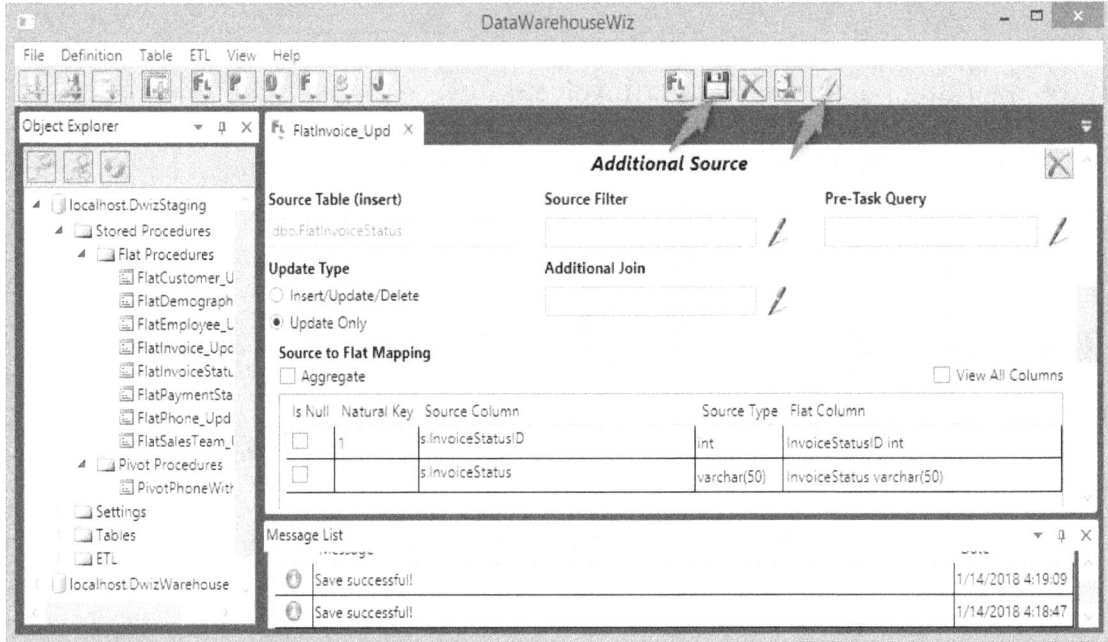

Illustration 89: Alter or Create a Stored Procedure

Now press Save (Floppy-Disk) to re-save the modified page. Next we will generate the stored procedure, by pressing the Create/Alter Procedure button. After the code is displayed, press the Save Procedure button (Lightning Over Floppy icon).

Now go back to the tab shown above (FlatInvoice_upd) so you can repeat these steps to add PaymentStatus:

- Press Define Additional Source button

- Select FlatPaymentStatus to be added and press OK

- Scroll down to reveal the new Additional Source section

- Put a "1" in the Natural Key of column PaymentStatusID

- Uncheck "View all columns" button

- Press Save Page button (Floppy-Disk)
- Press Alter Procedure button
- Press Save Procedure button

Design of the Junk Dimension Procedure

We need to make one more procedure, that of the Junk Dim itself. The Junk Dim is part of the warehouse DB, so the procedure will reside there as well. DWiz will write the Junk Procedure for you, based on your inputs to the Junk Procedure Definition Page; however, DWiz will always give you an opportunity to view and modify the code if you wish.

Perform the following steps to create an ETL stored procedure for JDimInvoice:

- Expand **DWizWarehouse**-->Stored Procedures-->**Junk**, right-click the Junk folder, and select New Junk.

- Create Junk Definition Page with Stored Procedure Name = JDimInvoice_upd, Source Table = FlatInvoice, and Junk Dim Table = JDimInvoice. Then press OK.

- In the Junk Dim Definition Page, select ETL Group = TutorialGroup, and UnCheck "View All Columns". This should leave only the two new columns in the display: InvoiceStatus & PaymentStatus. Press the **Save** icon.

- Press the Create/Alter Procedure button (Lightning/+ icon).

- After the code is displayed, press the Save Procedure button (Lightning over Floppy icon).

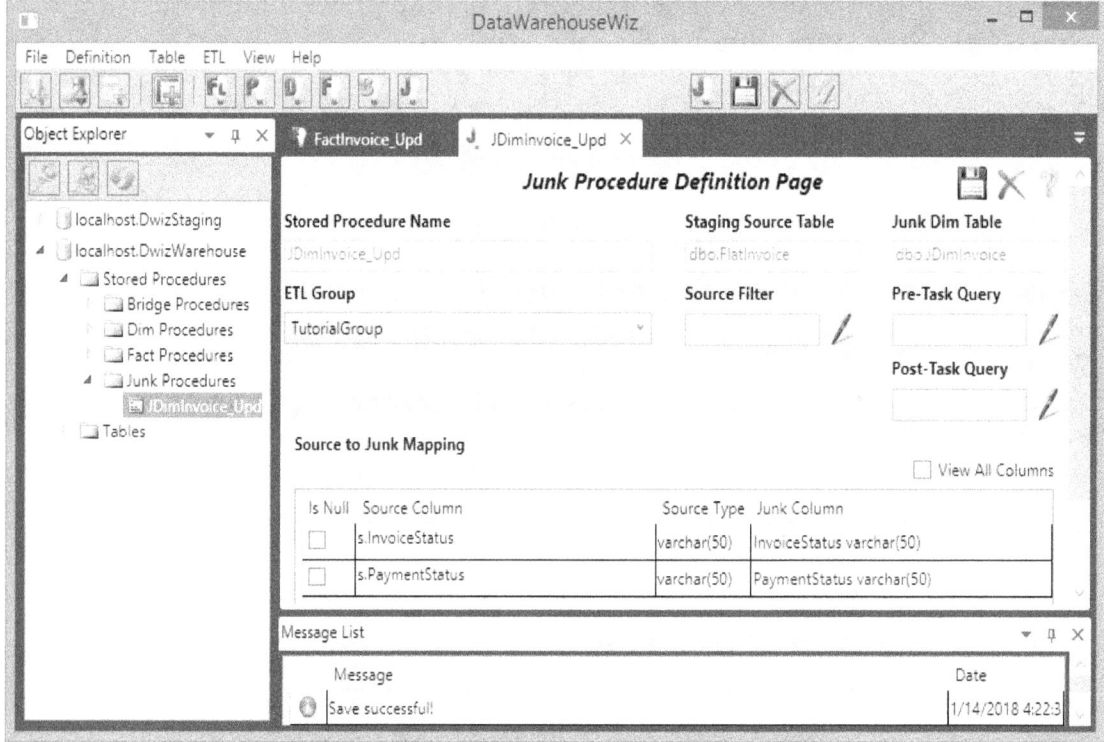

Illustration 90: Junk Procedure Definition Page

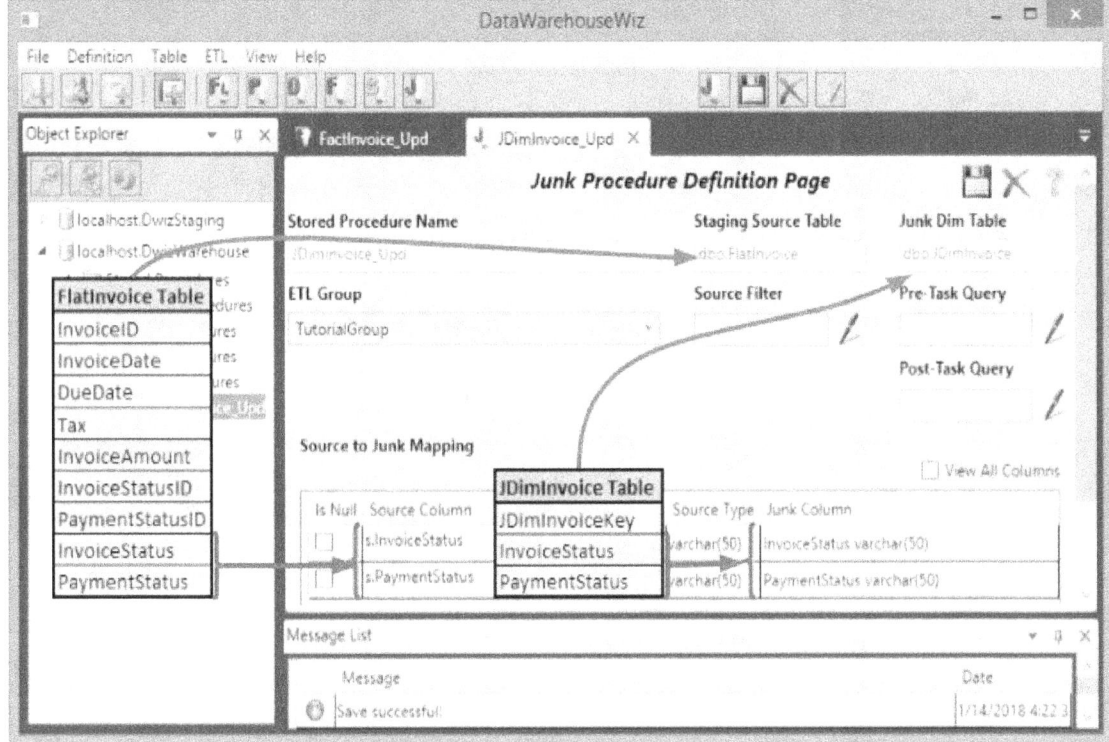

Illustration 91: Junk Procedure Uses Tables of the Junk Subsystem

Add Foreign Key for the Junk Dimension to the Fact Table

Expand DWizWarehouse->Tables->Fact, and double-click FactInvoice to open it. Append the column JDimInvoiceKey (type = int) to the table and Save it.

Add New Junk Column ETL to the Fact Procedure (FactInvoice_upd)

In Object Explorer, double-click FactInvoice_upd (DWizWarehouse->Stored Procedures->Fact) to open it:

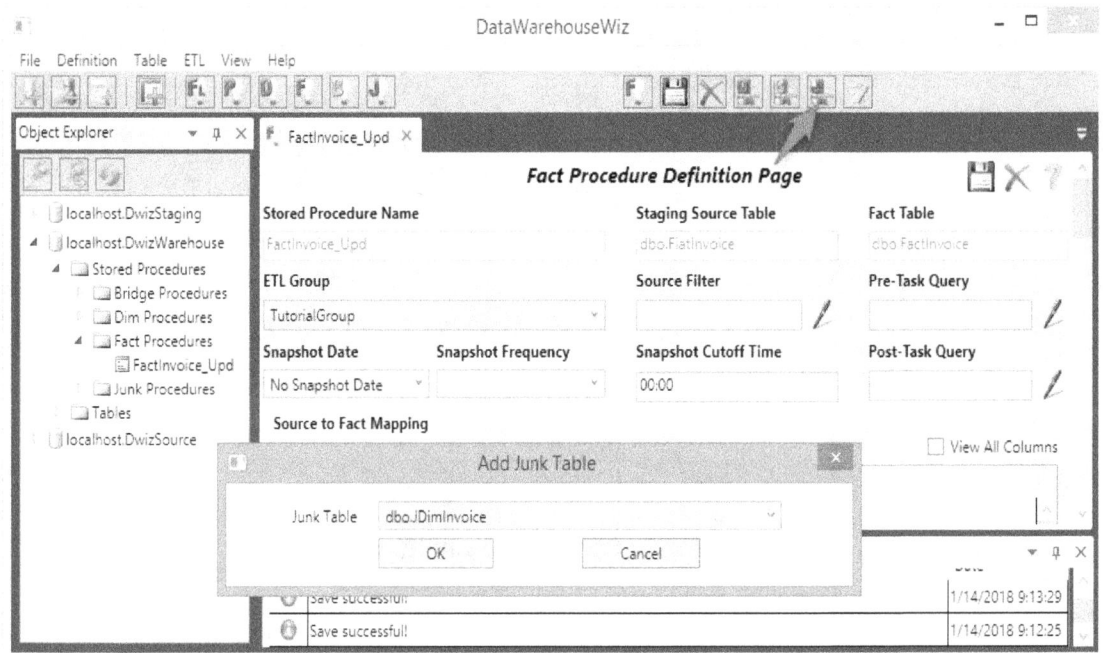

Illustration 92: Adding a Junk Table to a Fact Table Update Procedure

Press the Define Junk button (as shown above). From the pop-up, select JDimInvoice, and press OK:

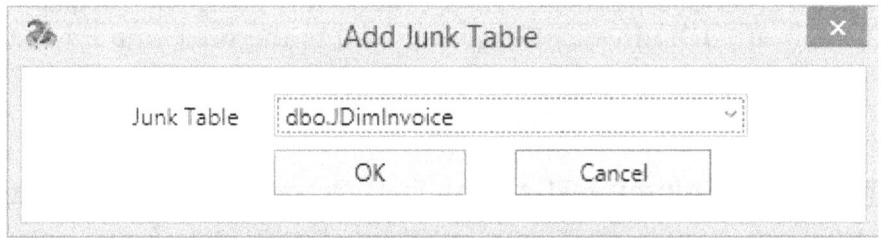

Illustration 93: "Add Junk Table" Pop-Up

Perform the following:

- Scroll down to reveal the new Fact To Junk section

- Set Fact Table Key to "JDimInvoiceKey"

- Set Junk Table Key to "JDimInvoiceKey"

- Press Save

Recompile ETL Package

With all the tables and procedures done, we can now re-create the ETL Package, in a similar fashion to the steps from chapter "Compiling an ETL Group".

Our choices are 1) to compile an ETL Group Procedure, or 2) to compile an ETL SSIS Package. The first option is simple, just open the ETL Definition Page and compile the ETL Group Procedure. The second option (higher performance) entails the following steps:

- Expand **DWizStaging**-->ETL-->Definitions, right-click the Definitions folder, and double-click on TutorialETL

- Review ETL Definition Page (no changes are necessary), and press the Save button

- Press the Create BIML button (Scroll+Pen icon on top right)

- Open your TutorialETL project in SQL Data Tools for Visual Studio, and double-click the BimlScript.biml file to open it

- Copy (cut-and-paste clipboard) the new BIML from DWiz to overwrite the BimlScript in Visual Studio

- Save All in Visual Studio

- Right-click BimlScript.biml (under Miscellaneous in Solution Explorer) and click "Generate SSIS Packages". This may take a few minutes. Visual Studio may ask if you want to overwrite the package TutorialETL.dtsx; click on Yes.

- Afterward, you may view the data flow by double-clicking on the TutorialETL.dtsx package

- You may run the ETL Package by pressing the Start button on the top menu. Afterward, you can see the filled warehouse tables in SSMS.

This concludes the mods to add a Junk Dimension to an existing warehouse. The augmented warehouse is "finished" and usable. In the next chapter, we will add a Bridge Dimension.

18. Bridge Dimension Design

During the design of your warehouse, you may encounter certain dimensions which have a many-to-many relationship with the grain of your Fact table, which poses a problem for your design because a single transaction in your Fact table can have multiple simultaneous values of this certain dimension type. Some common scenarios are:

- A patient receives multiple diagnosis codes for a single hospital visit
- An account has multiple owners or beneficiaries
- A sale or account is serviced by a team of employees

Bridge Dimension tables are a very tidy solution to this problem, without breaking the ease-of-use or efficiency of the Fact table. The many-to-many values are collected into groups, and only the group key is added to the Fact table. The bridge dimension then makes the many-to-many relationship of groups to individual values. The following illustration shows two good approaches to making a Bridge subsystem which solves the problem of linking an unpredictable number of employees that contribute to a single sale. In the top approach, we see that the employees are grouped into (perhaps ad hoc) sales teams such that each unique combination of employees that has ever contributed to a single common sale becomes one record of a "sales team", whether or not that "sales team" has any other significance in the business. This solves the many-to-many problem because each Fact record will then need to reference only one DimSalesTeam record. Any descriptive info about the sales team can be collected in its DimSalesTeam record. Then we need to create the many-to-many Bridge table BridgeSalesTeam, which links which employees comprise each sales team. If we decide that the ad hoc sales teams have no other relevance, then we can take the bottom approach and dispense with the DimSalesTeam table altogether. The rest of the subsystem works exactly the same as before, with the BridgeSalesTeamKey defining the unique combination of employees on an otherwise un-described ad hoc sales team.

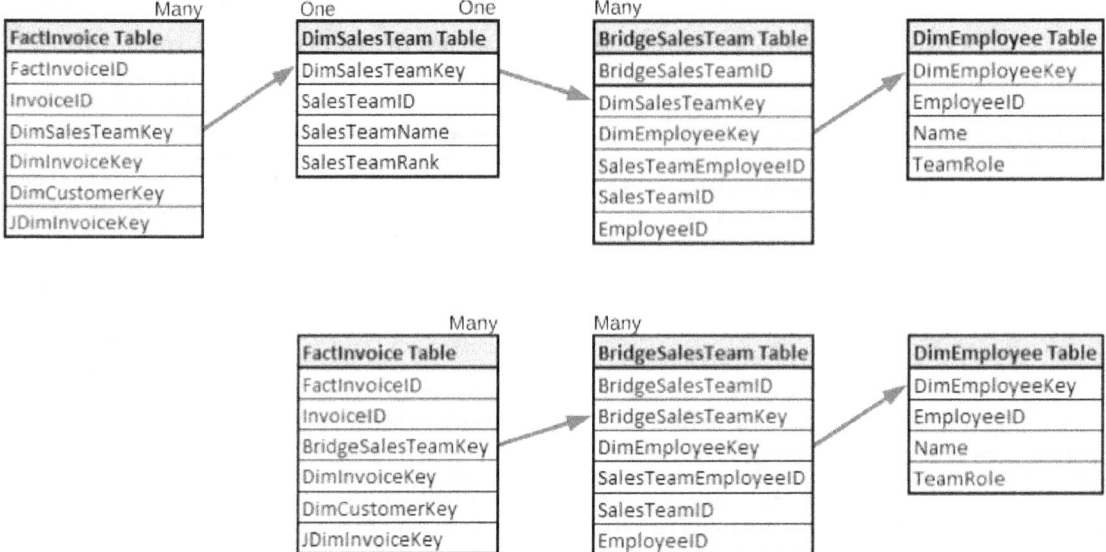

Illustration 94: Typical Tables in a Bridge Subsystem

However, Bridges should not be used when the situation can be solved by pivoting a small number of columns (see BAD Bridge illustration). The Pivot solution will be much more efficient for the cases where ten columns or less will be created.

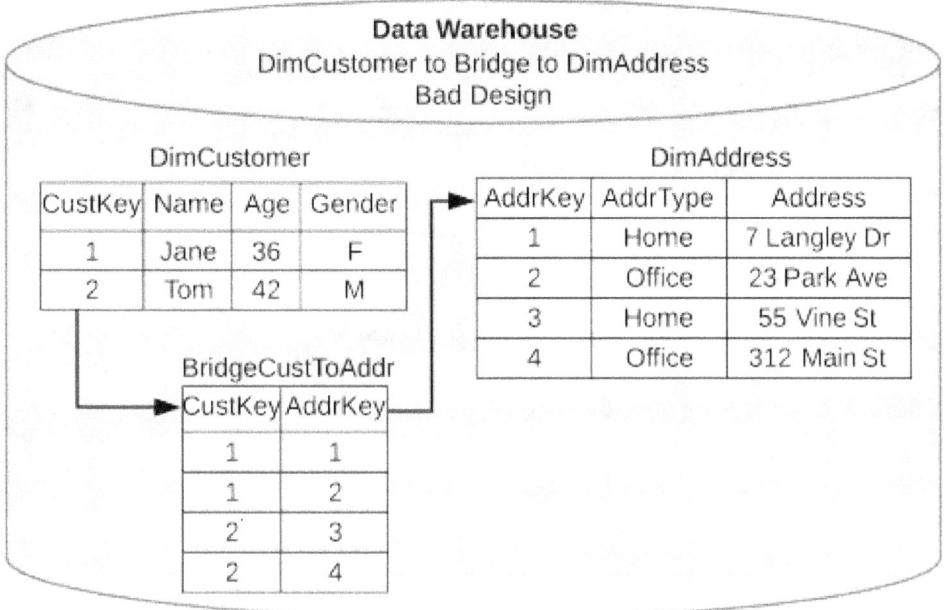

Illustration 95: BAD Bridge Design (Use Pivot Table Instead)

Bridge Procedure Definition Page

DWiz will write the Bridge Procedure for you, based on your inputs to the Bridge Procedure Definition Page; however, DWiz will always give you an opportunity to view and modify the code if you wish. A Bridge Procedure Definition Page is shown in the following illustration. Each of the fields will be described in detail. Afterward, we will demonstrate the design of a Bridge Dimension by adding a Bridge to our rapid prototype.

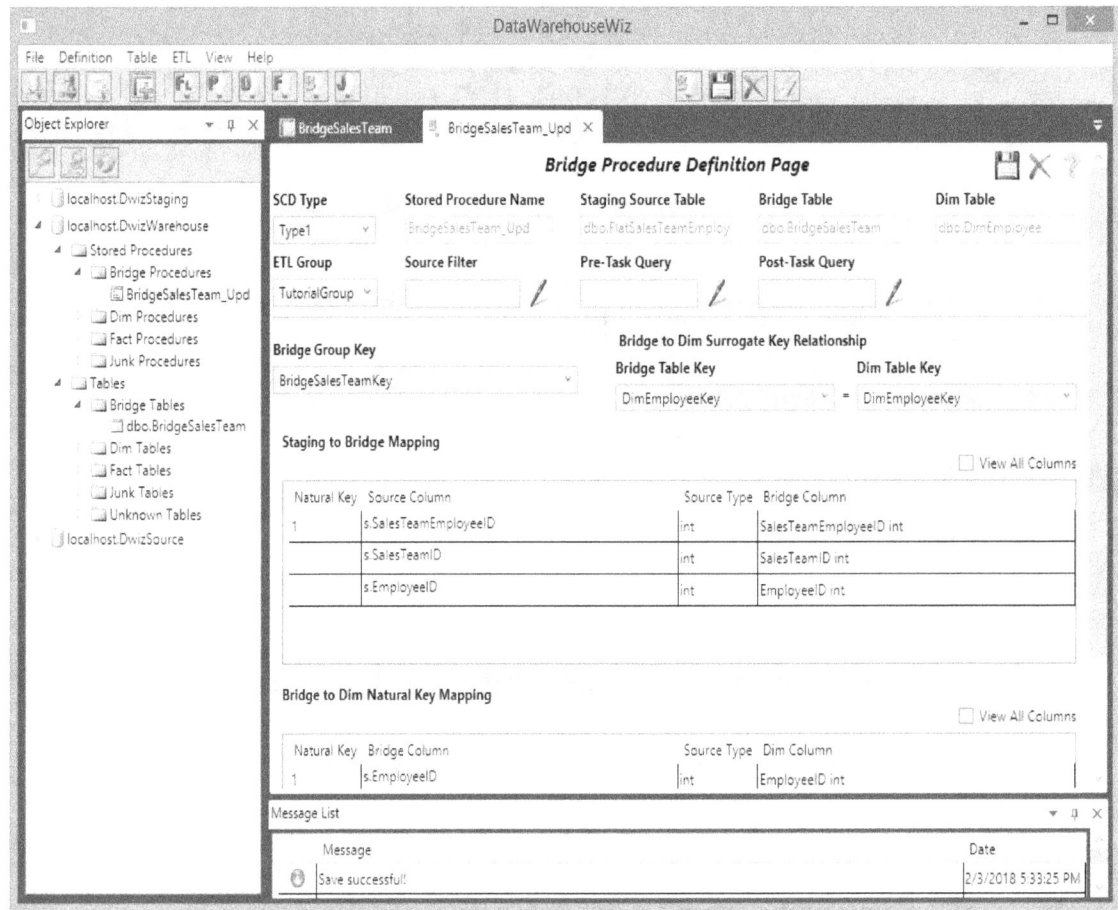

Illustration 96: The Bridge Procedure Definition Page

SCD Type

The "SCD Type" indicates the desired type of slowly-changing dimension handling, as defined by Kimball et al[2]. DWiz directly supports SCD Types 1 and 2, by selecting the type in this SCD Type column.

SCD 1 is "Overwrite". If a non-key attribute of a Dimension changes, then the new value overwrites the previous value in the Dimension table, with no change to the primary key.

SCD 2 is "New Record". If a non-key attribute of a Dimension changes, this causes a new record to be created in the Dimension table, with a new value of the primary key. However, a maximum of one new record per day will be created for a given Dimension entry. Any further changes to the same entry within the same day are handled as SCD 1 Overwrites. This is the behavior that most warehouse designers want for Type 2 dimensions, as it captures slowly changing dimensions without accumulating trash from transient changes within a day.

Stored Procedure Name

This field contains the exact name of the stored procedure that will be created/altered in the staging DB. The default is `<name of the flat table to be updated>` + `"_upd"`. If desired, these default settings can be changed in the Settings folder under the staging DB of the Object Explorer. You can change any of these global settings for your own purposes, but if you do so, then you must re-compile any stored procedures that made use of the previous setting values.

Staging Source Table

This field identifies the primary source of data from the Flat tables, that will be used for raw data going into the transforms. Within the stored procedure, this table will have the alias "s" (for source). In other input fields below (Source Filter, Source Column), you may reference any primary source column by using the prefix "s.". Note that the Source Table is a Flat table in the staging DB, **not** the original table of the Source DB. The following illustration shows the relationship and mapping of the Source and Target tables.

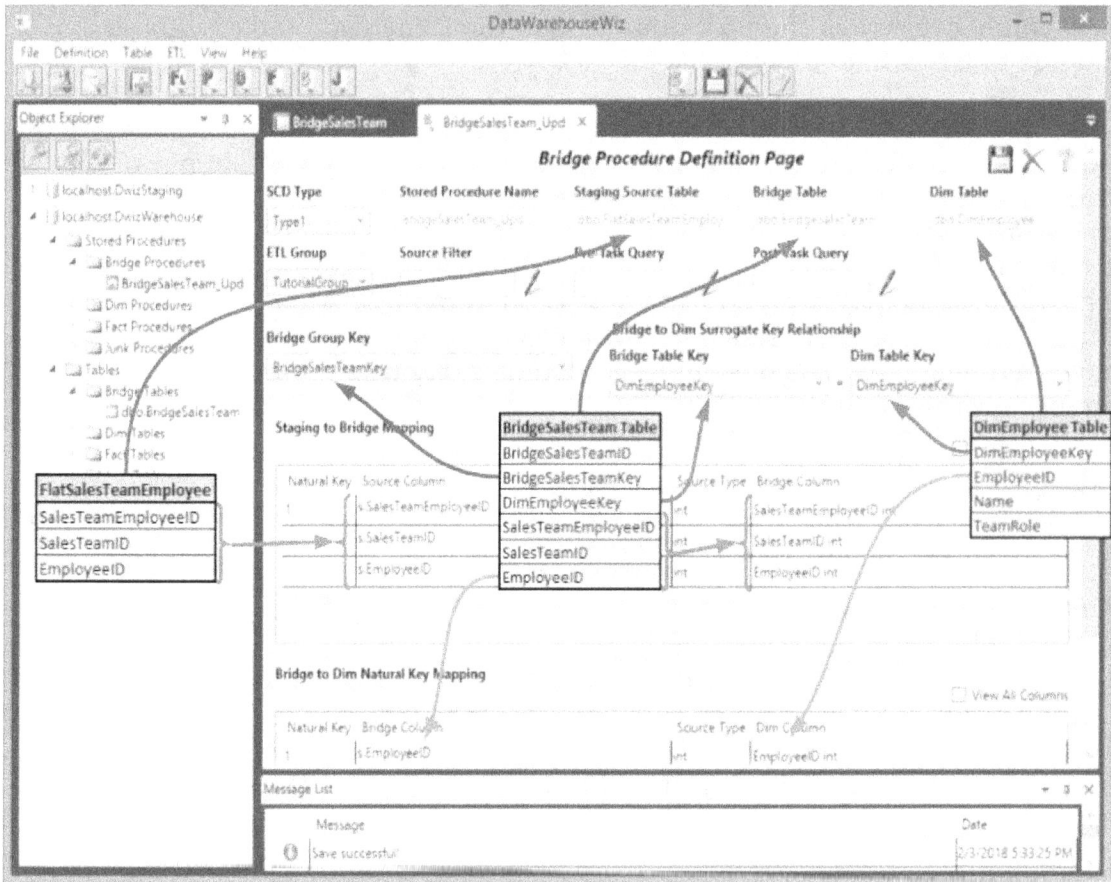

Illustration 97: The Source and Target Tables of the Bridge Procedure Definition Page

Bridge Table

This identifies the Bridge table, the "target", that will be updated by this stored procedure. Within the stored procedure, this table will have the alias "t" (for target). In other input fields below (Source Filter, Source Column), you may reference any target column by using the prefix "t." .

Dim Table

This identifies the Dimension table. This table is not updated by this stored procedure, but the table must be indicated so that DWiz can create the Bridge code.

ETL Group

This field indicates which ETL Group that this stored procedure will be included into. It should be the same ETL Group that includes the primary source table. If the ETL Group is changed in the future, then the primary source table should also be moved to the new group.

Source Filter

This field allows you to specify a filter that will be applied (in a SQL WHERE clause) when the procedure queries the primary source table. Do not include the "WHERE" nor the closing ";". An example is "`s.MyFlag = 1`", which will then be included in the WHERE clauses, causing all the procedure's queries to be limited to rows where the primary source table has column MyFlag = 1. If your desired source filter has multiple lines, such as a CASE statement, then simply click the InkPen button to the right of the Source Filter input box--this will pop-up a convenient multi-line box for you.

Pre-Task Query

This field specifies a SQL statement that will be executed immediately *before* the queries of this Flat Stored Procedure run in the ETL process. It is a catch-all to allow you to do any kind of processing that you cannot easily implement through the other fields. An example is "`exec MySpecialPreProcessor_SP`", where MySpecialPreProcessor_SP is a stored procedure that you have written from scratch and placed into the staging DB. We recommend that this be used only as a last resort, after use of the other input fields has proved insufficient; using the other powerful input fields is easier, more readable, and more maintainable. To enter a multi-line query, press the InkPen button to the right of the input box.

Post-Task Query

This field specifies a SQL statement that will be executed immediately *after* the queries of this Flat Stored Procedure run in the ETL process. It is a catch-all to allow you to do any kind of processing that you cannot easily implement through the other fields. An example is `"exec MySpecialPostProcessor_SP"`, where MySpecialPostProcessor_SP is a stored procedure that you have written from scratch and placed into the staging DB. We recommend that this be used only as a last resort, after use of the other input fields has proved insufficient; using the other powerful input fields is easier, more readable, and more maintainable. To enter a multi-line query, press the InkPen button to the right of the input box.

Bridge Group Key

This drop-down field is used to select the surrogate primary key of the Bridge table.

Bridge to Dim Surrogate Key Relationship

These drop-down fields, both "DimEmployeeKey" in the illustration, relate the Bridge Table Key (a foreign key in the Bridge) to the Dim Table Key (the surrogate primary key of the Dimension). This tells DWiz how to map the foreign key in the Bridge.

Staging to Bridge Mapping: View All Columns

Checking this field allows the user to see all columns of the target Bridge table schema. When unchecked, after Saving the Definition Page, DWiz will display only the columns being updated by the queries. This field does not affect the actual queries in any way.

Staging to Bridge Mapping: Natural Key

This field is used to indicate the Natural Key(s) of the source table. These Natural Keys are generally the primary key(s) of the original table in the Source DB, with a "1" indicating the first part, and a "2" indicating the second part (if existing), etc.

Staging to Bridge Mapping: Source Column

This field holds the transform for the data to be loaded into the Bridge Table Column, as shown in the following illustration. For a simple copy of a source column, it might be similar to "s.Cost". For an aggregation, it might be similar to "SUM(s.Cost)". For a more lengthy transform, click on the Source Column, and then on the InkPen that appears to the right--this will pop-up a multi-line space for you to enter a CASE statement or other lengthy element. The transform may reference any source columns with "s.", any target columns with "t.".

Staging to Bridge Mapping: Source Type

This field indicates the SQL variable type of the original source column. If the Source Column is changed to a transformation (such as "SUM(s.Cost)"), then DWiz will blank this field.

Staging to Bridge Mapping: Bridge Column

This field indicates the target column into which the transform of Source Column will be loaded.

Bridge to Dim Natural Key Mapping: View All Columns

Checking this field allows the user to see all columns of the Bridge/DIm table schema. When unchecked, after Saving the Definition Page, DWiz will display only the columns being updated by the queries. This field does not affect the actual queries in any way.

Bridge to Dim Natural Key Mapping: Natural Key

This field is used to indicate the Natural Key(s) of the Dimension table. This Natural Key is generally the primary key(s) of the original table in the Source DB, with a "1" indicating the first part, and a "2" indicating the second part (if existing), etc.

Bridge to Dim Natural Key Mapping: Source Column

This field holds the transform for the data to be loaded into the Bridge Table Column, as shown in the following illustration. For a simple copy of a source column, it might be similar to "s.Cost". For an aggregation, it might be similar to "SUM(s.Cost)". For a more lengthy transform, click on the Source Column, and then on the InkPen that appears to the right--this will pop-up a multi-line space for you to enter a CASE statement or other lengthy element. The transform may reference any source columns with "s.", any target columns with "t.".

Bridge to Dim Natural Key Mapping: Source Type

This field indicates the SQL variable type of the original source column. If the Source Column is changed to a transformation (such as "SUM(s.Cost)"), then DWiz will blank this field.

Bridge to Dim Natural Key Mapping: Dim Column

This field indicates the Dimension table Natural Key column which corresponds to the Natural Key column in the Bridge.

204

Bridge Table Example (BridgeSalesTeam)

This will be illustrated by adding a Bridge to our rapid prototype. In this example, we have an existing invoice Fact table of high-end sales, and we wish to add the (multiple) employees that contributed to each sale. To avoid the inherent problems with this many-to-many relationship, we will group the employees into ad-hoc "sales teams", creating a"team" for every combination of employees encountered in the sales. Now we can add a single foreign key DimSalesTeamKey to the Fact table. Separately, we create an DimEmployee dimension that includes all sales employees. Finally, the BridgeSalesTeam table will contain the mappings of employees (from DimEmployee) to each group (DimSalesTeam).

Design Download Tables

We will create download tables, called DownloadSalesTeam and DownloadEmployee in DWizStaging to facilitate the downloading of the "SalesTeam" and "Employee" table data from the Source DB. We will use the same method as we did for DownloadCustomer.

Right-click the SalesTeam table under DWizSource and select Copy Table to define the new DownloadSalesTeam. Fill in the definition page, being certain to select the ETL group "TutorialGroup" and to specify the DWizSource Connection. Make sure that column ID is indicated as the Source Primary Key with a "1", then press the Save icon (Floppy-Disk).

Repeat these steps for DownloadEmployee: Right-click the Employee table under DWizSource and select Copy Table to define the new DownloadEmployee. In the definition page, select the ETL group "TutorialGroup", specify the DWizSource Connection, indicate EmployeeID as the Source Primary Key with a "1", and press Save.

Design Flat Tables

We will create Flat tables, called FlatSalesTeam and FlatEmployee, in DWizStaging by using the same method as we did for FlatCustomer. Right-click the DownloadSalesTeam table under **DWizStaging** and select Copy Table to define the new FlatSalesTeam with Table Type = **Flat:**

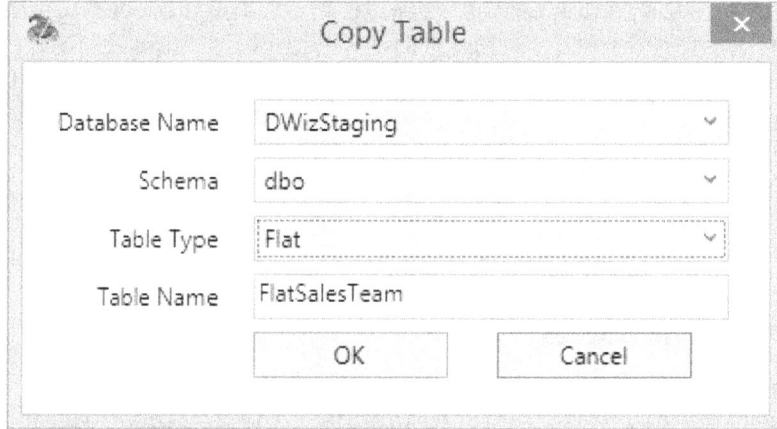

Illustration 98: "Copy Table" Pop-Up for FlatSalesTeam

In the definition page, indicate ID as the Source Primary Key with a "1", and press Save.

Do the same for FlatEmployee: Right-click the DownloadEmployee table under DWizStaging and select Copy Table to define the new FlatEmployee with Table type = Flat. In the definition page, indicate EmployeeID as the Source Primary Key with a "1", and press Save.

Design Dimension Table

We will create a DimEmployee table in DWizWarehouse by using the same method as we did for DimCustomer. Right-click the FlatEmployee table under **DWizStaging** and select Copy Table to define the new DimEmployee with:

- Database Name = DwizWarehouse <or your warehouse name>
- Schema = dbo <or your pre-existing alternate Schema>
- Table type = Dim
- Table Name = DimEmployee <or your chosen table name>

In the definition page, indicate EmployeeID as the Natural Key with a "1", and press Save.

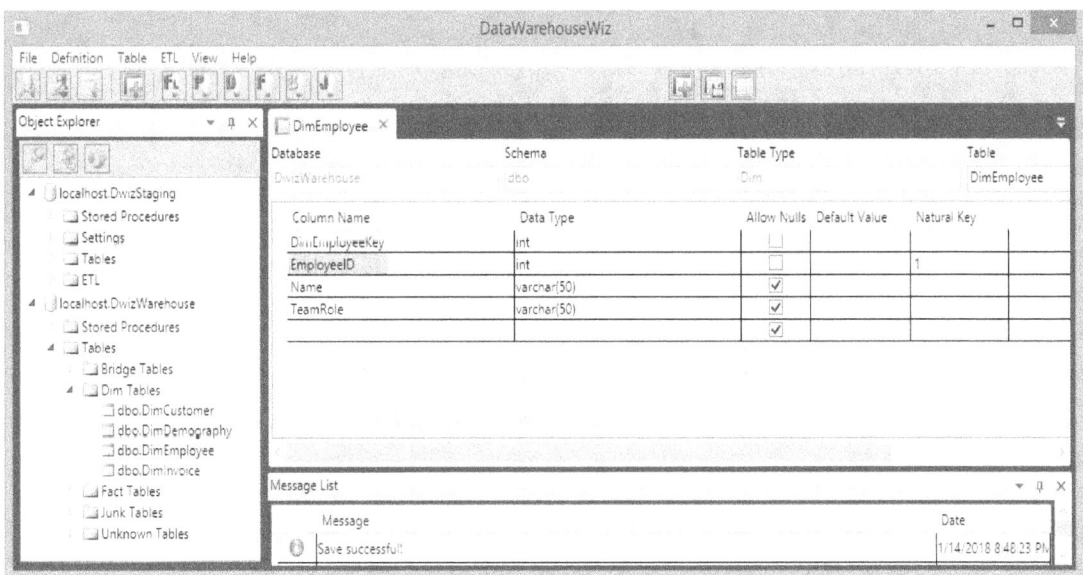

Illustration 99: The DimEmployee Table Definition Page

Define Bridge Table

Now we are ready to define the Bridge table proper, BridgeSalesTeam, in the Warehouse DB. Right-click the FlatSalesTeam table under DWizStaging->Tables->Flat, and select Copy Table:

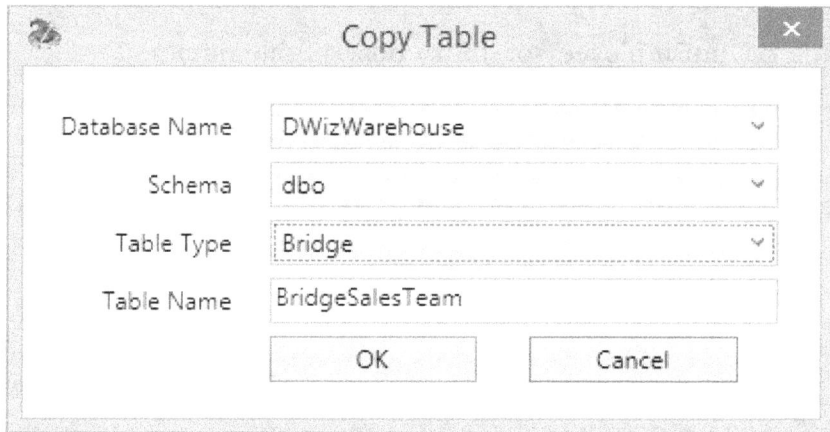

Illustration 100: "Copy Table" Pop-Up for Defining a Bridge Table

Make sure to set:

- Database Name = DwizWarehouse <or your warehouse DB>

- Schema = dbo <or your pre-existing alternate Schema>

- Table Type = Bridge

- Table Name = BridgeSalesTeam <or your chosen Bridge Table name>

In the BridgeSalesTeam definition page, append two new columns at the bottom, BridgeSalesTeamKey and DimEmployeeKey. Also indicate "ID" as the Natural Key with a "1", as this was the primary key of the FlatSalesTeam table that feeds this new bridge table. DWiz needs the primary key of the Flat table in order to maintain sync with it. Then press the Save button:

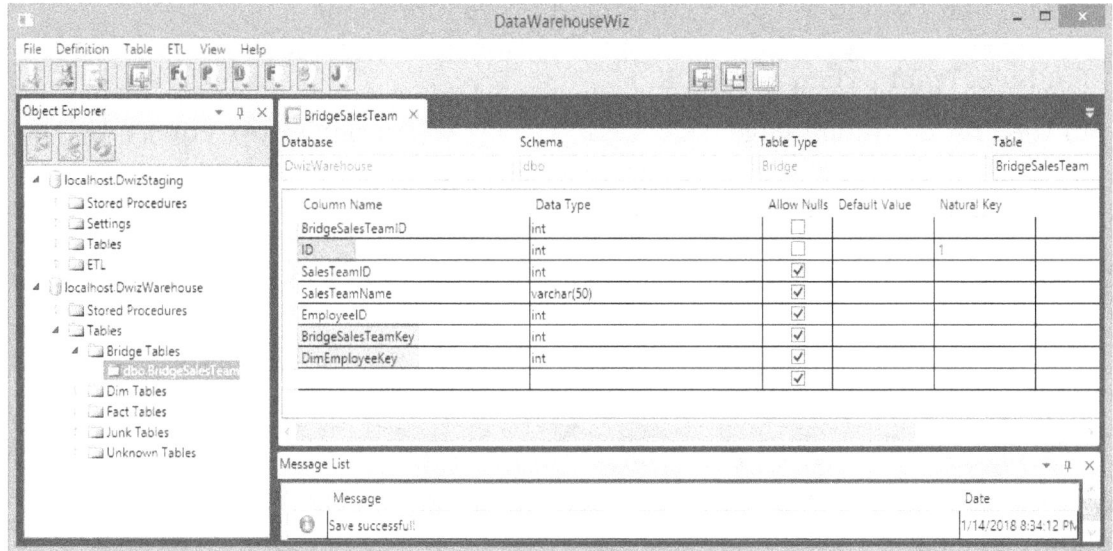

Illustration 101: "Bridge Table" Definition Page

Don't forget to Save the definition page! Note that DWiz silently creates the new table primary key, BridgeSalesTeamID.

Add New Bridge Foreign Key Column to the Fact Table

In Object Explorer, double-click FactInvoice (DWizWarehouse->Tables->Fact) to open it. In the definition page, append column BridgeSalesTeamKey (int); then press Save at the top of the definition page. With the tables all set, we are ready to define the stored procedures to load them.

Design Procedure for Flat (SalesTeam)

Next we will create an ETL stored procedure for FlatSalesTeam. Perform the following steps:

- Expand DWizStaging-->Stored Procedures-->Flat, right-click the Flat folder, and select New Flat.

- Create Flat Definition Page with Stored Procedure Name = FlatSalesTeam_upd, Source Table = DownloadSalesTeam, and Flat Table = FlatSalesTeam. Then press OK.

- In the Flat Definition Page, select ETL Group = TutorialGroup, enter a "1" in the Natural Key box of column ID, and then press the **Save** icon.

- Press the Create Procedure button (Lightning/+ icon).

- After the code is displayed, press the Save Procedure button (Lightning Over Floppy icon).

Design Procedure for Flat (Employee)

Next we will create an ETL stored procedure for FlatEmployee. Perform the following steps:

- Expand DWizStaging-->Stored Procedures-->Flat, right-click the Flat folder, and select New Flat.

- Create Flat Definition Page with Stored Procedure Name = FlatEmployee_upd, Source Table = DownloadEmployee, and Flat Table = FlatEmployee. Then press OK.

- In the Flat Definition Page, select ETL Group = TutorialGroup, enter a "1" in the Natural Key box of column EmployeeID, and then press the **Save** icon.

- Press the Create/Alter Procedure button (Lightning/+ icon).

- After the code is displayed, press the Save Procedure button (Lightning Over Floppy icon).

Design Procedure for Dimension (Employee)

Next we will create an ETL stored procedure for DimEmployee. Perform the following steps:

- Expand DWizWarehouse-->Stored Procedures-->Dim, right-click the Dim folder, and select New Dim.

- Create Dim Definition Page with Stored Procedure Name = DimEmployee_upd, Source Table = FlatEmployee, and Dim Table = DimEmployee. Then press OK.

- In the Dim Definition Page, select ETL Group = TutorialGroup, enter a "1" in the Natural Key box of column EmployeeID, and then press the **Save** icon.

- It is not necessary to compile the procedure (with the Create/Alter Procedure button) just yet. We will compile each of the warehouse procedures (Fact, Bridge, and Dim) only after all three have been defined and SAVED. The reason for this is that DWiz needs the definition info from all three before writing the code for any of them.

Design Procedure for Bridge

We will create an ETL stored procedure for BridgeSalesTeam. As Bridge tables reside in the Warehouse, our stored procedure will reside there also. The Bridge Procedure will take data that has already been processed and prepared in a Flat table, and use this data to update the Bridge table. DWiz will write the Bridge Procedure for you, based on your inputs to the Bridge Procedure Definition Page; however, DWiz will always give you an opportunity to view and modify the code if you wish.

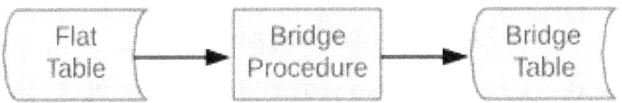

Illustration 102: Flow of a Bridge Procedure

Perform the following steps:

- Expand **DWizWarehouse**-->Stored Procedures-->Bridge, right-click the Bridge folder, and select New Bridge.

- Create Bridge Definition Page with Stored Procedure Name = BridgeSalesTeam_upd, Source Table = FlatSalesTeam, and Bridge Table = BridgeSalesTeam, and Dim Table = DimEmployee. Then press OK:

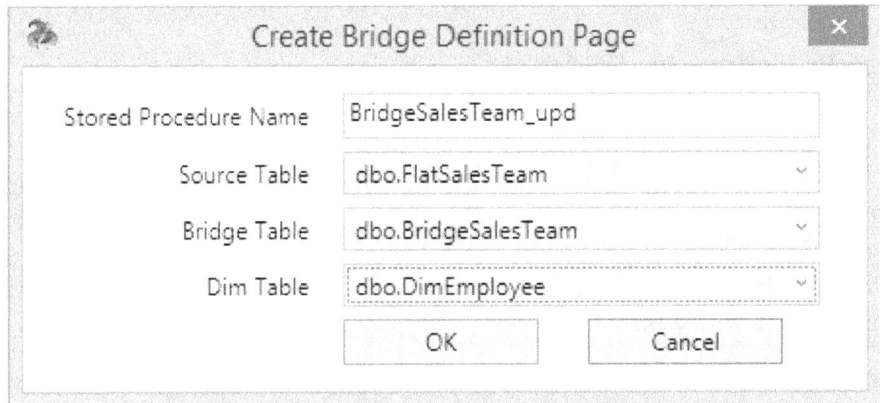

Illustration 103: "Create Bridge Definition Page" Pop-Up

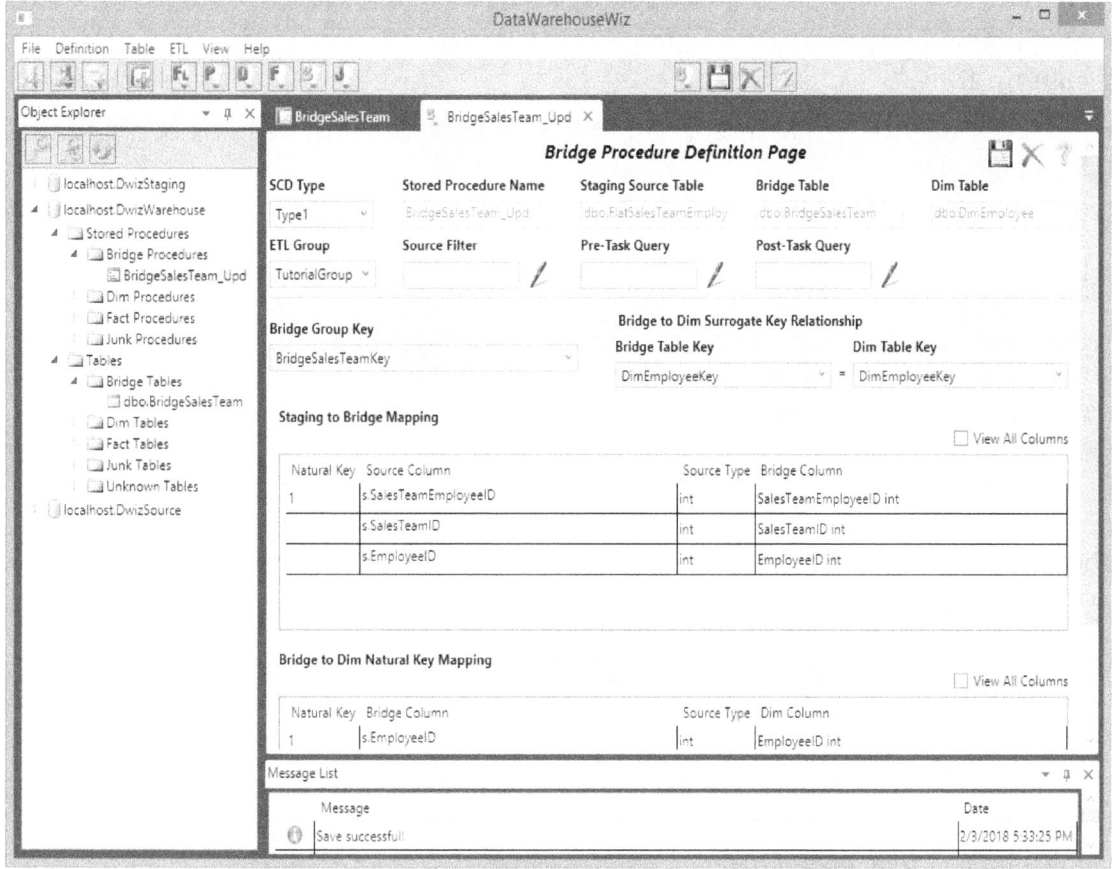

Illustration 104: Bridge Procedure Definition Page

In the Bridge Definition Page that appears in the page area, perform the following steps:

- Select SCD = Type1

- Select ETL Group = TutorialGroup

- Select Bridge Group Key = BridgeSalesTeamKey

- Select Bridge Table Key = DimEmployeeKey

- Select Dim Table Key = DimEmployeeKey

- In the Staging to Bridge Mapping, enter a "1" in the Natural Key box of column ID

- In the Bridge to Dim Mapping, enter a "1" in the Natural Key box of column EmployeeID

- Press the **Save** icon.

- It is not necessary to compile the procedure (with the Create/Alter Procedure button) just yet. We will compile each of the warehouse procedures (Fact, Bridge, and Dim) only after all three have been defined and SAVED. The reason for this is that DWiz needs the definition info from all three before writing the code for any of them.

The following illustration shows how the Bridge Procedure uses the tables of the Bridge subsystem.

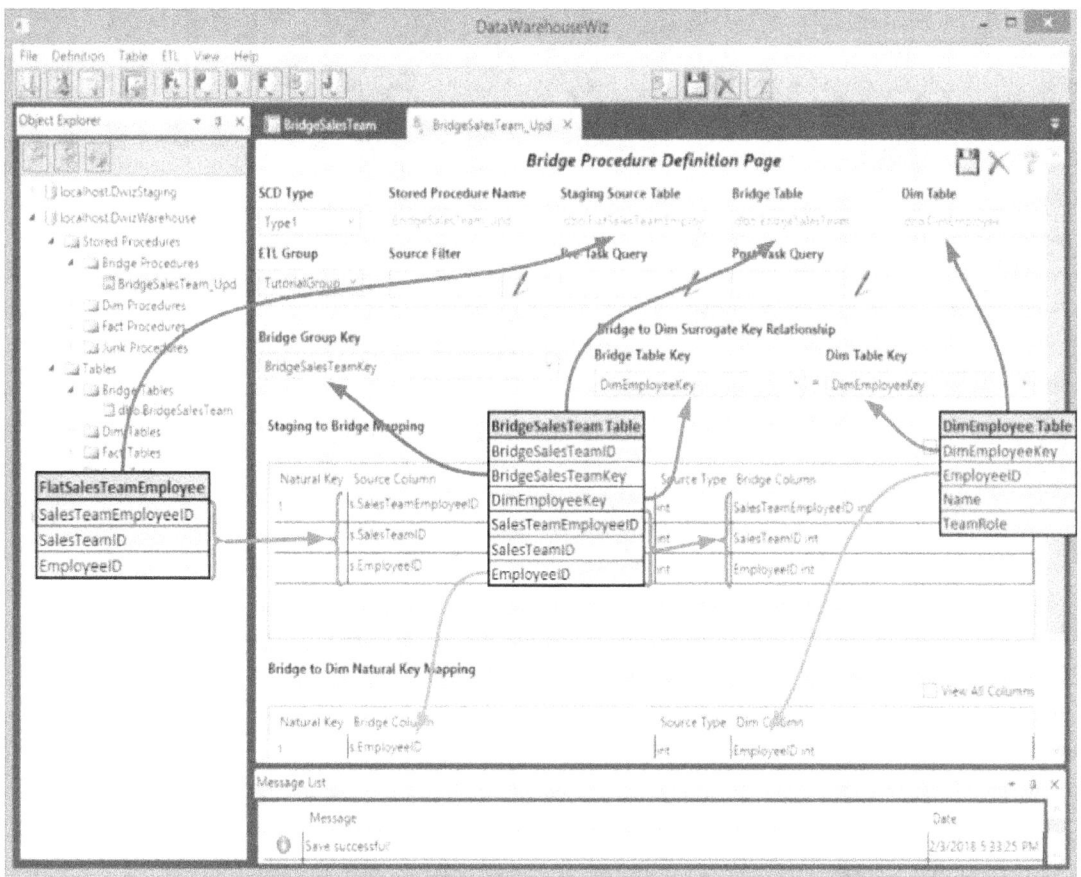

Illustration 105: Table Relationships in the Bridge Procedure

Add New Bridge Foreign Key Column to Fact Update Procedure

In Object Explorer, double-click FactInvoice_upd (DWizWarehouse-->Stored Procedures->Fact) to open it. In the top Tab Button Bar, press Add Bridge:

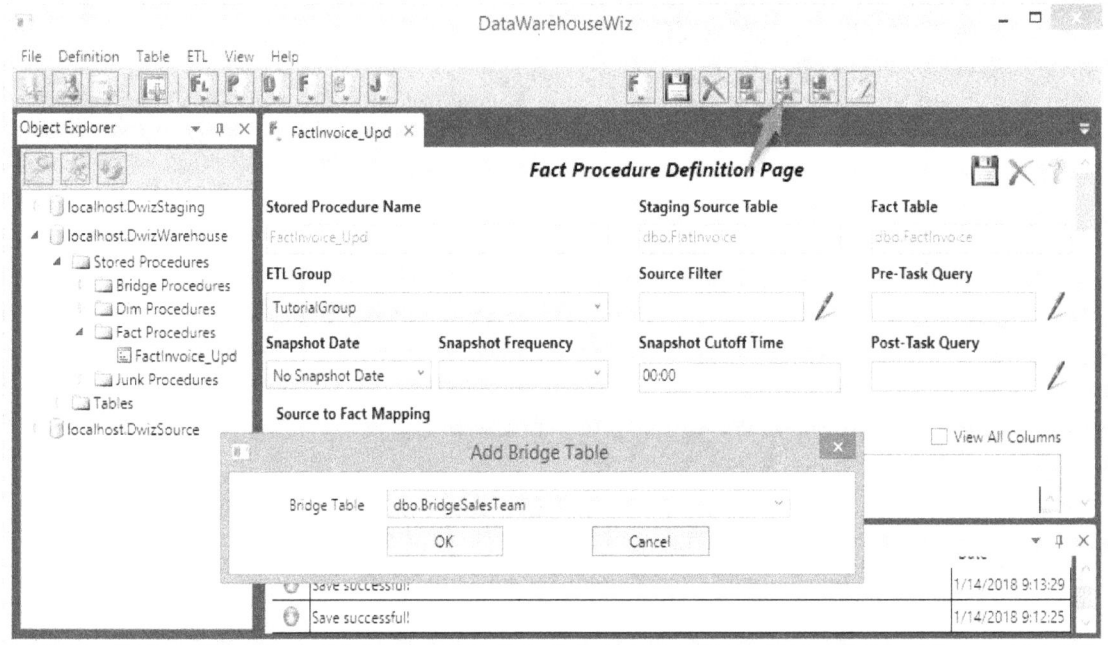

Illustration 106: Adding a Bridge Table to a Fact Update Procedure

In the resulting pop-up. select BridgeSalesTeam:

Illustration 107: "Add Bridge Table" Pop-Up

In the definition page, scroll down to reveal the new section at the bottom, "Fact To Bridge", and perform the following steps:

- Select Fact Table Key = BridgeSalesTeamKey

- Select Bridge Table Key = BridgeSalesTeamKey

- Put a "1" in the Natural Key of column SalesTeamID. This section should look like the following figure:

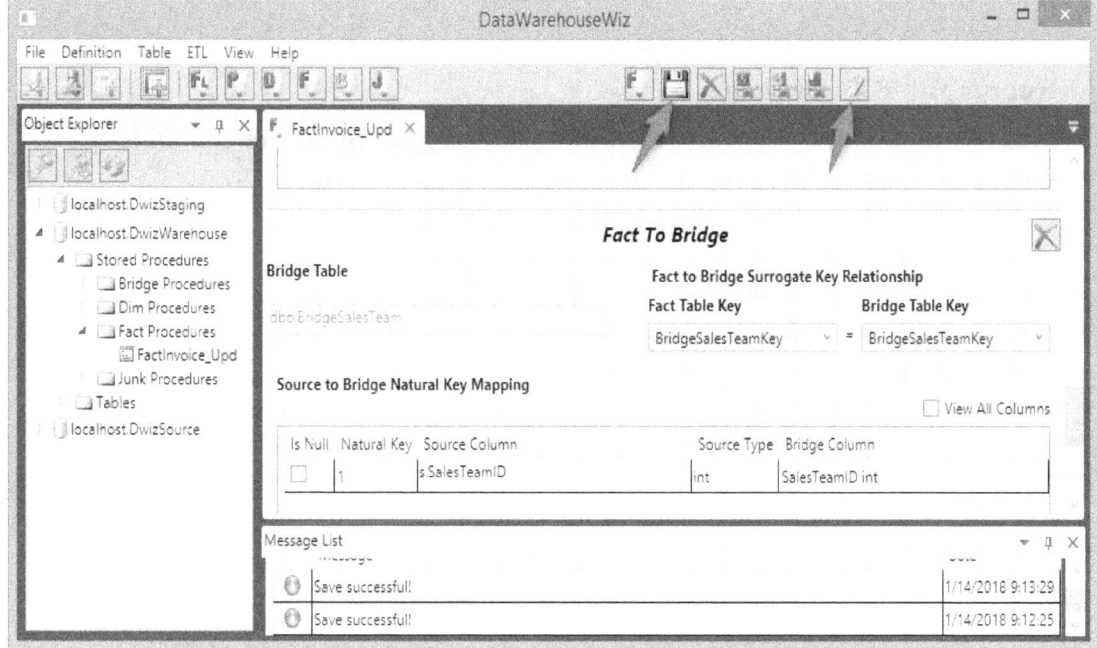

Illustration 108: Scrolling Down to View the Fact-To-Bridge Section

Now press Save (Floppy-Disk) to re-save the modified page. Next we will generate the stored procedure, so press the Create/Alter Procedure button. After the code is displayed, press the Save Procedure button (Lightning Over Floppy icon).

Now return to the BridgeSalesTeam_Upd procedure page, and compile it by pressing the Create/Alter Procedure button, followed by the Save Procedure button. Then do the same for the DimEmployee_Upd procedure. When designing a bridge, it is important to compile/recompile all warehouse procedures (Fact Update, Bridge Update, and Dim Update) after all three have been defined and SAVED.   So first define and save each of these procedures, then go back and compile each of them with the Create/Alter Procedure button followed by the Save Procedure button. This is necessary because DWiz needs the definition info of all three before it can correctly write code for any of them.

Recompile ETL Package

With all the tables and procedures done, we can now re-create the ETL Package, in a similar fashion to the steps in chapter "Compiling An ETL Group".

Our choices are 1) to compile an ETL Group Procedure, or 2) to compile an ETL SSIS Package. The first option is simple, just open the ETL Definition Page and compile the ETL Group Procedure. The second option (higher performance) entails the following steps:

- Expand **DWizStaging**-->ETL-->Definitions, right-click the Definitions folder, and double-click on TutorialETL

- Review ETL Definition Page (no changes are necessary), and press the Save button

- Press the Create BIML button (Scroll+Pen icon on top right)

- Open your TutorialETL project in SQL Data Tools for Visual Studio, and double-click the BimlScript.biml file to open it

- Copy (cut-and-paste clipboard) the new BIML from DWiz to overwrite the BimlScript in Visual Studio

- Save All in Visual Studio

- Right-click BimlScript.biml (under Miscellaneous in Solution Explorer) and click "Generate SSIS Packages". This may take a few minutes. Visual Studio may ask if you want to overwrite the package TutorialETL.dtsx; click on Yes.

- Afterward, you may view the data flow by double-clicking on the TutorialETL.dtsx package

- You may run the ETL Package by pressing the Start button on the top menu. Afterward, you can see the filled warehouse tables in SSMS.

This concludes our example of adding a Bridge Dimension to an existing warehouse. The augmented warehouse is "finished" and usable.

19. Outrigger Dimension Design

An Outrigger Dimension links to another Dimension instead of (or in addition to) a Fact table. Outriggers are particularly useful when you want to search one of your dimensions, such as Customers, by a category such as Demographics. Henceforth you can add a foreign key (DimDemographyKey) to Customers, which points to an Outrigger table (DimDemography), through which you can then do fast searching of the Customers table.

The following steps are needed to design an Outrigger Dimension:

1. Identify the sub-category within a base Dimension that could constitute a separate Outrigger Dimension. Create the normal staging elements for the source tables of this new Outrigger dimension: Download table, Flat table, Flat Procedure to feed the Flat table.

2. Create the new Outrigger Table proper. This table catalogs a sub-dimension, and is pointed to by a foreign key within the base Dimension table.

3. Create an Outrigger Procedure to feed the new Outrigger Table.

4. Add the foreign key (the Outrigger table's surrogate primary key) to the base Dimension table. Use the "Add Outrigger" button to define this relationship in the Dimension Procedure Definition page.

5. Recompile the ETL Process.

Outrigger Table Example (DimDemography)

In this chapter, we will use an example from the Tutorial to demonstrate the design of Outriggers. We will add an Outrigger Dimension to the existing dimension "DimCustomer".

Design Download Table

We will create a download table, called DownloadDemography in DWizStaging to facilitate the downloading of the "Demography" table data from the Source DB. We will use the same method as for DownloadCustomer.

Right-click the Demography table under DWizSource and select Copy Table to define the new DownloadDemography. Fill in the definition page, being certain to select the ETL group "TutorialGroup" and to specify the DWizSource Connection. Make sure that column DemographyID is indicated as the Source Primary Key with a "1", then press the Save icon (Floppy-Disk).

Design Flat Table

We will a create Flat table in DWizStaging by using the same method as for FlatCustomer. Right-click the DownloadDemography table under **DWizStaging** and select Copy Table to define the new FlatDemography with Table Type = **Flat.**

In the definition page, indicate DemographyID as the Source Primary Key with a "1", and press Save.

Design Outrigger Dimension Table

We will create a DimDemography table in DWizWarehouse by using the same method as for DimCustomer. Right-click the FlatDemography table under **DWizStaging** and select Copy Table to define the new DimDemography with:

- Database Name = DWizWarehouse   <or your warehouse DB>
- Schema = dbo   <or your pre-existing alternate Schema>
- Table type = Dim
- Table Name = DimDemography   <or your chosen Outrigger Table name>

In the definition page, indicate DemographyID as the Natural Key with a "1", and press Save. Notice that DWiz silently adds surrogate primary key DimDemographyKey.

Add New Outrigger Foreign Key Column to Existing Dimension (Customer)

In Object Explorer, double-click DimCustomer (DWizWarehouse->Tables->Dim) to open it. In the definition page, append column DimDemographyKey (int); then press Save at the top of the definition page. With the tables all set, we are ready to define the stored procedures to load them.

Design Procedure for Flat (Demography)

Next we will create a Flat Procedure for FlatDemography. Perform the following steps:

- Expand DWizStaging-->Stored Procedures-->Flat, right-click the Flat folder, and select New Flat.

- Create Flat Definition Page with Stored Procedure Name = FlatDemography_upd, Source Table = DownloadDemography and Flat Table = FlatDemography. Then press OK.

- In the Flat Definition Page, select ETL Group = TutorialGroup, enter a "1" in the Natural Key box of column DemographyID, and then press the **Save** icon.

- Press the Create/Alter Procedure button (Lightning/+ icon).

- After the code is displayed, press the Save Procedure button (Lightning Over Floppy icon).

Add New Outrigger Relationship to Existing Dimension Update Procedure

In Object Explorer, double-click DimCustomer_upd (DWizWarehouse-->Stored Procedures->Dim) to open it. Make sure that there is a "1" in the Natural Key column of CustomerId. In the top Tab Button Bar, press Add Outrigger:

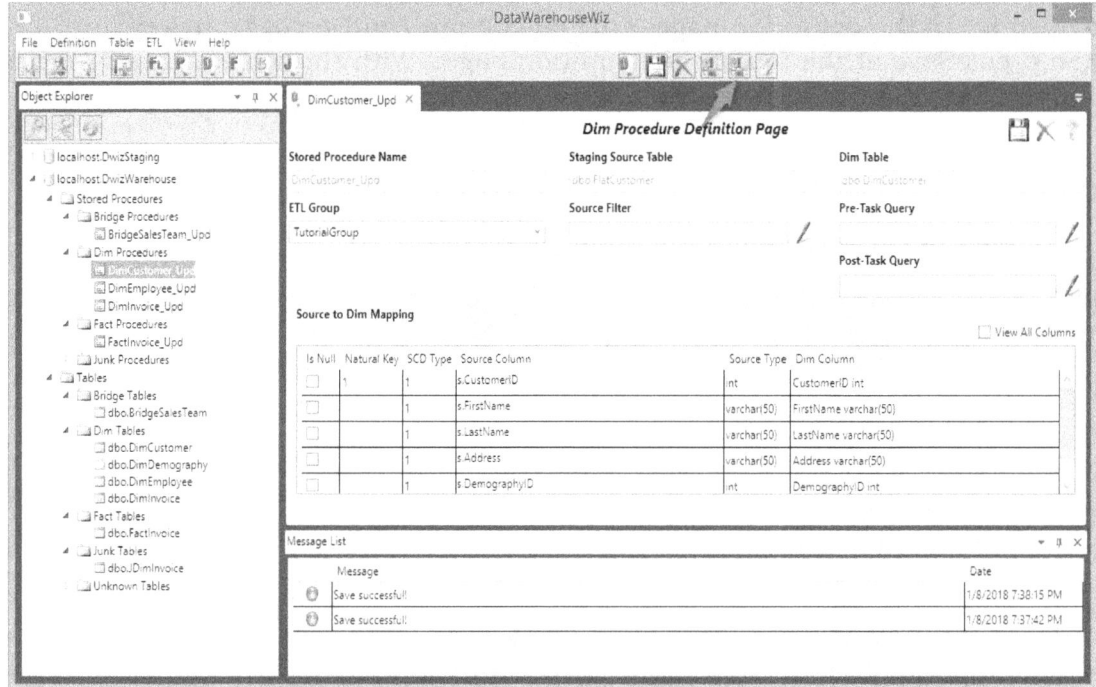

Illustration 109: Adding an Outrigger Table to a Dim Table Procedure

In the resulting pop-up. select DimDemography:

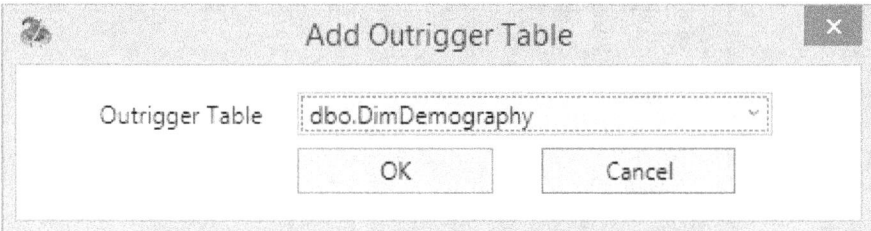

Illustration 110: "Add Outrigger Table" Pop-Up

In the definition page, scroll down to reveal the new section at the bottom, "Dim To Outrigger", and perform the following steps:

- Select Dim Table Key = DimDemographyKey

- Select Outrigger Table Key = DimDemographyKey

- Put a "1" in the Natural Key of column DemographyID. This section should look like the following figure:

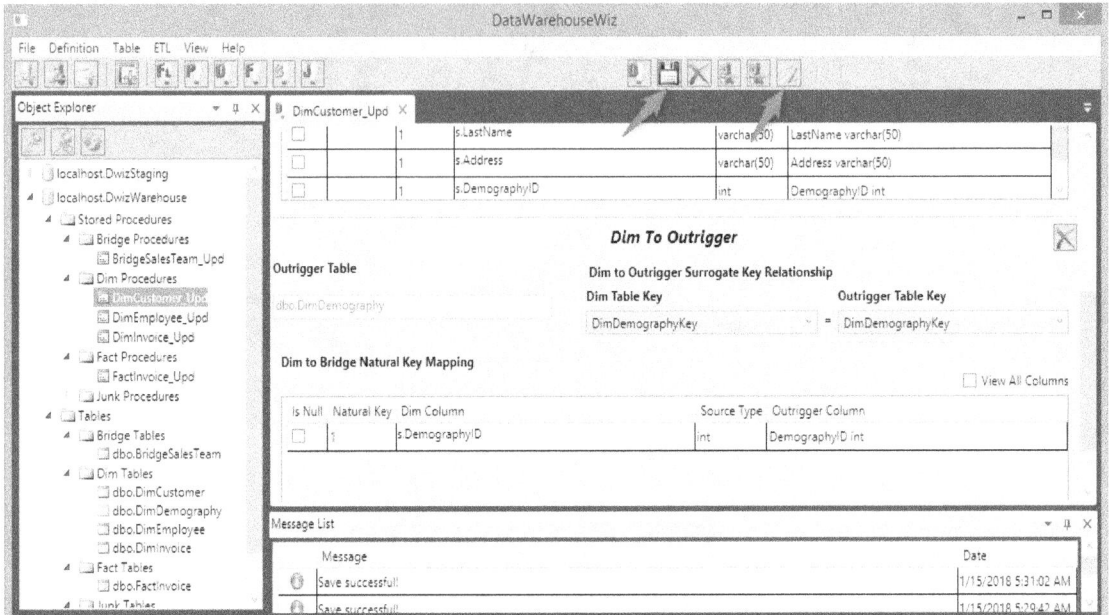

Illustration 111: Scrolling Down to View the "Dim To Outrigger" Section

Now press Save (Floppy-Disk) to re-save the modified page. Next we will generate the stored procedure, so press the Create/Alter Procedure button. After the code is displayed, press the Save Procedure button (Lightning Over Floppy icon). The following illustration shows the way that the DimCustomer_upd procedure makes use of the tables of the Outrigger subsystem.

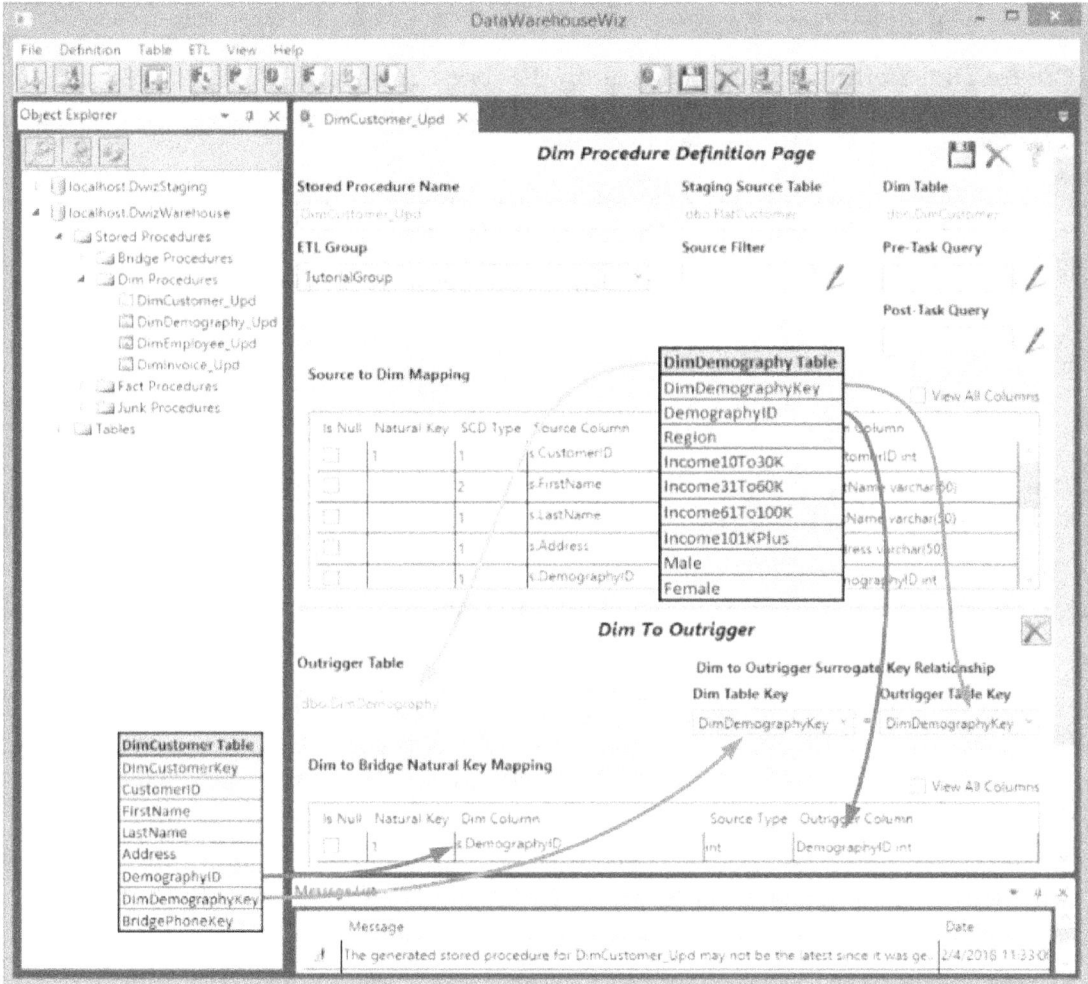

Illustration 112: The Tables of the Outrigger Subsystem are Used in the Dim-To-Outrigger Section

Design Procedure for Outrigger Dimension (Demography)

We will make a stored procedure for the new DimDemography. The Dim is part of the warehouse DB, so the procedure will reside there as well. Perform the following steps to create an ETL stored procedure for DimDemography:

- Expand **DWizWarehouse**-->Stored Procedures-->**Dim**, right-click the Dim folder, and select New Dim.

- Create Dim Definition Page with Stored Procedure Name = DimDemography_upd, Source Table = FlatDemography, and Dim Table = DimDemography. Then press OK.

- In the Dim Definition Page, select ETL Group = TutorialGroup, and put a "1" in the Natural Key column of DemographyId. Press the **Save** icon.

- Press the Create/Alter Procedure button (Lightning/+ icon).

- After the code is displayed, press the Save Procedure button (Lightning over Floppy icon).

Recompile ETL Package

With all the tables and procedures done, we can now re-create the ETL Package, in a similar fashion to the steps in chapter "Compiling An ETL Group".

Our choices are 1) to compile an ETL Group Procedure, or 2) to compile an ETL SSIS Package. The first option is simple, just open the ETL Definition Page and compile the ETL Group Procedure. The second option (higher performance) entails the following steps:

- Expand **DWizStaging**-->ETL-->Definitions, right-click the Definitions folder, and double-click on TutorialETL

- Review ETL Definition Page (no changes are necessary), and press the Save button

- Press the Create BIML button (Scroll+Pen icon on top right)

- Open your TutorialETL project in SQL Data Tools for Visual Studio, and double-click the BimlScript.biml file to open it

- Copy (cut-and-paste clipboard) the new BIML from DWiz to overwrite the BimlScript in Visual Studio

- Save All in Visual Studio

- Right-click BimlScript.biml (under Miscellaneous in Solution Explorer) and click "Generate SSIS Packages". This may take a few minutes. Visual Studio may ask if you want to overwrite the package TutorialETL.dtsx; click on Yes.

- Afterward, you may view the data flow by double-clicking on the TutorialETL.dtsx package

- You may run the ETL Package by pressing the Start button on the top menu. Afterward, you can see the filled warehouse tables in SSMS.

This concludes our example of adding an Outrigger Dimension to an existing warehouse. The augmented warehouse is "finished" and usable.

20. Pivot Tables

Pivot Tables are a special type of Flat table, wherein certain data from rows in the source table (a Flat) is pulled out to become separate columns in the resulting pivot (flat) table. Thus the data is "pivoted" from rows into columns. The Pivot table can then be used to provide data for warehouse tables such as Dimensions. As shown in the figure, this allows you to de-normalize many-to-one data (such as customer addresses) by pivoting the info to multiple new columns in the main dimension table (e.g., DimCustomer). This makes for an efficient warehouse, and is recommended when the pivot will generate ten columns or less.

For example, in the Tutorial Source DB, we have a Phone table that may have multiple records for a given customer, with each record labeled as a "HomePhone", "CellPhone", or "OfficePhone". In keeping with best practices of data warehousing, we want our Customer Dimension to have only one row per distinct customer, and for that one row to have columns of "HomePhone", "CellPhone", and "OfficePhone". In this example, we will accomplish this desired result easily using DWiz's Pivot Table feature.

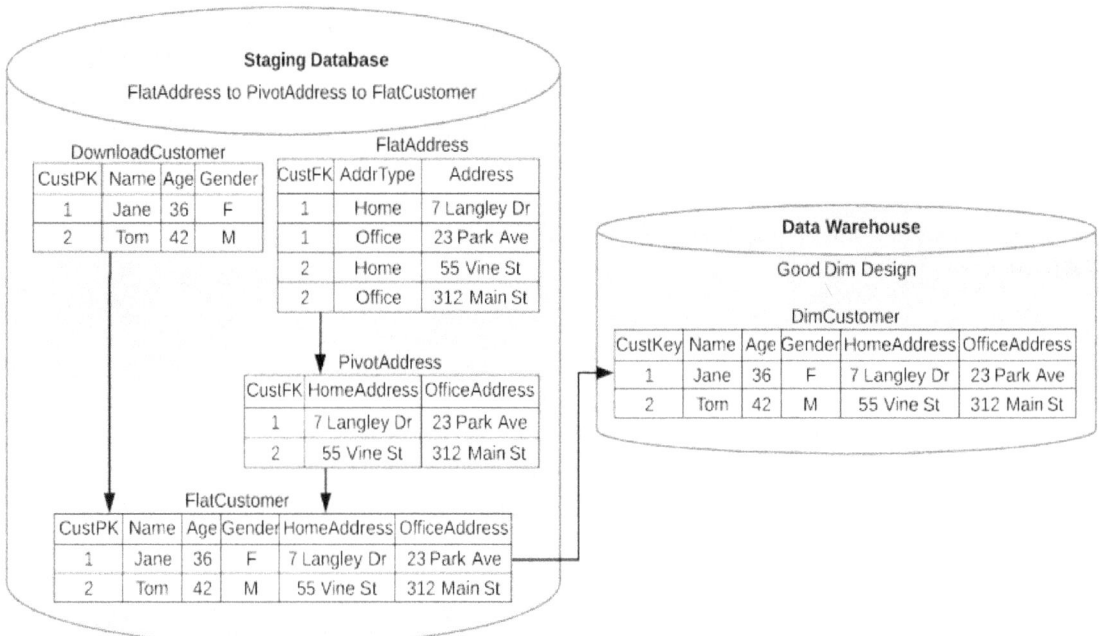

Illustration 113: Typical Use of a Pivot Table

Note that the input source for a Pivot is a normal Flat table. The output is a Pivot table, which is a special type of Flat.

Pivot Table Example

We will use an example from the Tutorial to demonstrate the design and use of a pivot table. In this example, the Source has a table with multiple *rows* of phone numbers per customer. We wish to design a pivot table that pivots these phone numbers into multiple *columns* in a single record per customer, as shown in the following figure.

Unpivoted Data — Phone numbers in rows

PhoneID	CustomerID	Phone Type	Phone Number	Extension
1	1	Cell	4073334444	NULL
2	1	Home	4071232345	NULL
3	1	Office	3131112222	423
4	2	Cell	4445558888	NULL
5	2	Home	1112223333	NULL
6	3	Home	2223334444	NULL
7	3	Office	6665554444	5322
8	4	Cell	8883335555	NULL
9	4	Office	2227779999	623

Pivoted Data — Phone numbers in columns

CustomerID	Home Phone	Cell Phone	Office Phone	Office Extension
1	4071232345	4073334444	3131112222	423
2	1112223333	4445558888	NULL	NULL
3	2223334444	NULL	6665554444	5322
4	NULL	8883335555	2227779999	623

Illustration 114: Example of Pivoted Data

The following steps are needed to design a pivot table:

1. Identify a source table that would benefit from pivoting. Create the normal (un-pivoted) staging elements for this source table: Download table, Flat table, Flat Procedure to feed the Flat table.

2. Create the new pivot table proper. This is a special pivot flat table with new columns for the pivoted data. Later, data will be drawn from the Flat table of step (1.), pivoted, and placed into the Pivot table.

3. Create a Pivot Procedure to feed the new pivot table.

4. Finally, use the pivot table results by adding the pivoted columns to a

warehouse table (usually a Dimension), and also to the Flat table that feeds the selected warehouse table. Update the procedures that feed this Flat table and the warehouse table, so that they will fill the new columns.

Design Download Table

We will create a download table, called DownloadPhone, in DWizStaging to facilitate the downloading of the "Phone" table data from the Source DB.

Right-click the Phone table under DWizSource and select Copy Table to define the new DownloadPhone. Fill in the definition page, being certain to select the ETL group "TutorialGroup" and to specify the DWizSource Connection. Make sure that column PhoneID is indicated as the Source Primary Key with a "1", then press the Save icon (Floppy-Disk). Note that the Phone table has columns "PhoneNumber" and "PhoneType"--this latter column will specify whether the phone is Home, Cell, or Office.

Design Flat Table

Create a Flat table, called FlatPhone, in DWizStaging by using the normal method for Flat tables (see "Flat Table Design"). Right-click the DownloadPhone table under **DWizStaging** and select Copy Table to define the new FlatPhone with Table Type = **Flat.**

In the definition page, indicate PhoneID as the Source Primary Key with a "1", and press Save.

Design Pivot Table (PivotPhoneWithExt)

Now we are ready to create the Pivot Table proper. Create the Pivot table in DWizStaging as follows. Right-click the FlatPhone table under **DWizStaging** and select Copy Table to define the new PivotPhoneWithExt with Table Type = **Pivot.**

In the definition page, add and delete columns so that the resulting table has only:

- CustomerId int, Allow Nulls = No, Primary Key = 1

- HomePhone varchar(10), Allow Nulls = Yes

- CellPhone varchar(10), Allow Nulls = Yes

- OfficePhone varchar(10), Allow Nulls = Yes

- OfficeExtension varchar(4), Allow Nulls = Yes

Note that our primary key will now be CustomerID, not PhoneId. After the pivot, we will have one row per CustomerId, which is what we wanted. Be sure to indicate CustomerID as the Primary Key with a "1", and mark it as non-nullable, and press Save:

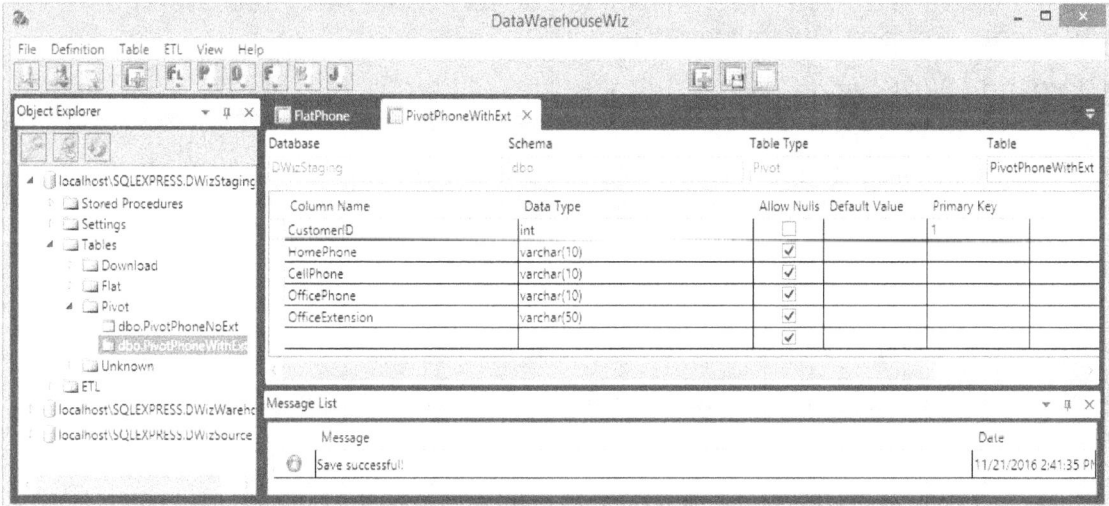

Illustration 115: "Pivot Table" Definition Page

Add New Pivoted Columns to Existing Flat and Dimension Tables (Customer)

In Object Explorer, double-click DimCustomer (DWizWarehouse->Tables->Dim) to open it. In the definition page, append the following column:

- HomePhone varchar(10), Allow Nulls = Yes

- CellPhone varchar(10), Allow Nulls = Yes

- OfficePhone varchar(10), Allow Nulls = Yes

- OfficeExtension varchar(4), Allow Nulls = Yes

Then press Save at the top of the definition page. Do the same for FlatCustomer (DWizStaging->Tables->Flat).

Design Procedure for Flat (Phone)

In a similar fashion as before, we will create an ETL stored procedure for FlatPhone. Perform the following steps:

- Expand DWizStaging-->Stored Procedures-->Flat, right-click the Flat folder, and select New Flat.

- Create Flat Definition Page with Stored Procedure Name = FlatPhone_upd, Source Table = DownloadPhone and Flat Table = FlatPhone. Then press OK.

- In the Flat Definition Page, select ETL Group = TutorialGroup, enter a "1" in the Natural Key box of column PhoneID, and then press the **Save** icon.

- Press the Create/Alter Procedure button (Lightning/+ icon).

- After the code is displayed, press the Save Procedure button (Lightning Over Floppy icon).

Design Procedure for Pivot Table

Here is where the actual pivoting happens. We will make a stored procedure for the new PivotPhoneWithExt. The Pivot is part of the Staging DB, so the procedure will reside there as well. DWiz will write the Pivot Procedure for you, based on your inputs to the Pivot Procedure Definition Page; however, DWiz will always give you an opportunity to view and modify the code if you wish.

Perform the following steps to create an ETL stored procedure for PivotPhoneWithExt:

1. Expand **DWizStaging**-->Stored Procedures-->**Pivot**, right-click the Pivot folder, and select New Pivot.

2. Create Pivot Definition Page with Stored Procedure Name = PivotPhoneWithExt_upd, Source Table = FlatPhone, and Pivot Table = PivotPhoneWithExt, then press OK.

   ○ In the Pivot Definition Page, select the following:ETL Group = TutorialGroup <or your chosen ETL Group>

   ○ Source Natural Key = PhoneID <the primary key of the Flat table that feeds>

   ○ Aggregate Function = max <in other scenarios, perhaps min, sum, or avg>

   ○ Pivot-On Column = PhoneType <the column that determines the pivot>

3. Put a "1" in the Natural Key column of CustomerId. This causes the pivot data to be Grouped By the column CustomerId.

4. Then enter the Pivot-On Values as shown in the following illustration. The Pivot-On values determine when the source PhoneNumber is entered into a destination column; for example, when the source PhoneType = 'Home', then the source column PhoneNumber will be copied into the HomePhone column. When the source PhoneType = 'Office', then the source PhoneNumber will be copied to OfficePhone, while the source Extension will be copied to OfficeExtension.

5. Press the **Save** icon.

6. Press the Create/Alter Procedure button (Lightning/+ icon).

7. After the code is displayed, press the Save Procedure button (Lightning over Floppy icon).

As shown below, the Pivot Procedure Design page also offers the other transform features of a normal Flat Procedure Definition page (source filter, pre- and post-queries, etc.). For a detailed description of these features, see the chapter "Flat Procedure Design".

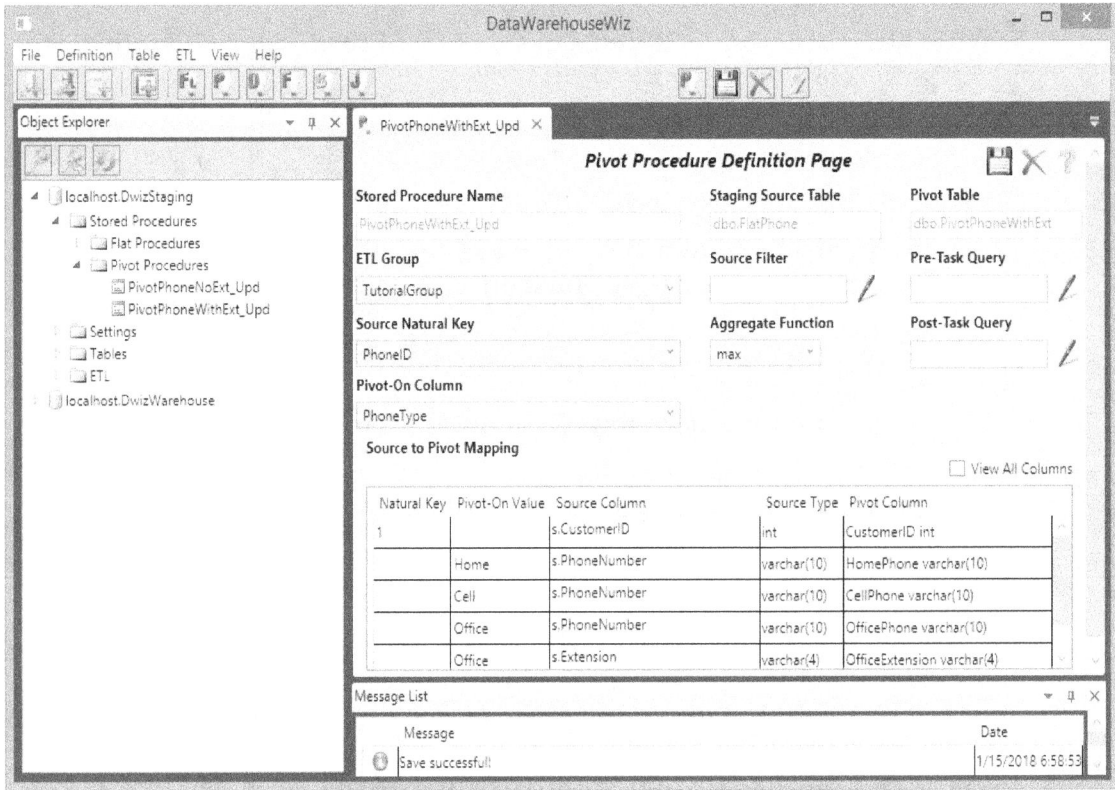

Illustration 116: Defining Pivot-On Values in the Pivot Update Procedure

The following illustration shows the input and output tables of the Pivot Procedure and how the data is "pivoted".

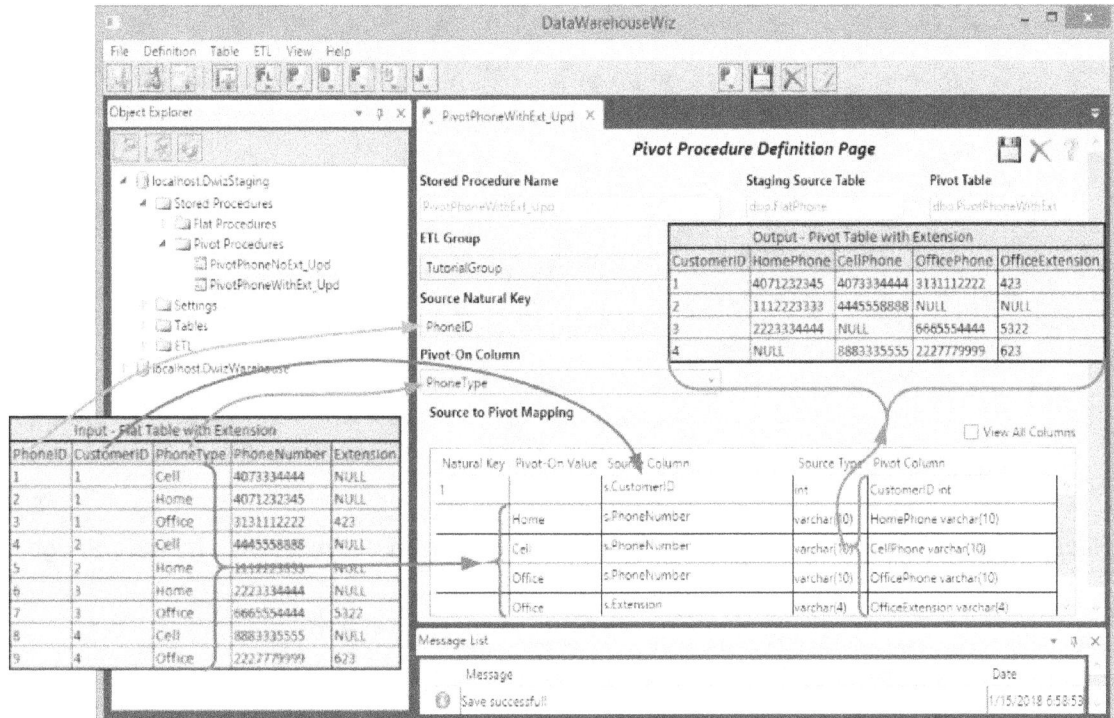

Illustration 117: Input and Output Tables of a Pivot Procedure

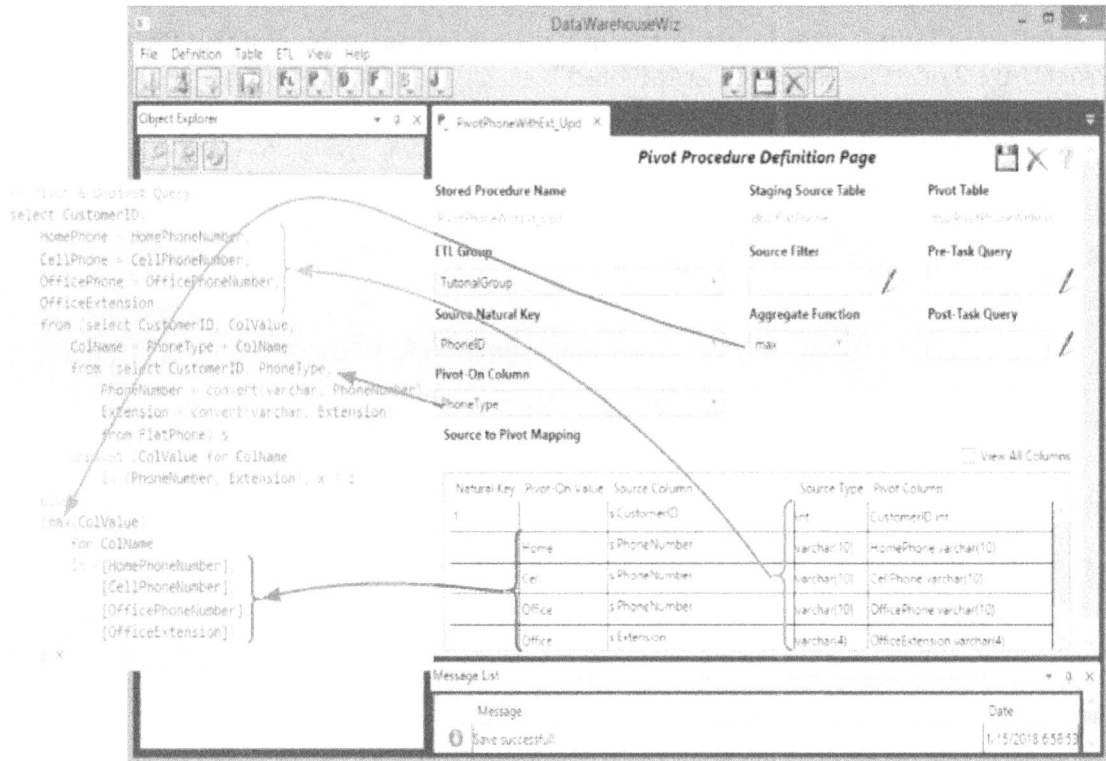

Illustration 118: DWiz Creates Pivot Code Based on the Pivot Procedure Definition Page

Update the Existing Procedure for Flat (Customer)

Now we can use the new pivot table by updating the existing ETL procedures to fill the new columns in FlatCustomer and DimCustomer. Double-click the FlatCustomer proc DWizStaging-->Stored Procedures-->Flat-->FlatCustomer. Above the Flat Definition page, click the Additional Source button and select "PivotPhoneWithExt":

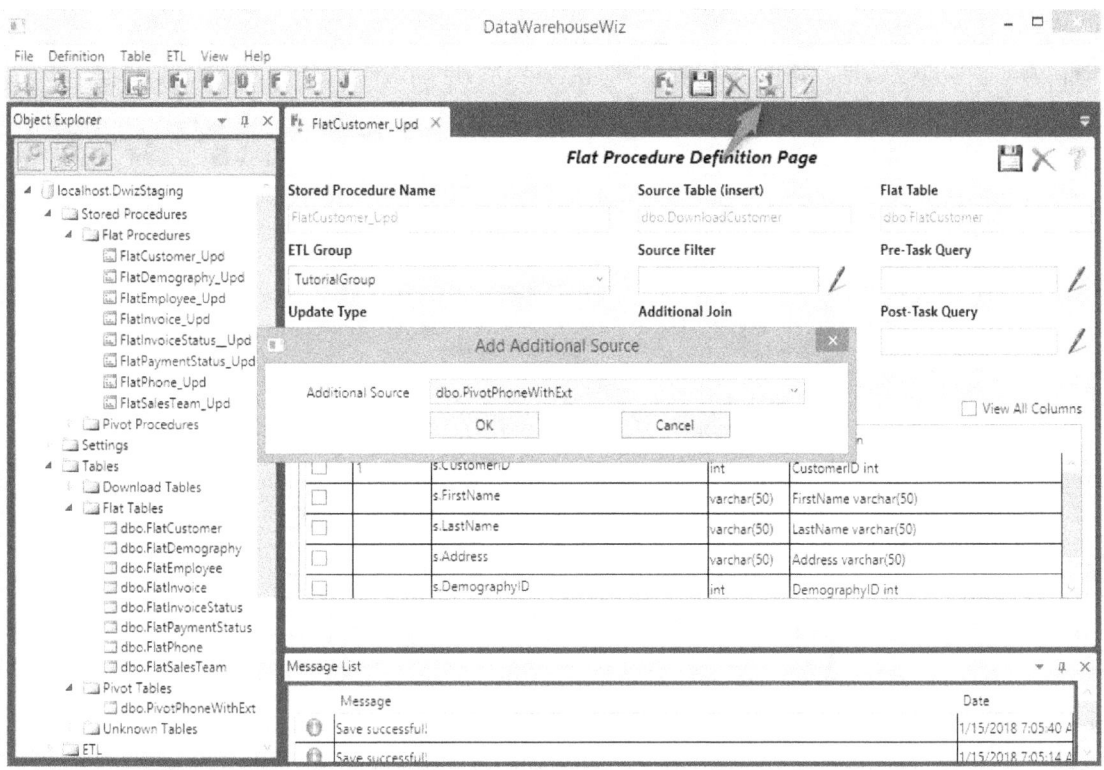

Illustration 119: Adding a Pivot Table to a Flat Update Procedure

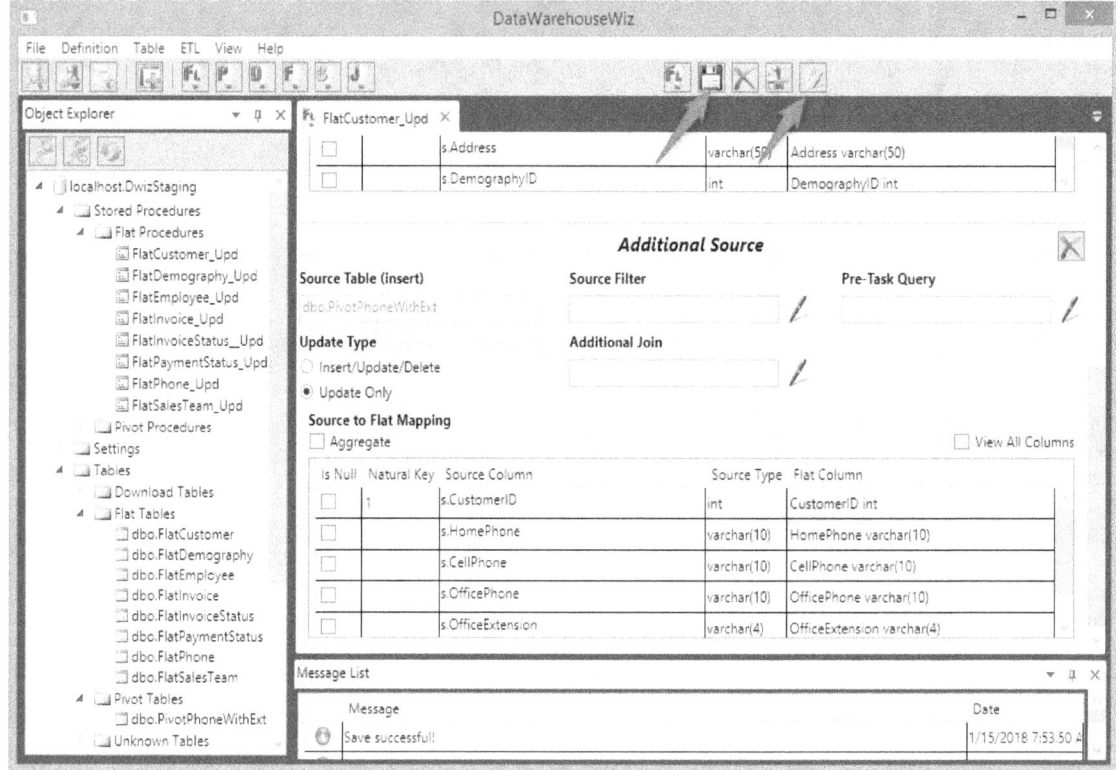

Illustration 120: Scrolling Down to View the Additional Source Section

Then scroll down in the page to view the new Additional Source section. This section should look like the following illustration:

Perform these steps:

- Press the **Save** icon.

- Press the Create/Alter Procedure button (Lightning/+ icon).

- After the code is displayed, press the Save Procedure button (Lightning Over Floppy icon).

Update the Existing Procedure for Dimension (Customer)

Now we can update the DimCustomer_upd procedure to fill the new columns. Double-click the DimCustomer proc DWizWarehouse-->Stored Procedures--> Dim-->DimCustomer_upd. Verify that the new columns have been sensed (HomePhone, CellPhone, OfficePhone, OfficeExtension), then press the Save button. Finally, press the Create/Alter Procedure button and lastly the Save Procedure button.

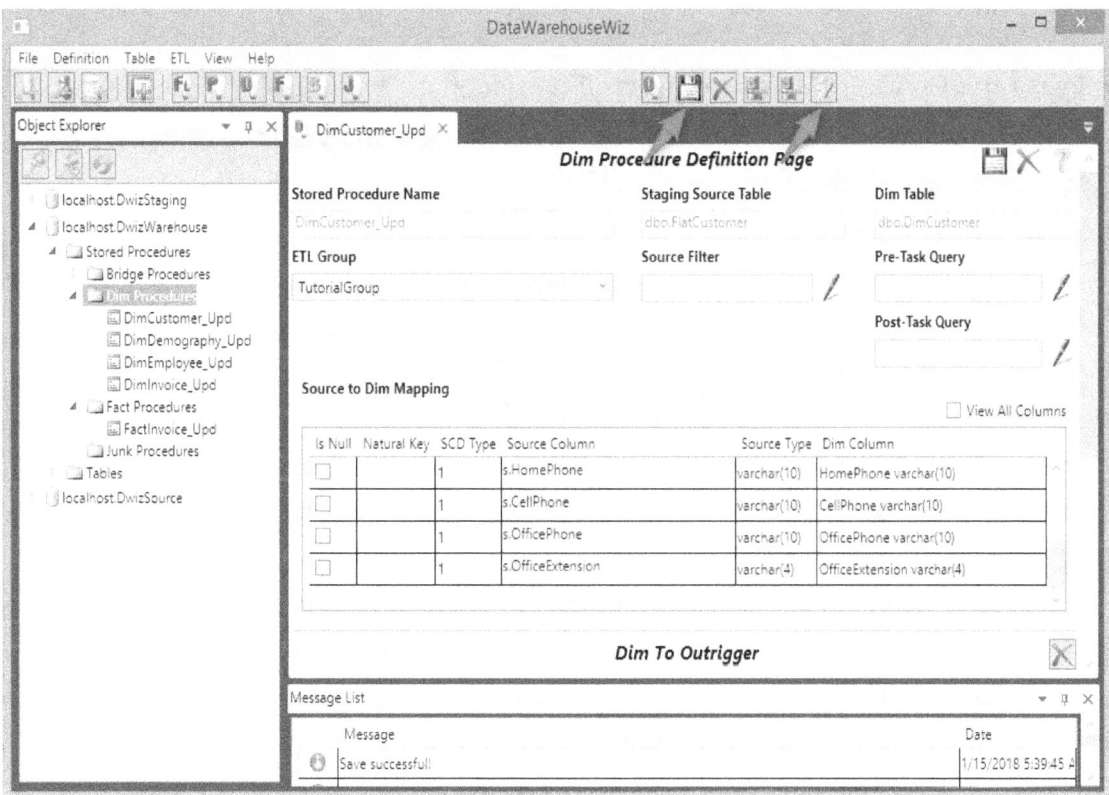

Illustration 121: Adding New Columns to the DimCustomer_upd Procedure

Recompile ETL Package

With all the tables and procedures done, we can now re-create the ETL Package, in a similar fashion to the steps in "Compiling An ETL Group".

Our choices are 1) to compile an ETL Group Procedure, or 2) to compile an ETL SSIS Package. The first option is simple, just open the ETL Definition Page and compile the ETL Group Procedure. The second option (higher performance) entails the following steps:

- Expand **DWizStaging**-->ETL-->Definitions, right-click the Definitions folder, and double-click on TutorialETL

- Review ETL Definition Page (no changes are necessary), and press the Save button

- Press the Create BIML button (Scroll+Pen icon on top right)

- Open your TutorialETL project in SQL Data Tools for Visual Studio, and double-click the BimlScript.biml file to open it

- Copy (cut-and-paste clipboard) the new BIML from DWiz to overwrite the BimlScript in Visual Studio

- Save All in Visual Studio

- Right-click BimlScript.biml (under Miscellaneous in Solution Explorer) and click "Generate SSIS Packages". This may take a few minutes. Visual Studio may ask if you want to overwrite the package TutorialETL.dtsx; click on Yes.

- Afterward, you may view the data flow by double-clicking on the TutorialETL.dtsx package

- You may run the ETL Package by pressing the Start button on the top menu. Afterward, you can see the filled warehouse tables in SSMS.

This concludes our example of adding a Pivot Table to an existing warehouse. The augmented warehouse is "finished" and usable.

21. Classifying Unknown Tables

In the Object Explorer, under the Staging database, DWiz shows the staging tables of your projects under the three folders Download Tables, Flat Tables , and Pivot Tables. If a table is created in the Staging DB but outside of the DWiz app, then DWiz will show this "Unknown" table under the fourth folder, Unknown Tables.

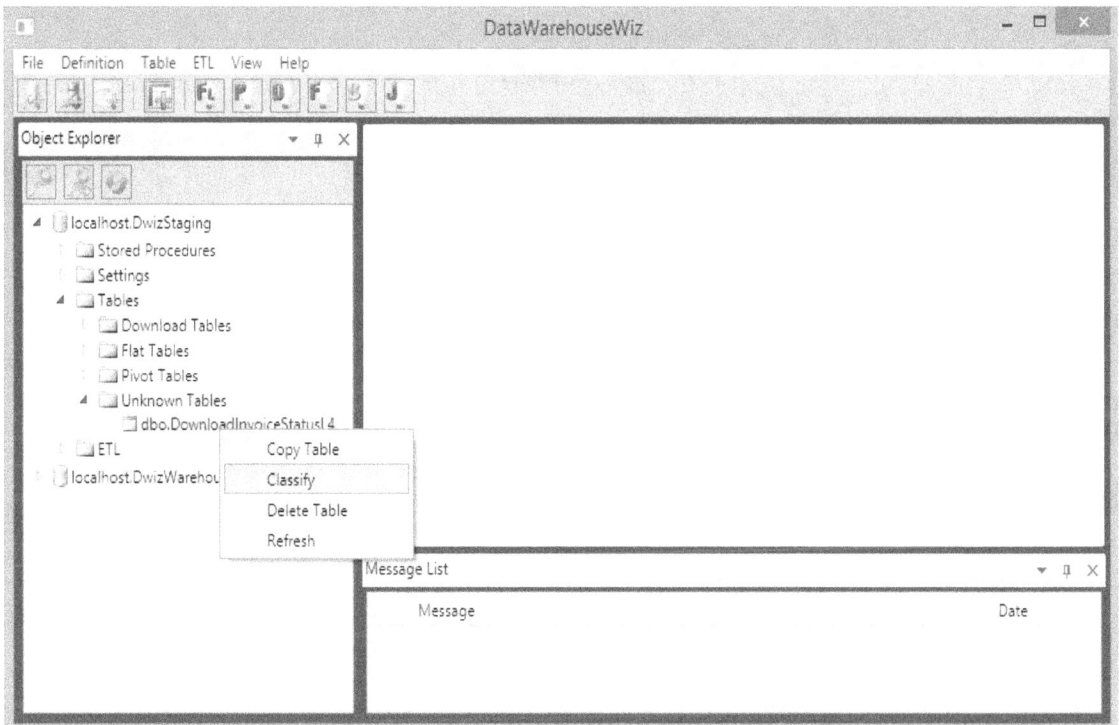

Illustration 122: Staging Tables Created Outside of DWiz are Shown in the Unknown Folder

If you wish to use this Unknown table in a DWiz project, you must first Classify it as a Download, Flat, or Pivot table. To do this, simply right-click the table name and select "Classify". For example, you may want to create a lookup table outside of DWiz, but then use your lookup table as part of a Transform in DWiz. You can do this by selecting "Classify" and then classifying your lookup table as a Flat table.

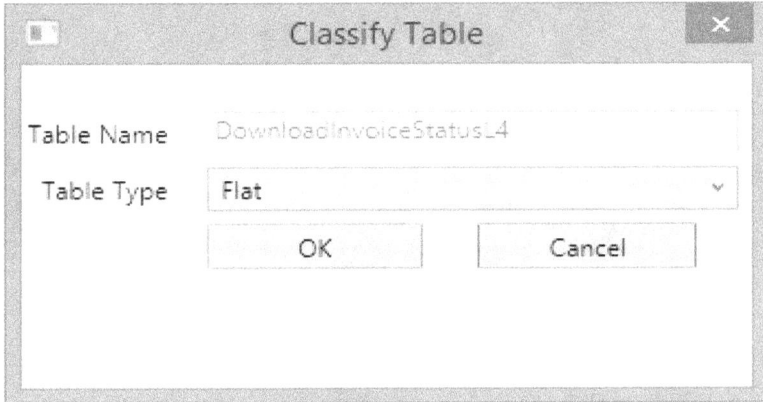

Illustration 123: The "Classify Table" Pop-Up Window

When you Classify an Unknown table, DWiz adds appropriate metadata columns to the table, and thereafter the table will be listed under the desired Download, Flat, or Pivot folder.

22. You Can Build A Data Warehouse On a Small Budget, Completely In-House

By following the steps in this book, you can develop *any* data warehouse. Let's summarize the high-level tasks.

If this is a new data warehouse, work through the Strawman exercise of Chapter 3 before diving into your rapid prototype.

Start your first build by creating empty Staging and Data Warehouse databases. Run DWiz and connect to your operational Source DB (or clone thereof). Create an ETL Group.

Use DWiz to view the Source DB, and select a source table (such as Sales) to provide facts for a new Fact table in your first new data mart. DWiz will design a Download table in the Staging DB to capture the data changes of this table. If possible, set up the Source to use Change Tracking or Change Data Capture, which will minimize the amount of data necessary to download on each run of the ETL Group. Note that no data will be downloaded until the ETL Group is compiled and run as the ETL Process.

Next, decide on the grain, which is the lowest level of detail that will exist in your new Fact table. Note that often you will need to join multiple Source tables together to produce one de-normalized Fact table. For example, many company Source transactional DBs have separate tables for SalesInvoices and SalesInvoiceLineItems. These will be joined together to produce one de-normalized SalesInvoiceFact table, which will have the grain at the lowest detail available: each table row will correspond to a single line-item of an invoice.

Now, view your Source DB again and choose what tables will be needed to flesh out your Fact table and also to form the related Dimension tables for your star-schema data mart. Then use DWiz to quickly form Download tables and ETL for all your chosen tables. For example, if you have chosen Sales for your fact table, then you will also want to Download tables related to Sales, such as customer & customer info tables, sales employee tables, product info tables, and vendor info tables.

Next, use DWiz to form Flat tables in Staging that will have the de-normalized (flat) schema that will be needed for your warehouse Dimension tables. You can use DWiz to create these Flat tables by clicking the closest Download table, to use as a template, and then filling-in a simple form for the Flat table design. DWiz automatically adds meta-data columns needed for tracking changes. In the same way, create a Flat table for your fact table, making sure to include a foreign key column for each of your dimension tables. Ensure that each Dimension maintains consistency with the grain of the Fact table.

Now use DWiz to design the "Transform" part of your ETL, which takes the differential input from the Download tables, applies transforms as needed (joins, filters, format changes, cleaning, and any other desired processing), and stages the output to your Flat tables. DWiz will design a SQL stored procedure for each Flat table, based upon your selections and inputs to a form called a "Flat Procedure Definition Page". After writing the code for a stored procedure, DWiz will display the entire source code (with nothing hidden) and even allow changes, before committing the new stored procedure to the Staging DB. DWiz automatically handles all meta-data columns and writes efficient code for the differential updates to the Flat tables. DWiz offers powerful options in the Definition Page, so that it can write robust and efficient code for you. DWiz can even write code to pivot tables for you—a common need for data marts.

Next, use DWiz to design and create your warehouse tables, starting with the Dimensions, and ending with the Fact table. You create these warehouse tables by clicking the closest Flat table, to use as a template, and then filling-in a simple form for the warehouse table design. DWiz automatically adds meta-data columns needed for tracking changes.

Now use DWiz to design the "Load" part of your ETL, which takes the differential changes from the Flat tables and loads the updates to your warehouse tables. DWiz will design a SQL stored procedure for each warehouse table, based upon your selections and inputs to a form. After writing the code for a stored procedure, DWiz will display the entire source code (with nothing hidden) and even allow changes, before committing the new stored procedure to the Warehouse DB. DWiz automatically handles all meta-data columns and writes efficient code for the differential updates to the warehouse tables.

Finally, use DWiz to assemble all the ETL code into one efficient SQL Server Integration Services (SSIS) package. This package is your "ETL Process". [As an alternative option, DWiz instead can create a single ETL group stored procedure instead, which serves as the ETL Process.] When designing this ETL Process, DWiz automatically sequences all the parts of the ETL, from "Extracting to Download Tables" through carefully ordered "Loading to the Warehouse Tables". Congratulations, you have completed a first data mart of one business area. However, there is no data in the warehouse yet, as the ETL Process has not yet run for the first time.

The first time that you run the ETL Process (SSIS package or group stored procedure), it will download the entire contents of your selected Source tables, and completely fill the new Data Warehouse/Data Mart. Later runs of the ETL Process will extract only new/changed data from the Source, transform the staged data to formats conducive to data warehousing, and efficiently load the differential data into your Data Warehouse to keep it up-to-date. However, this first run will need to catch up all the history currently in your source tables, so it will be much larger in comparison. Therefore, unless your source database is small (a few GB or less), you should use the following procedure to accomplish the first run of the ETL Process:

- On the production Source Database, enable Change Tracking.

- Run a backup of this Source DB. Note: Do not start the backup until you are ready to perform this entire procedure: For best results, the remaining steps of this procedure should be performed in a timely fashion.

- Make a clone by restoring the backup to a new location.

- In DWiz, create a connection string to the new clone.

- In the ETL DefinitionPage, point the connection strings to the clone. Set the download method to Change Tracking. Choose your largest table (usually the fact table), and enter it as the Huge Table in this page, and set the chunk size to about 200000. It is OK if the table is not actually huge. This nice feature streamlines the ETL to work in chunks, rather than doing a resource-hungry grab of an entire huge table.

- In the ETL Definition Page, press Save, and then compile it as in Chapter 15. If you are using the SSIS option, check the connection string displayed at the top of the SSIS code view, to ensure that it points to the clone.

- Now run the ETL Process for the first time. As previously described, this first run may take a long time for a big existing database. Afterward, check the results and check the warehouse tables, make sure everything ran OK.

- Now go back to the ETL Definition Page, and change the connection strings to the production Source DB. Save and re-compile, making sure that the connection string now point to the **production** Source.

- Run the newly-compiled ETL Process. On this pass, it will process all delta changes that occurred in the Source DB after it was backed-up for the clone.

- Schedule the ETL Process to run on a regular schedule, such as nightly, hourly, or every 15 minutes. Check the results and durations of the first few scheduled runs. Experiment with the schedule, looking for a sweet-spot. Do not assume that if a nightly run takes over an hour, then a 15-minute update is prohibited: there is much less data to process in a 15-minute period (although the process will not be linear, hence experimentation for the sweet-spot).

Test and experiment with your data mart. Deploy it to your production platform. Open your first small data mart to actual data consumers as early as possible. Encourage your support group to use the new DW and welcome suggestions. Data warehouses tend to be most successful when data consumers participate early in the agile development cycles.

In fine agile style, you can make improvements and expand to cover other business areas—DWiz will assist you at every point, making the design changes easier, and automatically downloading/processing the minimal data necessary to accommodate the design changes. For each new Fact table that you create, you must define the grain and maintain consistency with any relationships to existing Fact tables. You should conform the dimensions such that, when a dimension is related to multiple Fact tables, the exact same Dimension table (and its keys) can be used by the various Fact tables and in each case "mean the same thing". So, for example, if both the Sales fact table and the Inventory fact table use a "product" dimension, then you should use one single Product Dimension table which is shared by both and which is accurate in both cases.

As you build out and expand your DW, you may find it beneficial to add advanced warehouse structures such as Bridges, Junks, and Outriggers. DWiz can guide you through (and write code for) the use of these advanced structures.

Alphabetical Index

Illustration Index

Bibliography

1: Christopher Adamson, Star Schema: The Complete Reference, First Edition, 2010 McGraw-Hill, 978-0071744324
2: Ralph Kimball and Margy Ross, The Data Warehouse Toolkit: The Definitive Guide to Dimensional Modeling, Third, 2013 Wiley, 978-1118530801

###

www.ingramcontent.com/pod-product-compliance
Lightning Source LLC
Chambersburg PA
CBHW080824220526
45467CB00008B/2188

* 9 7 8 1 7 1 7 8 2 9 9 0 0 *